"Damned Notions of Liberty"

Other titles in the Diálogos series available
from the University of New Mexico Press:

SERIES ADVISORY EDITOR: LYMAN L. JOHNSON,
UNIVERSITY OF NORTH CAROLINA AT CHARLOTTE

"Damned Notions of Liberty"

Slavery, Culture, and Power in Colonial Mexico,
1640–1769

FRANK T. PROCTOR III

University of New Mexico Press ✢ Albuquerque

15   14   13   12   11   10   1   2   3   4   5   6

LIBRARY OF CONGRESS CATALOGING-IN-PUBLICATION DATA

Proctor, Frank T., 1970–

Damned notions of liberty : slavery, culture, and power
in colonial Mexico, 1640–1769 / Frank T. Proctor III.

p. cm. — (Diálogos series)

Includes bibliographical references and index.

ISBN 978-0-8263-4966-8 (cloth : alk. paper)

1. Slavery—Mexico—History. 2. Blacks—Mexico—History.
3. Blacks—Mexico—Social conditions. 4. Blacks—Race identity—Mexico.
5. Mexico—Race relations—History. 6. Mexico—History—
Spanish colony, 1540–1810. I. Title.

HT1053.P76 2010

306.3′620972—dc22

2010023986

Composed in 10/13.5 Janson Text Lt Std
Display type is Bernhard Modern Std

For my daughter

Taylor E. H. Proctor

La luz en la oscuridad

Contents

Figures, Tables, and Maps

Acknowledgments

The process of researching and writing a book may at times feel like a solitary process, and yet without the support and assistance of countless people and institutions this project would have been impossible to complete. I owe a tremendous debt of gratitude to my many excellent teachers and colleagues. Susan M. Socolow, Peter Bakewell, Kevin Gosner, Donna Guy, Michael C. Meyer, and James Roark have done much to shape the historian that I have become. Special thanks to B. J. Barickman for putting me on the path of New World slavery and to Charles Walker, who urged me to pursue history as a life's work when I was an undergraduate. I have been equally fortunate to be surrounded by supportive and engaging colleagues at Denison University, as I was during my time at Whitman College.

Countless friends and collogues have made important contributions to this work. D. Michael Bottoms, Patrick Carroll, Mitchell Snay, and Nanette Thrush read drafts of the manuscript and made thoughtful suggestions for improvement. Jennifer Marian Frances Miller, Christopher Curtis, and Tabitha Sparks slogged through drafts of the dissertation it is based on. Stimulating conversations with Ben Vinson III and Bianca Premo have shaped this work in fundamental and incalculable ways. My interactions with Jeffrey Shumway, Timothy Boyle, Curt Enderle, and Jeffrey Voris have enriched my life, personally and academically. Finally, to William Connell, I will never forget our frequent coffee breaks and constant discussions during our time at the Archivo General de la Nación de México. MJ Devaney's careful copyediting and helpful suggestions improved the manuscript significantly. Special thanks go out to the editor of the Diálogos series, Lyman Johnson, for his assistance and guidance in shepherding this project to completion. He and the anonymous readers from the University of New Mexico Press gave excellent advice on polishing the arguments herein. Thank you. You all have been terrific friends and intellectual role models.

I am particularly grateful for the assistance and support from the Seminario sobre la presencia Africana en México and in particular María Elisa Velásquez Gutiérrez, María Guevara Sanginés, Adriana Naveda Chávez-Hita, and Juan Manuel de la Serna H. The administrators and staff of the Archivo General de la Nación de México and the Archivo Histórico de Notarias, both in Mexico City, and the Archivo Histórico de Guanajuato were generous with their time and assistance.

This research was made possible through the generous financial assistance from a William J. Fulbright / García Robles Dissertation Grant; a graduate fellowship in residence at Emory University's Center for Humanistic Inquiry; a graduate fellowship from the Department of History at Emory; a grant from the Denison University Research Fund; and research funds from the History Department at Whitman College and Denison University.

Parts of chapters 1 and 6 appeared as "Afro-Mexican Slave Labor in the Obrajes de Paños of New Spain, Seventeenth and Eighteenth Centuries," *The Americas* 60, no. 1 (2003): 33–58, and "Gender and the Manumission of Slaves in New Spain," *Hispanic American Historical Review* 86, no. 2 (2006): 309–36, respectively. In addition, portions of chapter 5 appear in "Slave Rebellion and Liberty in Colonial Mexico," in *Black Mexico: Race and Society from Colonial to Modern Times*, edited by Ben Vinson III and Matthew Restall (Albuquerque: University of New Mexico Press, 2009), 21-50. My thanks to the journals and press for permission to use the material here.

Finally, I would have never completed this without the loving support of my parents, Jill and Wes, Frank and Ann, and the rest of my family. Megan Threlkeld has brought a new joy to my life, and I look forward to growing old together. A tremendous debt of gratitude is owed my daughter, Taylor Eden, who has given up far too much time with her father during the years it has taken to research and write this study. She has been, and will always remain, my inspiration.

Introduction

An Invitation

✣ ON MAY 26, 1728, A LARGE GROUP OF SLAVES ARMED WITH KNIVES
and machetes surrounded a colonial official on the road and threatened
to burn the *ingenio* (sugar plantation) where they lived to the ground,
"sending all those who lived there to the Devil," if he would not intervene on their behalf. The slaves were motivated to such extremes, they
later testified, by their fear that neighboring planters would take control
of the ingenio and subsequently break up their families and community
in retribution for an alleged theft.[1] On August 9, 1763, nearly fifty armed
and panicked slaves fled this same plantation, en masse. This group did
not lash out violently at their oppressors. Nor did they escape into the
countryside to establish a *palenque* (runaway community). Rather, they
made their way to Mexico City to lodge a formal protest before high-
ranking colonial officials about living and working conditions on the
hacienda.[2]

The questions that these two moments in time within a single slave
community provoke are at the core of *"Damned Notions of Liberty"*: *Slavery,
Culture, and Power in Colonial Mexico, 1640–1769*. The central goal of
this study is to explore slavery from the perspective of slaves themselves,
to reveal how the enslaved understood their own actions in the specific
geographical and chronological context of New Spain in the middle colonial period (roughly 1630–1760s). Four core themes that appear in these
two accounts prove central to the slaves' appreciation of their own social
position. Both of these incidents reveal slaves' complicated understanding

of the nature of their labor, communities, identities, and agency, all of which fall under the larger rubric of the cultures of slavery.

This study approaches the cultures of slavery in New Spain from two overlapping perspectives grounded in the idea that culture is best defined as a "complex of attitudes, beliefs, and codes of behavior" created, maintained, and ever altered by the experiences of living within the confines of structures of power.[3] First, *"Damned Notions of Liberty"* reconsiders the ability of slaves (and eventually free Afro-Mexicans) to construct and maintain families and distinctive cultural communities within the culturally complicated milieu of Catholic New Spain.[4] Second, because slaves persistently struggled to mitigate the oppressive nature of slavery, this study also investigates the nature of master-slave relations. In combination, these themes allow for a better understanding of the cultures of slavery in New Spain from the perspective of slaves themselves.

A planter complaint from the sugar-producing jurisdiction of Córdoba in 1735 illuminates another key set of issues that also falls under the rubric of cultures of slavery and points to another important theme that informs this study. In that complaint, masters charged that local runaway slaves (*cimarrones*) had attempted to foment a slave rebellion by "pouring their damned notions of liberty" into the slave quarters.[5] This allegation raises important questions regarding the relationship between slavery and freedom with respect to the enslaved in New Spain. It prompts both a reconsideration of slaves' conceptions of liberty and an exploration of the relationship between slaves' potential pursuit of freedom and their notions of identity and agency.

The planter testimony demonstrates that colonial elite clearly feared that a desire for liberty drove slave rebelliousness. Yet the voluminous documentary base that speaks to master-slave relations in New Spain suggests that much more mundane issues led to master-slave conflicts and to slave rebelliousness.[6] Slaves' testimonies on issues such as master-on-slave violence, flight, and rebellion, and the operation of manumission suggest that conceptions of liberty *may not* have been central to slave identity. In the 1728 and 1763 rebellions, neither group of slaves pressed for liberation, nor did either group suggest that their position in the social hierarchy was unjust.

Central New Spain provides a compelling context for an investigation of how slaves envisioned their own oppression and what role liberty played in those visions. It represents one of the few settings where the enslaved population was surrounded by a much larger indigenous majority and where the growth of the free population of African descent outpaced that of slaves. By the second half of the seventeenth century, there were more free Afro-Mexicans than slaves in the colony (it's worth observing, by way of contrast, that there were not more ex-slaves than slaves in most other slaveholding societies until the nineteenth century).[7] Both of these demographic conditions had profound implications with respect to the nature and operation of slavery; they had an effect on both the cultural communities inhabited by slaves and on how slaves envisioned their struggles against their oppressors.

MAP 1. New Spain. By author

Chronologically, this study begins with the termination of the regular slave trade to New Spain in 1640 and ends in the 1760s.[8] Prior to 1640
the colony was the second largest importer of slaves in the Americas. In
that year, the nearly fifty thousand to sixty thousand slaves of African
descent in New Spain made it the second largest slaveholding society in
the New World, behind only Brazil.[9] Even so, slavery never supplanted
indigenous labor in the colony but rather only supplemented it. And, at
the very moment when slavery began to expand throughout the rest of the
Americas, Spain lost direct control of the slave trade to its colonies owing
to the dissolution of Spanish and Portuguese crowns. Imports to colonial
Mexico slowed to a trickle thereafter as Spain redirected slave imports to
its other American colonies. Traditional chronologies of Mexican slavery
suggest that the 1640s also marked the beginning of a long period of quantitative and qualitative decline of slavery in the colony.[10] On the surface it
appears logical to assume that the ancillary importance of slavery to the
colonial economy compared to that of native labor and the increasingly
large free majority among Afro-Mexicans after 1650 may have created a
situation ripe for slaves to reject their subordinated social position. This
study reexamines and recasts those assumptions.

Two significant moments of slave resistance in the 1760s—the mass
flight of 1763 and the foundation of the free town of Amapa by runaway
slaves in 1769—mark the endpoint of this study. Ending my exploration in the 1760s allows me to consider slavery in a context that predates
the social, cultural, and ideological impact of the Bourbon reforms,
the Atlantic revolutions, and nineteenth-century abolitionism.[11] Many
studies explore slavery during the late eighteenth and nineteenth centuries, at a time when the Atlantic revolutions and abolitionist rhetoric had
provided slaves a "lexicon of liberation" with which to challenge their
social position in new ways.[12] How might slaves have conceptualized and
contested their oppression before this language of liberty was available is
a key question considered herein.

A Model of Master-Slave Relations

A fundamental question in slave studies is how to reconcile the extent
of the master's power with the ability of slaves to influence and limit the
application of that power. That tension between master power and slave
agency informs the history of slave labor, slave community formation,

and master-slave relations that are at the heart of this study. A reconsideration of Gramscian notions of cultural hegemony allows for the treatment of master-slave relations as a part of a larger process of the negotiation of both mastery and servitude in New Spain.[13] According to T. J. Jackson Lears, cultural hegemony is presumed to be the spontaneous consent given by subordinate groups to the general direction imposed on social life by the powerful. The use of the term "consent" may convey the impression that subordinate or dominated groups were passively resigned to their situation. Lears, however, understands cultural hegemony as providing a means by which to resolve the apparent contradiction between the power wielded by dominant groups and the relative cultural autonomy of the subordinate groups they victimize. Additionally, it allows for the reconciliation of dissent and discontent on the part of subordinated groups with other actions that appear to undergird power structures and reinforce their own subordination.[14] The question becomes, however, if, and if so, how, dominated groups like slaves influenced power in practice.

James Scott, for one, questions the applicability of hegemony to discussions of slavery on the grounds that it reduces the enslaved to a position of submissive acquiescence to their own domination. He hypothesizes that the lack of public displays of dissent and discontent on the part of subordinate classes, which could be construed as strong evidence of the pervasiveness of elite power, does not mean that such dissent did not exist. Rather, he argues that in the case of slavery, the power differential between masters and slaves was so great that such public displays would likely result in harsh punishment, disruption of families, and potentially even death. Slaves, knowing this, hid their frustrations from their masters. Scott cites an example of a slave woman who watched in silence as her master viciously beat her daughter. In this instance the slave's silence was evidence of the extreme power of the master. Her recognition that any reaction would likely have resulted in increased violence against herself or her child determined her response. According to a white governess, once her master had left the room, the slave woman condemned the attack as unwarranted and said that her master would face eternal damnation for his cruelties. For Scott, her outburst highlights slaves' ability to reject master power (albeit through the imposed discourse of Christianity). The threat of violence did not negate the possibility of this woman, or any other slave for that matter, rejecting the legitimacy or justice of their masters' actions in their hearts and minds.[15]

Scott, in his critique of hegemony, proposes a new theoretical approach for the study of extreme power relations through the exploration of what he calls "public" and "private" transcripts. Public transcripts constitute the public performance of mastery and subordination. This includes "rituals of hierarchy, deference, speech, punishment, and humiliation" and ideological justification for inequalities such as the "public religious and political worldview of the dominant elite." Private, or hidden, transcripts comprise the offstage responses and rejoinders to the public transcripts articulated and expressed within the cultural autonomy described by Lears. Private transcripts occupy a continuum from simple criticisms about the oppression(s) inherent in relations of power on the one hand to revolutionary ideologies or counterhegemonies on the other.[16]

The creation of private transcripts was possible precisely because masters weren't capable of compelling the "passive resignation" of their slaves. While the elite does determine, in large part, what is acceptable on the public stage it is rarely successful in completely imposing its cultural vision on subordinated groups. Further, the dominated never completely internalize ideologies imposed on them. For example, Carlo Ginzburg argues that in premodern Western Europe, imposed dominant cultural frameworks were filtered through the materialism of the experiences of daily life in the construction of subaltern cultural visions. This "filtering" process led to the articulations of elite and nonelite cultural understanding.[17] Similarly, slaves reinterpreted imposed systems of power through their lived experiences. These inconsistencies, then, highlight the potential for struggle between unequals to flesh out rule in the dynamics of everyday relations.

Yet even if we allow for complete public deference in the face of power in one instance (i.e., the public transcript) and complete or partial repudiation of the social order on the other (i.e., the private transcript), such actions and ideologies cannot coexist without interacting.[18] In Scott's example, the slave mother's apparently passive response to the beating of her daughter represents the operation of the public transcript. Her subsequent outburst is evidence of slaves' ability to privately reject the application of power. The existence of such private transcripts highlights the lack of complete ideological domination by the elite, but in Scott's construction they do not appear to provide the subordinate groups with agency to affect the nature of rule.[19] How then can we explain the willingness of the slaves whose stories open this introduction to publicly reject what they considered to be the illegitimate use of master power? That question can be answered by following Michel Foucault in treating power as dynamic and relational rather than as something exercised or imposed. Power relations are inherently imbued with "innumerable points of confrontation, focuses of instability, each of which has its own risks of conflict, of struggles, and of an at least temporary inversion of power relations."[20] Thus, "power is not something possessed or wielded by powerful agents, because it is co-constituted by those who support and resist it."[21] Slaves proved perfectly capable of challenging the applications of power in public. They understood that their masters also lived within structures of power (law and religion, for example) that constrained their actions. Slaves and masters also had distinctive and often contradictory visions of legitimate social behavior for both. The unequal interactions of those differing conceptions resulted in an ambiguous and ever-changing consensus on what constituted acceptable actions for slaves and their masters.[22] This is not to deny that master-slave relations were a form of personal rule that included great latitude for "arbitrary and capricious" behavior by masters but rather to say that slaves helped to define what was arbitrary and capricious.[23] Thus, the cultural hegemony of slavery could be understood as the unequal interaction between the private transcripts of the oppressor and the oppressed in a public space bounded, in this case, by the loose confines of Spanish imperial law and Catholic religious tradition.[24]

Slave owners vigorously protested any attempt by colonial authorities to interject themselves into master-slave relations. They saw such interventions as violations of their right to dominion over their slaves granted by Spanish imperial law. Therefore, we might begin with the supposition that in their most private thoughts masters longed for a slavery that fits Orlando Patterson's model of "social death." Patterson describes slavery as "one of the most extreme forms of domination, approaching the limits of total power from the viewpoint of the master, and of total powerlessness from the point of view of the slave."[25] While he speaks of slavery as *approaching* total domination, he defines slaves as possessing no power, no independent social existence outside that of their master.

We might be tempted to assume that slaves, for their part, longed for the freedom to reap the fruits of their labor and for control over their physical mobility, over the form and nature of their families, and their cultural beliefs and that they desired to escape their servitude.[26] Such a vision of what slaves wanted largely rejects the idea that slaves were ideologically dominated, however, since it was only in the late eighteenth-century Atlantic world, with the fluorescence of Enlightenment ideologies on liberty, that an abstract notion of freedom became dominant. Therefore it may be more fruitful to treat their private transcripts as a representation of their desire to *expand* their control over labor, family, cultural beliefs, and even access to manumission and as aimed at working the system to their "least disadvantage."[27] Slave agency, therefore, should not be measured against attempts to challenge the ideological justifications of an institution that few people, slaves and nonslaves alike, had yet decided was wrong or immoral anywhere in the Atlantic world.[28] The dynamics of power between masters and slaves played out through the unequal interactions of these private transcripts.

"*Damned Notions*" relies heavily on trials from civil, ecclesiastical, and Inquisition courts. Although testimonies and petitions in such cases were made in contexts where language, tone, and style were framed to meet official expectations, they provide important access to the everyday experiences of colonial subjects precisely because they include the (filtered) voices of average members of colonial society, including slaves. These sources are multivalent and multivocal. By investigating the differing viewpoints of the various actors within them, we can begin to demonstrate the articulation of an unspoken, ambiguous social consensus on the treatment of slaves, labor expectations, the limits of master power, and acceptable behavior for both masters and slaves. These sources allow for the combined exploration of the history of race and identity *and* of the specific lived experience of slavery for bondspeople. The confrontations between masters and slaves over work, marriage, community, and cultural identity were as much disputes over boundaries as were master-slave conflicts over physical punishment, flight, rebellion, and access to freedom.

Organization of the Book

What follows is a series of detailed explorations of the lived experience of slavery as it relates to such concerns as labor, family, cultural community, individual and collective agency, and liberation. The nature of the sources prevents the establishment of a single overarching narrative that would unite all of these concerns seamlessly, yet each element provides insight into the experiences of slaves as individuals and as a group, and collectively they provide a more integrated picture of slavery in colonial Mexico.

Because labor so profoundly shaped the slave experience, I begin in chapter 1 by examining changes in the demand for slaves following the end of the regular slave trade in 1640. In New Spain, the primary demand for slaves between 1600 and 1750 came from two very different industries—sugar and woolen textiles produced in *obrajes* (woolen textile mills). Both were fundamental to the health of the colonial economy, although they largely serviced internal, rather than export, markets.[29] The nature of the labor demands of these two industries fundamentally affected the lives of slaves. This chapter also explores the demographic changes within the slave population and considers whether it could have reproduced at rates high enough to continue to meet colonial demand for slaves after the close of the slave trade in 1640.

Chapters 2 and 3 take up the question of the extent to which slaves across the colonial period were able to create and maintain distinctive cultural communities. The two chapters in combination complicate a major theme in the cultural history of Mexico—*mestizaje* (miscegenation)—and further clarify larger debates on slave ethnic and racial identities in the African diaspora. Ever since the publication of José Vasconcelos's influential *La raza cósmica*, which argues that racism and discrimination would lose force as a result of miscegenation, the cultural history of Mexico has largely been understood as the intermixture of Spanish and Indian cultural traits resulting in the racially mixed population and hybrid culture that make Mexico distinct.[30]

That vision has shaped much of the scholarship on the cultural history of New Spain and the place of *negros* (blacks) and *mulatos* (mulattoes) within it. Afro-Mexicans were the second largest nonindigenous racial group in New Spain throughout much of the colonial period. In the middle of the eighteenth century nearly one in nine colonials and one in three non-Indians were of Afro-Mexican heritage.[31] Yet Vasconcelos viewed their contributions to the construction of Mexican culture as negligible.[32] Most scholars have assumed that blacks and mulattoes, like all other lower-class Mexicans with the exception of Indians, shared a single mestizo culture.[33] These studies do not consider the possibility that Afro-Mexicans saw themselves as a culturally distinct part of the great *casta* (racially mixed, non-Spanish) middle.[34] On the other hand, there has been a dramatic increase in attention paid to the themes of ethnicity, race, and identity within the African diaspora and particularly in New Spain in the recent past. Through the consideration of popular culture and Afro-Mexican engagement with colonial institutions like marriage, confraternities, and militias, these works explore of the implications of blackness in the colony, adding much to our understanding of the distinct experiences of blacks and mulattoes.[35] *"Damned Notions of Liberty"* engages and extends these considerations of identity by exploring the evolution of Afro-Mexican slave cultural communities.

Chapter 2 traces the construction of, and transformations within, the distinct Afro-Mexican cultural community through slave marriage in Mexico City and the silver mining cities of Guanajuato and San Luis Potosí. Marriage and the selection of *testigo/padrino* (wedding witnesses) by slaves highlight the creation and evolution of social networks based first in the ethnic and later in the racialized identities of Afro-Mexican slaves. Chapter 3 considers the creation of a distinctively Afro-Mexican cultural vision. Inquisition records for *curanderismo* (curing magic) from the eighteenth century provide evidence of variations within *novohispano* (New Spanish) popular culture. Those variations, largely unexplored in the ethnohistory of New Spain, correspond to the racialized social networks found in the marriage patterns discussed in chapter 2. A comparison of the beliefs and practices among black and mulatto curers with those of their mestizo and Spanish counterparts suggests that Afro-Mexican curanderismo represented a variant of popular Mexican cultural beliefs that was fundamentally influenced by West Central African conceptions of magic, illness, and healing, even as European and indigenous elements were clearly incorporated into it.

Specific considerations of slavery and the experiences of the enslaved are the focus of the second half of the book. For although one cannot underestimate the importance of race and identity in the African diaspora, as Stuart Schwartz reminds us, the slave community was like no other, and we must take into account "the essential and distinctive facts of the slaves' lives that served as a backdrop to all their actions and constrained their lives."[36] To date only Colin Palmer's *Slaves of the White God: Blacks in Mexico, 1570–1640*, published in 1976, has focused exclusively on slavery in New Spain. Therefore, the final three chapters take up the specific exploration of slave identity and the negotiation of mastery and slavery in the colony.

Testimony from Inquisition records relating to blasphemy and witch-craft, explored in chapter 4, highlight that slaves recognized their deni-grated social position and some of the various legal, religious, and social norms that limited master authority. Because trial transcripts include testimony from masters, slaves, and other witnesses, it is possible to compare the perspectives of various groups and thereby learn what their idealized notions of master-slave relations were. This allows us to envision how the power of masters operated in practice and how it was mitigated by slave agency. The extreme level of physical violence described in these case files underscores its centrality to master-slave relations and demonstrates a power differential that favored masters. Despite this brutality, however, slaves were seldom beaten into submission. Rather, they continued to press back against their masters, by and large calling into question even the legitimate employment of physical coercion.

Chapter 5 considers cases of individual runaways alongside two exceptional cases of collective slave resistance from the 1760s to explore the causes and implications of slave flight and rebelliousness. The mass flight of 1763 frames this discussion, which also includes an exploration of a series of slave rebellions and the creation of runaway-slave communities in Córdoba between 1735 and 1769 that culminated with the formation of Amapa, a free town populated by runaway ex-slaves. The issues that led to flight or rebellion were very similar to those that animated the master-slave conflicts I discuss in chapter 4.

Finally, chapter 6 builds on the foundations established in the pre-ceding chapters to explore the complicated relationship between slavery and freedom for the enslaved before the Atlantic revolutions introduced a lexicon of liberation into master-slave relations.[37] The consideration of some seven hundred individual manumissions from Mexico City and Guanajuato suggests that the motivating factor behind the liberation of a significant majority of bondspeople was the nature of the long-term and personal (though not necessarily sexual) relationship between slaves and their masters. These manumissions were typically imitated by mas-ters rather than achieved by slaves pursuing or purchasing their own liberation. A full account of manumission, it is thus revealed, must take into consideration the complicated realm of master power and master-slave relations.

Spanish law circumscribed the sociopolitical implications of manu-mission by defining it as a possibility, not a right, and by making access to freedom almost solely the prerogative of mastery. Thus, chapter 6 also explores the extent to which Spanish colonial institutions prevented slaves from pressing for their own liberation. It assesses the ideological implications of the boundaries established by those institutions with respect to the ability of slaves to conceptualize and articulate a fully developed notion of freedom. The lawsuits initiated by slaves to force their masters to free them illuminate the limited nature of the vocabulary about freedom available to slaves in pressing for their own personal liberation. Those limitations of vocabulary and the lack of institutional spaces available to slaves within which to proclaim a general desire for liberation, in turn, help to explain why slaves who challenged master authority in other contexts did not identify "freedom" as a primary motivation for their exercise of agency.

Our basic modern Western assumption that liberty, as the antithesis of slavery, is natural, innate to all human beings, potentially clouds our understanding of slaves' agency in the sixteenth, seventeenth, and early eighteenth centuries.[38] We must resist situating the history of the enslaved narrowly within the larger metanarratives of how Atlantic slavery was superseded by freedom. In so resisting, we can avoid treating slave agency as part of a broader history of attempts of the enslaved to gain their freedom.[39]

CHAPTER I

Slave Labor
Demand, Demography, and Work Experiences

✣ IN 1650, DIEGO DE LA CRUZ, AN ENSLAVED MULATTO, FACED charges before the Holy Office of the Inquisition for falsely accusing another slave of practicing Judaism. In the course of his trial, Diego testified about the range of occupations in which his various owners had employed him. His experiences provide an excellent preview of the multiple areas of the colonial economy where slaves could be found. He had worked in a variety of *tiendas* (small shops or plaza stands) selling wine, peanuts, and cacao and as an *aguador* (water vendor) selling potable water on the streets of the viceregal capital. He had also pooled his resources with another slave to open a clothing stall on the main plaza. His previous owner had also threatened to send Diego to an ingenio as a reprimand for being a thief, a liar, and a drunkard. Instead, that owner sold Diego to Padre Bartolomé de Valfermoso, who subsequently placed Diego in a textile mill as punishment for running away. Obrajes were like jails; workers, both slave and free, were locked in and not permitted to leave after hours.[1] The structured regimen and harsh working conditions of obraje life as well as the inability to leave were unbearable for Diego after having enjoyed mobility and control over his own labor. Thus, he falsely accused Pascual de Rojas of practicing Judaism to gain a chance to plead his case before the Inquisition. He hoped to use that audience to beg to be removed from the obraje and sold back to Mexico City to be near his wife.[2]

The experience of slavery was largely defined by the nature and quality of work. The working lives of slaves—the various occupations they filled, the structure of the work they performed, and locations and locales where they labored—fundamentally shaped the lived experience of individual bondsmen and bondswomen.[3] Therefore, the logical starting point for any inquiry into slaves' perspectives on slavery in New Spain must be the workplace. Providing a slave's-eye view of the institution requires an exploration of the demand for enslaved labor in the colony and of the work experiences of slaves in those industries that relied on them. Supplying such an analysis will also allow us to begin to assess the ideological strength of slavery after the close of the slave trade in 1640. The three most important areas in which slaves could be found within the colonial economy after 1640, which Diego's story highlights, were sugar plantations, woolen textile mills, and urban labor markets.

Demand

The growth of the importance of slaves to the colonial economy is generally tied to a late sixteenth-century labor crisis created by a significant dwindling of the indigenous population in New Spain. The simultaneous expansion of silver mining, the early stages in the development of the sugar and woolen textiles industries, and the growth of urban centers made access to a dependable labor force a central concern. The Spanish initially relied on Indian laborers. However, the native population experienced a precipitous decline from between nine to twenty-five million prior to conquest to a nadir of approximately one million somewhere between 1605 and 1630.[4] In response, colonial authorities increasingly restricted access to forced indigenous labor over time. The enslavement of Indians was prohibited in 1542. Shortly thereafter, in 1549, the crown also abolished the labor requirement of the *encomienda*. Under the encomienda, a labor grant given to meritorious Spaniards by the crown, native villages were required to supply the *encomendero* with a fixed number of workers for certain days during the year. Following the abolition of personal service, the crown continued to require native communities to provide a portion of their labor to the state. This forced labor, known as the *repartimiento de labores*, was then allocated by colonial authorities to sugar production, mining, and public works.[5] In 1599, the crown prohibited sugar producers from receiving repartimiento labor.[6] Similarly, two royal decrees dated November 24, 1601, and May 27, 1603, attempted to ban Indians from obrajes and suggested that *obrajeros* (obraje owners) replace them with slaves.[7] Thus, the earliest forms of labor recruitment used by sugar and obrajes had been restricted or eliminated by 1605.

Spanish attempts to stem the indigenous demographic decline coupled with their long-term experience with African slavery in Iberia led them to import African slaves to meet growing labor needs. Demand for slaves in New Spain increased gradually between 1519 and 1580 and then meteorically between 1580 and 1640. Slave labor facilitated the expansion of silver, sugar, and woolen textile production. These industries proved central to the transition from a subsistence to a market economy in New Spain prior to 1640.[8] Nearly 150,000 slaves were imported into the colony by that date, a number that was surpassed only by Brazil and that represented nearly half of all slaves introduced to Spanish America in this period.[9]

Contrary to the consensus that slavery began to decline shortly after the close of the slave trade in 1640, demand in central New Spain appears to have remained fairly constant well into the eighteenth century.[10] Sugar production, which was dependent on slavery prior to 1640, continued to be so for nearly a century following the close of the slave trade.[11] That demand was matched by the reliance on slave labor in the obraje sector that began in the early seventeenth and extended well into the eighteenth century as well.[12] Slaves also came to fill numerous roles in the urban economies of New Spain, either remitting *jornales* (day wages) to or working directly for their masters. Unlike slaves in most of the Americas, slaves in New Spain did not become the primary labor force in the dominant export economy—silver.[13]

The novohispano nonslave labor market was defined by a complicated timeline in which "private employment" in the form of debt peonage came to supplant forced indigenous labor by the mid-seventeenth century. Historians agree that "the sequence of agricultural labor—encomienda, repartimiento, and private employment [debt peonage]—may be understood as a progressive adjustment to a shrinking labor supply" over time.[14] The inability of sugar planters and obrajeros to draw sufficient workers via wages forced them to turn to debt peonage "to control the scarce free-labor force."[15] Debt peonage, the final stage in the evolution of the Indian labor market, became dominant in the seventeenth and eighteenth centuries.[16] Similarly, obrajes also turned to coercion in the form of enclosure (they would lock workers in factories and deny them the freedom to leave at the end of the workday) in response to the weak free labor market.[17] The importance of African slavery as a bridge between forced indigenous labor in the sixteenth century and the creation of a free labor market that favored employers that characterized the late colonial period has been underappreciated up to this point.[18]

A complex combination of forces was required to create that late colonial "buyers' market" for labor. By the eighteenth century, hacienda expansion and population growth had produced a land shortage for the peasant population, which drove free workers into the labor market in numbers large enough to change conditions in favor of employers.[19] Only when that transition occurred were sugar and woolens producers in central New Spain able to abandon slavery. Producers who had come to rely on slaves before 1640 continued to do so longer than it has generally been believed precisely because of the weakness of the free labor market.

The most persistent demand for African slave labor came from the sugar sector, which was produced on two scales in New Spain. Most common were smaller units called *trapiches*. These relied on animal-powered mills and averaged approximately three to ten slaves.[20] Ingenios, which were larger producers, used much more productive water-powered mills. The haciendas associated with them cultivated much more sugarcane and used larger numbers of slaves. The use of African slave labor in large-scale sugar production began in earnest in Jalapa and Orizaba in the modern state of Veracruz. Sugar production then spread, first to central New Spain (predominantly the modern state of Morelos) and eventually to Córdoba, Veracruz, during the sixteenth- and early seventeenth-centuries.[21]

The three dominant sugar-producing regions in colonial Mexico—eastern Veracruz (Orizaba and Jalapa), western Veracruz (Córdoba), and central New Spain (largely Morelos)—followed distinct trajectories in terms of the general demand for slave labor and the timing of its decline in favor of Indian labor. Patrick Carroll persuasively argues that the growth of the indigenous and *casta* (racially mixed) populations in eastern Veracruz allowed sugar producers to transition to free labor prior to the middle of the seventeenth century.[22] In Córdoba, however, where the sugar industry was not in place until 1642, slaves constituted the primary labor force and would not be replaced by free workers until the late eighteenth century.[23]

Central New Spain took an intermediate path between eastern and western Veracruz. In Morelos, the number of ingenios in operation increased from thirteen in 1600 to forty-three in 1700.[24] As sugar production expanded in the seventeenth century, the demand for slave labor increased as well. Well into the eighteenth century, however, the average number of slaves on the ingenios of central New Spain remained fairly stable. Individual ingenio censuses from 1648 to 1686 suggest that plantations in central Mexico maintained 81 slaves on average, not including the 240 slaves from the Jesuit ingenio Xochimancas. From 1687 to 1724, plantations in the same region averaged 75 slaves. Those plantations still held approximately 68 slaves for the period from 1725 to 1763, excluding the sizable Jesuit holdings at Xochimancas (145 slaves in 1736), at Palapa (256 slaves in 1750), or at San Francisco Quautepec (302 slaves in 1729). What these figures imply is a slow decline in size of the slave labor forces associated with sugar production across the late seventeenth and eighteenth centuries in central New Spain.[25] Slaves there appear to have remained the core of ingenio labor forces, particularly among skilled workers, and were supplemented by free workers well into the eighteenth century.[26]

The other major colonial industry that came to rely on slaves was woolens production in obrajes, which were labor-intensive mills where workers processed, spun, and wove raw wool into textiles for sale in internal markets. Obrajes were essential to the colonial economy. The task of clothing the colony and providing all of the necessary textile goods (bags, blankets, etc.) for industries such as mining, ranching, and sugar fell to local industry until the arrival of English textiles near the end of the eighteenth century.[27] New Spain's obrajes did not experience technological innovations that significantly increased productivity. The mills served primarily as a means of stockpiling the materials and labor needed to produce textiles. That centralization served to cut costs and increase profitability.[28]

The consensus among historians is that slaves were too costly for obrajeros, and yet slavery proved essential to obrajes in the two most important centers of woolen textile production—Mexico City/Coyoacan and Querétaro.[29] Appraisals, censuses, and inspections of obrajes in central New Spain, while limited in number, reveal very few indigenous workers and fairly large and relatively stable slave populations in the great majority of obrajes.[30] For example, when colonial authorities inspected thirteen textile mills in Mexico City in 1670 to investigate abuses against indigenous workers they found only fifty Indians in total, an average of approximately four per obraje.[31] A similar *visita* (inspection) of obrajes in Coyoacan from 1703 listed only twelve Indian and convict workers in three inspected textile mills.[32] Relying on estimates that the average-sized obraje in central New Spain employed forty to sixty workers, we can conclude the Indians found in the 1670 and 1703 inspections represented less than 10 percent of workers in average-sized textile mills.[33] These visitas, therefore, do not suggest that obrajes relied on native workers in the middle colonial period.

In the 1670 visita of Mexico City's obrajes, inspectors examined an obraje owned by Baltasar de Sierra in the barrio of Santa María la Redonda. Whereas they found just six Indians working there, all convicts, an appraisal of the same property in 1679 found twenty-three slaves.[34] While neither document indicates the total size of the workforce, the two in combination suggest that slaves provided the bulk of that labor force, supplemented by Indians in the 1670s.

Colonial officials also inspected the six major obrajes in Coyoacan, on the outskirts of the viceregal capital, in 1660. Coyoacan was an important colonial woolens-producing region owing to its fertile soil, abundant waterpower, and proximity to the markets and finance capital of Mexico City.[35] Slaves were found in every obraje and, according to Gonzalo Aguirre Beltrán, accounted for 59 percent of all workers indentified in the visita.[36] In the obraje owned by Tomás de Contreras, 102 of the 125 workers were slaves. The remaining 23 laborers were apprentices, wageworkers, or convicts. At the turn of the eighteenth century, the Contreras obraje had 100 slaves.[37] Similarly, the inspectors reported that 92 of 114 workers in the obraje of Antonio de Ansaldo were slaves in 1660.[38] Inspections of the Ansaldo obraje in 1693 and 1695 listed 46 and 42 slaves, respectively. The sources do not indicate if changes in the number of slaves in these obrajes were due to the decreasing importance of slavery or a shrinking of the total labor force.[39]

The inspectors also visited the obraje owned by Juan Gallardo de Céspedes in 1660 but did not include a census of workers. The obraje employed some thirty-five slaves a year earlier when Gallardo de Céspedes purchased it. Although facing significant financial difficulties in 1666, the

Gallardo obraje still maintained twenty-one slaves.[40] Inspectors also visited the obraje belonging to Pedro de Sierra, the brother of the aforementioned Baltasar de Sierra. Again, the visita did not include a census of laborers. Yet when Sierra's heirs sold the obraje forty years later in 1700 the sale included thirty-four slaves.[41] Thus, four of the six obrajes inspected in Coyoacan in 1660 had sizeable slave workforces during the late seventeenth century.

Large-scale, slave-reliant obrajes also dotted other areas on the outskirts of Mexico City. In 1716 Capitán Francisco Pérez Novas employed fifty slaves in his Tacuba obraje. In 1703, Doña Agustina Álvarez de Casasola's Tacuba obraje, although smaller in scale, included fourteen slaves.[42] Three years later, Blas Mexía de Vera purchased thirty-six obraje slaves from the heirs of Regidor Domingo de Apresa y Gándara in Puebla and sent them directly in his mill in Mixcaoc.[43] A number of vertically integrated obraje/sheep-ranching enterprises found around Mexico City also relied on slave labor. Capitán Blas de Mata and his wife, Doña María Paray, established a sheep ranch and obraje that employed thirty-eight slaves in Huichiapa, Xilotepec, some twenty leagues from Mexico City in 1673.[44] Seventy-nine slave women and children worked within the obraje attached to Santa Lucía, a Jesuit ranching estate, in 1751.[45]

In medium to large-scale textile mills in and around Mexico City, therefore, slaves and not wage-earning Indians constituted the bulk of obraje workers by the 1630s, a pattern that extended well into the first half of the eighteenth century. A similar chronology with respect to reliance on enslaved labor applies for obrajes in Querétaro, the other major woolens-producing center.[46] The dominance of slaves after the 1630s was the result of a colony-wide transition away from the use of waged indigenous labor in obrajes through the mid-eighteenth century. Owing to slow population growth and the shortage of labor, "free wage labor and market incentives could not bring sufficient labor to most obrajes."[47] Slavery, therefore, proved an ideal match for the particular labor demands of obrajes until the rapid decline of slavery in the eighteenth century.[48]

Price trends for slaves throughout New Spain support the contention that demand remained fairly constant into the first half of the eighteenth century. Slave prices in the colony went through three distinct phases. Prices were highest during the first phase, (1580–1640), when adult slaves sold for over 400 pesos. Prices peaked in the 1630s and then settled at about 350 pesos for an adult in the 1650s, remaining fairly constant into the first decades of the eighteenth century. In the final phase, beginning sometime around the 1720s, prices decreased dramatically, falling to about 175 pesos for an adult male by 1750 in Mexico City. Prices in Guanajuato and in central New Spain seem to have been slightly higher than they were in the viceregal capital (see table 1.1).

While falling prices are often taken to indicate decreasing demand for slaves in New Spain, the market for slaves was much more complicated. Although slave prices declined across the seventeenth century, slaves in Morelos may have been more valuable to planters at the end of that century than at the beginning. Ward Barrett and Stuart Schwartz, comparing average slave prices to the market value of sugar in 1600, 1700, and 1800, found that the value of an adult slave was equivalent to 755 kilograms of sugar in 1600. By 1700, however, a similar slave was worth the equivalent of 1,564 kilograms of sugar. Based on data for Mexico City, the average price of an adult slave decreased from approximately 400–420 pesos in 1600 to 335–350 pesos in 1700. Although the average market

TABLE 1.1.   Unskilled Adult Slave Prices in New Spain (in Pesos), 1600–1750

	Mexico City		Guanajuato		Central New Spain	
	Men	Women	Men	Women	Men	Women
1600	420	400	--	--	--	--
1625	390	360	--	--	--	--
1650	350	380	--	--	--	--
1675	349	374	--	--	393	392
1700	335	370	321	340	305	308
1725	242	267	240	313	--	--
1750	175	220	170	246	222	222

Sources Mexico City: Bowser, "The Free Persons of Color in Mexico City and Lima," 336–37; Valdés, "The Decline of Slavery in Mexico," 172. The data for 1675 and 1725 represents every available slave sale in the AHN for those years. Guanajuato: the data includes all available slave sales in the AHG, PC for the periods 1699–1701 and 1748–50. The data for 1725 represents an average of data taken for 1719–21 and 1729–31. Central New Spain: table 1.4A in the appendix to this book. The 1675 data is taken from the 1670–99 dataset, the 1700 data from the 1700–29, and the 1750 data from the 1730–59. The Valdés and Bowser data is for black slaves, while that from Mexico City in 1675 and 1725, Guanajuato, and Central New Spain includes blacks and mulattoes.

price of a slave decreased nearly 20 percent, the value of that slave, cal-culated in kilograms of sugar, more than doubled in the same period. By 1800, however, the value of a slave had fallen to the equivalent of 615 kilo-grams of sugar, slightly less than what it had been in 1600.[49] The prices of slaves appear to have slowly decreased, while their value, vis-à-vis the products they produced, seems to have increased over time through the early eighteenth century, before declining thereafter. What these trends suggest is that by the time demand was increasing in the mid-seventeenth century from sugar plantations and obrajes in central New Spain, slave prices had normalized from their previous extreme high levels. That change was likely instigated by declining demand from silver mines and from sugar producers in regions like Orizaba and Jalapa.

Obrajes, in particular, did not have to purchase slaves in order to secure enslaved labor. In and around Mexico City, at least, there was a fairly active market in slave hiring. For example, eight of the eighteen slaves interviewed in the Melchor Díaz de Posadas obraje during the 1660 inspection of the Coyoacan obrajes were contracted. The estate of Baltasar de Sierra paid Francisco de Montes, the master of a slave named Andres, 72 pesos (calculated at 1.5 pesos per month) for four years of service upon the sale of the obraje in 1678. When Juan de Salas, a mulatto slave, was sentenced to ten years labor in an obraje by the Inquisition the obrajero, Diego de Contreras, signed a contract with Juan's owner that stipulated he would receive 2.5 pesos per month for the duration of Juan's sentence.[50] Thus, an obraje owner could supplement his or her own slave labor force with rented slaves at prices that were comparable to or even cheaper than free wage labor, which at the time cost about 3 pesos per month plus a food ration.[51]

On the surface, the continued reliance on slave labor by both sugar planters and textile producers after the end of the slave trade may seem illogical, particularly in light of the growth of the free casta and indig-enous population after 1640. The initial purchase price of slaves and the costs associated with maintaining them (food, clothing, etc.) would seem to make slaves an inefficient source of labor. Yet ingenios and obrajes kept sizable slaveholdings well into the eighteenth century, and that is in part because, as I've noted, the nature of the colonial wage economy was quite weak well into the eighteenth century. This meant that planters and obraje owners could not recruit sufficient numbers of dependable and skilled laborers through wages.[52] In that context, slavery may have been attractive because it guaranteed a comparatively immobile and skilled, or at least experienced, workforce. This recruitment problem, along with Spaniards' biases regarding the comparative value of slave and Indian labor and their sense that slaves could be worked harder than Indians, appears to have made slaves more attractive as laborers for longer than we might have expected.

Demography

The suggestion that demand for slave labor did not begin to decline simultaneously with the end of the slave trade creates a paradox—how was that demand met? The historiographical consensus is that "slavery in Mexico depended for its survival principally on the slave trade and not on internal reproduction [and that] the sexual imbalance of the slave population—a general ratio of three men to every woman—and the high infant mortality rate made the natural increase of the black population quite difficult."[53] While this might accurately describe the demographic experience of slaves during the era of the slave trade, after 1650 that population appears to have reproduced at rates high enough to meet continuing demand.

A scarcity of sources makes the question of whether the slave population in New Spain experienced natural increase quite difficult to answer. For example, no extant census enumerates the total colonial slave population. The problems created by the lack of such a census are exacerbated by the absence of other sources that speak specifically to general mortality and fertility rates for slaves in the colony. Available sources do allow one to calculate child-women ratios for rural slaves and urban birth rates and thereby provide an initial assessment of slave reproductivity, which in turn should permit the formulation of some hypotheses regarding the demographic fate of Afro-Mexican slavery, specifically whether or not slaves could have experienced long-term natural growth.[54]

The lethal combination of high morality and low fertility among slaves, particularly those on sugar plantations, often produced negative demographic growth.[55] Novohispano sugar-producing slaves, however, appear to have been quite extraordinary in their reproductive capacity. As might be expected, the slave population in central Mexico was marked by significant sex and age imbalances immediately following the end of the slave trade. Censuses from 1648 to 1686 show that the sex ratio was

155 males per 100 females. Children accounted for only 22.4 percent of ingenio slaves in this period. These demographic characteristics suggest a population shaped in large part by planters' preference for purchasing adult males. In the censuses from 1725 to 1763, the sex ratio had improved significantly to 125 men per 100 women, and children accounted for 34.8 percent of slaves on ingenios. This indicates a population shaped largely by natural reproduction. Yet improving sex ratios and the increasing importance of children within the population are not enough to conclude that slaves experienced long-term natural growth.[56]

Perhaps the best way to estimate the potential for natural growth among novohispano slaves is to compare fertility indices (the ratio of children to women of childbearing age) for that population with those of two other slave-owning regions that did experience natural growth in the seventeenth and eighteenth centuries, the Chesapeake region and South Carolina in British North America. The slave population of the tobacco-producing region of the Chesapeake was the first to experience natural growth in the Americas, indications of which can be discerned as early as the 1710s. South Carolina would not experience similar rates of sustained natural growth until the 1790s.[57] Figure 1 compares the slave fertility ratios in New Spain, the Chesapeake, and South Carolina across the seventeenth and eighteenth centuries. The trends evident in figure 1 suggest that slave fertility in New Spain compared favorably with that in the Chesapeake throughout the eighteenth century and was significantly better than that in South Carolina.[58] Therefore, if New Spain and the Chesapeake experienced similar levels of mortality, both adult and child, the slave population of New Spain could have experienced natural growth through reproduction.

Urban slave women in New Spain may also have been extraordinary in their reproductive capacity. Data on intervals between births for slave women from baptismal registers from San Luis Potosí, a major silver-producing region of northern New Spain, between 1652 and 1670 suggest that urban slaves did not suffer from depressed fertility (see table 1.2). In San Luis Potosí, unmarried mothers experienced an average interval between the baptisms of children of 35.7 months. These figures represent time between baptisms and not births. Stillborn children, those who died prior to being baptized, and those baptized in other parishes would not be included in the baptismal register. Because these figures do not record such births, they likely do not correspond precisely to the average interval

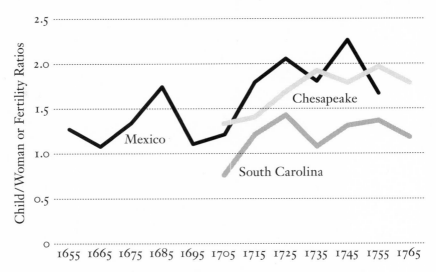

FIGURE I. Fertility Indices for New Spain, the Chesapeake, and
South Carolina. See tables 1.1A–1.3A in the appendix and Morgan,
Slave Counterpoint, 83.

between births. If we exclude all intervals over five years as anomalous,
unmarried slave women averaged 30.4 months between births in the mid-
seventeenth century.[59] Although the data is much less conclusive, married
slave women experienced even shorter intervals between births than did
unmarried women. Again, those patterns are similar to patterns found
among other slave populations that did experience long-term natural
growth.[60]

In summary, slave fertility in both the urban setting of San Luis
Potosí and on the sugar plantations of central New Spain compares
very favorably with that of other slave populations that exhibited natural growth. In fact, the data for New Spain closely mirrors that for the
Chesapeake region of the United States. These trends occurred within the
context of natural growth among the nonslave population. In New Spain,
the population—particularly Indians and castas—experienced an annual
growth rate of 0.39 percent between 1646 and 1742 and a rate of 0.84 percent between 1742 and 1792.[61] These similarities allow for the cautious
conclusion that the slave population *could* have grown naturally in New
Spain by the onset of the eighteenth century and at least reproduced at

TABLE 1.2. Intervals between Baptisms of Children of
Unmarried Slave Women, San Luis Potosí, 1652–70[a]

Interval in Months	No.	%	Cumulative %
12>	2	1%	1%
13–18	13	8%	10%
19–24	25	16%	26%
25–30	35	23%	49%
31–36	32	21%	69%
37–42	16	10%	80%
43–48	11	7%	87%
49–54	0	0%	87%
55–60	4	3%	90%
61–66	2	1%	91%
67–72	2	1%	92%
73–78	5	3%	95%
79–85	4	3%	98%
85+	3	2%	100%
TOTAL	154		

Average Interval 35.7 months

[a]Owing to the low numbers of married slave mothers in the baptismal registers they were not included herein.

Sources: AGN, AGH, Sagrario, San Luis Potosí, libros de bautismos de castas, roll 31593, vol. 1, 1652–78, roll 31593, vol. 3, 1678–89, roll 31614, vol. 2, 1713–24, roll 31615, vol. 6, 1742–52, roll 31616, vol. 6, 1742–52.

rates high enough to meet the ongoing demand for enslaved laborers and to prevent the premature death of slavery.[62]

Labor Experiences for Slaves

Where a slave labored was a primary determinant of the nature of his or her life and of what was expected of individual bondsmen and bondswomen with respect to their family and community. Thus, it is important to explore the nature of labor within the economies where slaves toiled, namely sugar production, textiles, and urban markets. Sugar was distinctive because it required two labor inputs, cultivation and processing, which created the need for two distinct, but often overlapping, workforces. Cultivation required a large labor force but not a significant amount of specialized skill. The processing of sugar in the boiling house, on the other hand, was very delicate and required a great deal of skill and experience. Slaves played key roles in the process of producing refined sugar in central New Spain, where planting and harvest were truly yearlong activities. The majority of slaves owned by sugar haciendas, including children over seven years of age, women, and unskilled men, worked in the fields through the middle of the eighteenth century. A select few adult male slaves, on the other hand, dominated skilled positions in the mill and boiling house.

The planting of cane intensified around November and continued apace through March. At that point, cane planting steadily decreased through to early July, when it reached its nadir. Harvest, on the other hand, was a more constant process, continuing at a fairly constant rate throughout the year.[63] Two sets of instructions for the operation of Jesuit ingenios in New Spain provide some indication of the division of labor among slaves and their daily, weekly, and seasonal labor patterns.[64] Other planters likely followed similar patterns in organizing their labor forces, and thus we can use these instructions to explore the labor patterns and rhythms of sugar slaves. In the face of the yearlong harvest the Jesuit instructions suggested that the mill only be operated three or four days per week. The staggering of planting, cutting, and processing in combination with the limited processing schedule allowed the workforce and necessary livestock to work throughout the year without becoming overtaxed.[65] This moderate and purposeful schedule may help explain why the ingenio slaves of central New Spain may have been fertile enough to experience natural growth.

Fields had to be plowed, planted, irrigated, and hoed a number of times prior to harvest, when mature cane was cut and transported to the mill/boiling house for processing. Once cut, the cane was processed quickly so as to extract maximum syrup and prevent spoilage. Slaves that did not work in the mill/boiling house were divided into four gangs. The first gang cut virgin cane, while a second cut *soca*, or shoots, from previously harvested sugar plants. Ingenios also processed soca, which did not have as high a yield as did virgin cane. The third gang cultivated the fields and presumably irrigated them as well. The fourth gang, composed largely of children, was responsible for planting new cane. Although sugar cultivation is often associated with gang labor, multiple sources indicate that fieldwork in New Spain was allocated by task, and after slaves completed their quotas they remained in the fields until dusk, assisting their compatriots to complete their daily work.[66]

The language of the instructions makes it clear that the majority of fieldworkers were women, reflecting an important transition following the close of the slave trade in 1640. In fact, the Jesuit instructions employed feminine nouns such as *escardadoras* (those who hoe), *cortadoras* (cane cutters), and *mandadoras* (female overseers placed in charge of the field-workers) to describe laborers.[67] The relative significance of women within the field gangs increased over time as they became more important within the general population, as was common throughout the Americas.[68] The relative value of adult women and unskilled men from sugar plantations highlights the central role that enslaved women played in sugar production. Assessed values of the two groups were nearly identical in the appraisals of sugar haciendas in central New Spain after 1670 (see table 1.1).[69] In most plantation societies prices for adult male slaves were approximately 10 percent higher than for females.[70] Yet in those regions that lacked an external supply of slaves, the relative value of women increased compared to that of men, largely owing to a combination of a growing emphasis on their productive and reproductive capacities.[71]

The complexity of sugar refining required skilled laborers, and slaves proved particularly important in filling those positions. "Hacendados preferred to train slaves rather than free workers for these demanding and highly skilled jobs" because planters simply could not afford a high turnover of skilled laborers.[72] Thus, as much as 40–45 percent of adult male slaves owned by sugar plantations had skilled occupations in the seventeenth and eighteenth centuries.[73] Nine censuses from central Mexico in the eighteenth century list the specific occupations of skilled slaves, providing a general sense of their importance within the sugar-making process. All nine had a least one slave *maestro de azúcar* (master sugar maker), who oversaw the entire sugar-making process from milling, boiling, and clarifying to refining. The quality of the sugar, and therefore the price it might fetch on the market, rested on the skill of the sugar master. Every hacienda also listed at least one slave *purgador*, who oversaw the

purification process, the separation of white sugar granules from uncrys-
tallized molasses. Eight of nine haciendas had at least one slave *calderero*,
the most common skill listed in the censuses, who oversaw the boiling of
sugarcane juice to remove water and other impurities. The *mayordomo*,
who supervised the overall operation of the ingenio, was another important position filled by a slave on four of nine haciendas. Similarly, slave
carpenters, who were responsible for the constant repairs required by the
mill and boiling house, were listed on four of nine haciendas. Slaves also
served as the *molinero/moledor*, also known as the *trapichero*, who oversaw
the grinding of cane. This was a delicate process, as overloading the mill
could damage it or at the very least prevent the optimal extraction of
juice. The value of these laborers to sugar production is evident from
average assessed prices for skilled and unskilled slaves. From 1671 to
1760, the average assessed value of a skilled male slave fifteen to forty-
four years of age was 133 percent of that of an unskilled adult male slave
of the same age.[74]

The Jesuits' instructions for Xochimancas outlined an average workday for skilled slaves. At 4 a.m. a bell called them to the mill/boiling
house to grind the cane harvested the previous day. Once milling was
complete, they washed the mill and the tubes that caught the extracted
juice and fed the *caldero* (caldron) used to boil the liquid. On particularly
hot days, slaves cleaned the mill and collection tubes twice to prevent the
extracted juice from spoiling.[75]

The distinction between skilled and unskilled labor had an important
impact on the transition from slave to free labor throughout the eighteenth century. Over time, the growth of the Indian and casta populations made it increasingly feasible to replace the nonskilled slave field
hands with temporary or resident nonslave laborers. Planters continued
to rely on skilled slaves because the level of expertise required in the
sugar-making process, achieved through years of experience, made the
transition to a wage labor force that was both skilled and free much
more difficult. Exactly when that the transition from slave to free skilled
labor took place is difficult to determine. However, "by the end of the
eighteenth century the growing numbers of skilled and disciplined free
workers had led most hacendados to abandon their seventeenth-century
predecessors' preference for slave labor."[76]

The labor needs of sugar production resulted in large, resident slave
populations with increasingly balanced gender ratios and increasing

numbers of children. Each plantation likely developed a distinct slave community, one that was in constant flux as slaves were bought and sold. If the Jesuit instructions speak to larger patterns, the planters of central New Spain did not work their sugar slaves as aggressively as did planters in other sugar-producing regions in the New World, such as Brazil or Barbados.[77] The nature of the various labor inputs required to produce sugar created a clear social hierarchy based on both skill and sex within these slave communities. Additionally, while the nature of work was fairly regimented, slaves were afforded some free time, particularly on Sundays and saints' days celebrated on the individual haciendas. In many ways then, the labor demands of sugar production determined the parameters of the lived experience of slaves who worked therein.

Cloth manufacture was similar to sugar production in that many tasks associated with the production process required a high degree of skill, making a permanent, specialized labor force a necessity. Most slaves over the age of fourteen preformed specific skilled labor in textile mills. Obraje censuses from Mexico City listed slaves as weavers (*tejedores*), weavers' assistants (*lanzaires*), cloth cutters (*tundidores*), dyers, stretcher makers, bobbin boys, tailors, fulling mill operators (*bataneros*), spinners (*hiladores*), *emborradores*, who carded the raw wool to ready it for spinning, *emprimadores* (specialized wool carders who carded for a second time wool that would be spun into fine yarn), and *percheros* (cloth inspectors).[78]

Obrajes earned a well-deserved reputation as loathsome places to live and work. Alexander von Humboldt remarked that visitors to obrajes

> were struck with . . . the unhealthiness of the situation and the bad treatment to which the workers are exposed . . . All appear half naked, covered with rags, meager and deformed. Every workshop resembles a dark prison. The doors . . . remain constantly shut and the workmen are not permitted to quit the house . . . All are unmercifully flogged if they commit the smallest trespass on the order established in the manufactory.[79]

Free and enslaved obraje workers testified on numerous occasions to the cramped, hot and humid, and dangerous work conditions. Vats of boiling dye released noxious chemicals into the air and created an environment that was often depicted as hellish.[80] In describing the normal work routine for obraje slaves, Juan Pablo, an Angolan slave who worked in one of the textile mills that dotted the urban landscape of Mexico City, testified that slaves labored from five o'clock in the morning until dark. Those who failed to finish their daily quota were beaten.[81] Numerous slaves swore that they were in effect prisoners who were prevented from leaving the confines of the obrajes even to see their families or visit their wives. Others complained about the lack of adequate food and clothing and of being forced to sleep in the rooms where they labored. Nearly all the slaves who testified about living conditions in obrajes spoke to the frequent beatings they suffered.

Obraje labor appears to have been particularly difficult for slaves. Obrajeros often attempted to augment production and therefore profits by increasing the workloads of their bondsmen. Free workers were expected to card ten *tareas* (task amount, equivalent to a *libra* or sixteen ounces) of raw wool each day. Carding entailed combing the wool with a wire brush to straighten, strip, and align the fibers of the fleece for spinning.[82] Various slaves testified that obrajeros like Gallardo de Céspedes, Andrés Álvarez de Pliego, and Tomás de Contreras, among others, imposed higher quotas on slaves, forcing them to card fifteen to twenty tareas each day.[83] Some obrajeros also attempted to increase production by forcing slaves to work on Sundays and saints' days despite church prohibition. In the 1650s and 1660s, Antonio Fragoso, Andrés Álvarez de Pliego, and Melchor Díaz de Posadas faced charges in Ecclesiastical or Inquisition courts that they worked their slaves on religious holidays. When similarly accused, Florián de Espinosa admitted working his slaves on religious holidays but defended his actions by insisting that he only required them to finish uncompleted tasks from the previous week and did not assign extra work, which seems unlikely.[84]

Obrajeros also appear to have felt that higher degrees of coercion could be employed against slaves than free workers. Slaves faced types of physical violence that it was not possible to impose on free wage laborers, especially Indians, as masters literally drove their slaves to work harder and faster with the whip. The reality that Afro-Mexican slaves were easier to exploit than Indians may have been due, in part, to the cumulative effect of royal and municipal attempts to curb abuses against the native population in the woolens sector highlighted by the 1601 and 1603 royal decrees. Obrajes were distinct from sugar plantations because the enslaved populations associated with the former were almost exclusively male. This made it much more difficult for the kind of family and community formation evident on ingenios to take place. Similarly, because obrajeros relied on enclosure, their slaves did not enjoy the same physical mobility as did even sugar slaves let alone urban slaves.

The last area of the colonial economy where significant numbers of slaves could be found was in the urban centers. While hard population figures are difficult to come by for the middle colonial period, Colin Palmer estimates that between five thousand and ten thousand slaves lived and labored in Mexico City by the 1640s.[85] There were also significant numbers of slaves in New Spain's provincial cities and mining centers—Puebla, Veracruz, and Guanajuato, for example. Urban slaves, like slaves everywhere in the Americas, were primarily laborers. Certain examples have led historians to conclude that such slaves represented forms of conspicuous consumption, but that does not contradict the fact that the fundamental purpose of owning a slave was to secure labor.[86] Slaves could and did serve as status symbols while making important economic contributions to the household economies of their owners and representing valuable investments at the same time. It is short sighted, perhaps, to see these functions as mutually exclusive. Slaves' labor became increasingly important to the personal economies of artisans, small-scale merchants, and widows, who occupied the middle sectors of the urban economy.

Urban slave labor can be divided into five categories that often overlap. Slaves served as domestic servants or worked as day laborers (*jornaleros*) (day laborers negotiated their own employment and remitted part of their wages to masters). Others labored alongside their owners in their professions or within their businesses. Some earned monies as marketers, and finally, some became skilled laborers, often after having been apprenticed in various trades. The opportunities open to urban slaves varied significantly based on their gender.

As on the sugar plantations, slave women in urban centers were largely excluded from skilled labor. They predominated among occupations traditionally associated with feminine roles and expectations, which included domestic service, wet-nursing and child care, laundry, and cooking.[87] Nearly all of the slaves who described themselves as domestics or personal servants (cooks, coachmen, pages, butlers, etc.) belonged to the elite of New Spain, principally the very wealthy, such as churchmen and state bureaucrats. Convents and nunneries also employed large numbers of slave women as personal servants. A slave could be owned by a convent or monastery and be assigned general domestic chores. Or they could

be owned by individual nuns or novices and serve as their personal servants. Nearly every professed nun and novice in the Convent of Santísima
Señora María de Gracia in Guadalajara had at least one slave servant in
the 1660s.[88] The wealthy often donated one or more of their slaves to
convents or monasteries to serve the confessants in their testaments. For
example, Pedro de Tejada bequeathed his slave Magdalena de Ribera,
and her one-year-old daughter, to Sister María de San Miguel, a nun in
the Convent of Santa Clara in Mexico City.[89] Outside domestic service
slave women were largely limited to vending, working in the tiendas of
their masters, and occasionally serving as unskilled labor in sombrero
and textile factories. There was a much greater variety of employment for
male slaves.

Slave women also served as nannies and wet nurses for the children
of their masters. Doña Catalina Rosel y Lugo rented Juana, a twenty-six-
year-old black slave, from Melchora de los Reyes to serve as a *chichigua*
(wet nurse) for her infant son, Don Joseph Rubiera de Valdez. In return
for Juana's loving care of her son, Doña Catalina purchased the freedom
of Juana's infant son, Juan Lorenzo, for 100 pesos in 1676.[90] As chapter 6
shows, some masters—particularly women—freed slaves in gratitude for
care provided to their children.

A large number of slaves who were not owned by the social and economic elite of New Spain testified that their *oficio*, or occupation, was
"to do what my master orders" or simply "to serve my master." These
responses suggest that slaves served a large number of functions within
their masters' households or businesses. For example, Juliana, the Angolan
slave of Doña María de Ribera, testified that although her primary job was
food shopping and cooking for her master's family, she was also required,
when she was not in the kitchen, to vend foodstuffs on the streets.[91]

It appears that numerous slave women may have turned, or have been
forced to turn, to prostitution, though there is not much direct evidence
of this. The crown certainly believed that masters were forcing slave
women into the streets in various states of undress to prostitute themselves, particularly in the empire's port cities, when it strictly forbade the
practice in 1710. That order charged local political officials and priests
to work to prevent the "scandalous" custom of masters prostituting their
slave women.[92]

Slaves, particularly women, found work vending in the streets and
plazas of New Spain. Clothing and food were among the most significant

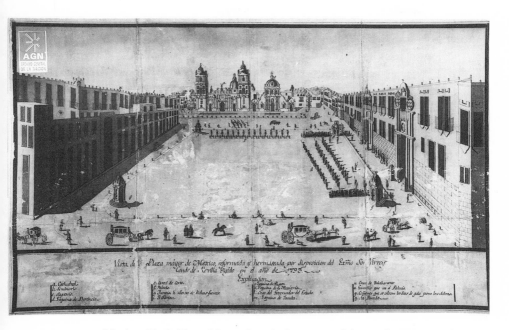

FIGURE 2. Mexico City's Plaza Mayor (1793). Courtesy of the Archivo General de la Nación, Mexico City.

items that slaves sold. María de la Cruz, for example, sold pork on the streets of Puebla de los angeles for her master, a butcher. Leonor Gauspin's slave Josepha sold honey from her home. In the city of Veracruz, Antonia de la Cruz sold candy in the streets. Pedro de Torres received a license for his slaves to sell general merchandise, while Juan Antonio, the slave of Alonso de Encinas, sold cacao and sugar on the streets of Mexico City. And lastly, Josepha de Avila, an orphan, received permission for her slave Simón to vend in the streets of Mexico City in order to support her and her two orphaned sisters.[93]

In addition to slaves who sold various goods in the streets and plazas were those who owned or operated his or her own business, usually a plaza stall. Juliana, a black slave, operated a food stand on the plaza mayor of Mexico City in the 1650s when she wasn't working in her master's home. Mariana de Aldana, a mulatta slave, sold fruit on the main plaza in Antequera, Oaxaca, in the 1650s.[94] Many slaves throughout New Spain operated clothing and blanket stands. Juan de la Cruz, a *chino* (Asiatic) slave, sold oriental silks on the plaza mayor of Mexico City in the 1650s. In the course of a lawsuit against him, Juan testified that he had rented the stall for the previous eight years from Juan Gutiérrez for 15 pesos per year. Before Juan, a black slave had rented this stall. Juan testified that he regularly paid an annual *alcabala* (sales tax) of 30–40 pesos. Given an average annual tax rate of 6 percent, it can be calculated that he sold between 500–670 pesos worth of silks from his plaza stand.[95] To give some perspective, free wage hacienda workers earned about 65 pesos per year, obraje workers earned approximately 36 pesos per year, and the value of a twenty-five-year-old black male slave was between 335 and 350 pesos during the second half of the seventeenth century (see table 1.1).[96] While Juan may have exaggerated the value of his yearly sales, cases such as his suggest that slaves could and did earn substantial wages as vendors and jornaleros in the cities of New Spain.

The occupations of slave jornaleros who were not contracted laborers or vendors are known only in outline. However, it is safe to assume that they filled any number of positions within urban economies. In one case, Agustín de la Cruz earned his jornal working as a peon on the construction of the Catedral Metropolitano in Mexico City.[97] Entertainment was another area in which slaves may have been able to earn their jornal. For example, Miguel Antonio de Luz purchased his freedom in 1742 using money he had earned as a musician.[98]

Slaves also provided crucial labor for masters who owned tiendas and plaza stalls. In 1660, Francisco López, a confectioner, employed his slave Nicolás Ramos in his tienda to sell candies. Similarly, Diego de la Cruz, whose story opened this chapter, worked in numerous types of tiendas for his different owners. Baltasar de los Reyes, a Congo slave owned by Carlos de la Fuente, labored daily without supervision in his master's tienda in Zacatecas.[99] The ability to work in a tienda or operate a plaza stand suggests a significant level of cultural integration on the part of slaves. They obviously had to speak Spanish and be knowledgeable about money and weights and measures.

One last example of a tienda slave underscores the value that such slaves could have for their masters and their families. In 1648, the Inquisition seized Margarita, Hernando Utrera's slave, pending a suit filed by Juan de Suaznabar y Aguirre. In his response to the suit Utrera begged that Margarita be released into his custody at once until the Inquisition decided the case. He explained that owing to his poverty,

failing eyesight, and old age, he and his family were completely dependent on Margarita's labor in his tienda in Mexico City. Utrera stressed
that without Margarita's labor his family would face financial ruin. The
weight of Utrera's testimony regarding the value of his slave to the economic viability of his family suggests the existence of a wider group of
masters who depended on the income or labor of their slaves.[100]

Slaves were also employed among the semiskilled and skilled crafts in
urban centers. For the period from 1673 to 1676 at least eleven slaves were
apprenticed in different trades in Mexico City—they served as tailors,
cobblers, coach makers, chair makers, and *doradors de agua* (tradesmen
who purified water for drinking).[101] These slaves were all between ten
and nineteen years of age, and their owners signed contracts with various
master artisans to train them as craftsmen. Slaves were also apprenticed
as master carpenters, candle makers, silversmiths, and hatmakers. Manuel
de Figueroa, a twelve-year-old mulatto slave, was apprenticed with a master carpenter named Manuel de Ontiveros for a term of four years in
1723. Slaves also appear to have been particularly visible as blacksmiths
throughout New Spain.[102] For example, Juan Núñez de Cabrera, a master
silversmith, sold his mulatto slave Juan Mateo, who was also a silversmith
(*oficial de platero*), in 1676.

Contracts specifically spelled out the terms of the apprenticeship for
slaves. For the most part, slaves were apprenticed for a period of three to
four years. The contract obligated the master artisan to train the slave
in the skill, provide him with room, board, and clothing, treat him well,
and cure his illnesses. Furthermore, the artisan agreed to pay the slave's
master the same wage a journeyman of the same trade would receive when
the slave's apprenticeship was complete. The contracts also stipulated that
the master artisan had to train the slave well enough to qualify him as a
journeyman in his craft. The contract became null and void if the slave
missed more than fifteen days work or fled the custody of the master with
whom he had been placed.

Such slave artisans proved quite valuable to their masters. A self-
described impoverished single woman, María de Salazar testified that the
arrest of her slave Sebastián de los Reyes by the Inquisition for blasphemy
had left her destitute. She explained that the loss of the "small daily wage"
she normally received from Sebastián, a *sombrerero* (a type of hatter) in
Mexico City, had reduced her to begging in the streets. María pleaded
with inquisitors to release him into her custody so that he might continue

to work and provide for her.[103] Much as was the case with jornaleros and vendors, the earnings of skilled slaves could be very important to the household economies of their masters.

It is hard to generalize about the nature of urban slavery because the experiences of domestic servants would have been distinctly different from those of jornaleros, street vendors, and artisans. Yet many urban slaves seemed to have had significant levels of physical mobility. They were able to walk the streets of the cities where they worked, to meet friends in *pulquerías* (which sold *pulque*, an indigenous alcoholic drink) or cantinas, to pursue love interests, and to visit family members. Slaves testified in no uncertain terms that they enjoyed that mobility and control over their own labor experiences. Diego de la Cruz spoke enthusiastically about the significant freedom he had to move about the city when not working. Urban slaves also had greater access to the courts and the church. And yet their experiences were not as ideal as they might sound. Many urban slaves were often required to feed, clothe, and house themselves while still providing a daily wage to their owners.[104]

Although Afro-Mexican slave labor was never central to the dominant export economy in New Spain—silver mining—traditional accounts undervalue the significance of this labor to the colonial economy. In the end, labor fundamentally shaped the possibilities for slaves, the communities they inhabited, and the myriad ways that they dealt with their degraded social position. While plantation slaves tended to live in small, isolated communities, perhaps with ties to neighboring plantations, many urban slaves were left to their own devices to create families and communities in New Spain's cityscapes, a topic taken up in the following chapter.

CHAPTER 2

"To Marry in the Holy Mother Church"
Marriage and Community Formation

✣ ON JANUARY 21, 1640, PEDRO SÁNCHEZ AND MARIANA PETITIONED
for the right to marry at the Catedral Metropolitano, which served the
main parish of Mexico City (see fig. 3). The prospective bride and groom
were slaves owned by Diego de Barrientos and Antonio de Almaraz
respectively. All such applicants were required to include their *calidad* or
personal status, which was generally expressed in racial or ethnic terms.
Pedro and Mariana both listed their calidad as Angola.[1] Juan de la Cruz
and Ana María, who appeared as their *testigos* (wedding witnesses), also
identified themselves as Angola slaves. According to Juan, he and Pedro
had been friends for over twelve years and he had known Mariana for
over six. Ana María testified she had been acquainted with the bride
and groom for over twelve and twenty-five years respectively.[2] Juan and
Ana María also testified that there were no legal or religious obstacles to
the marriage.[3]

Five years later in September, Lorenzo de la Cruz, an Angola slave,
and María de la Cruz, an Indian woman, sought license to marry in
the same parish. María's testigos, Bartolomé Fortuna, a Spaniard, and
Dominga de la Cruz, a free creole black woman, swore they had known
her for ten years. Juan Francisco, a creole black slave owned by Don

FIGURE 3. Metropolitano Cathedral, Mexico City. Construction began on
the Mexico City Cathedral, which served El Sagrario parish in the heart of
Mexico City, in the sixteenth century. Courtesy of Shutterstock.

Bernabé de la Vega y Amarilla, served as Lorenzo's witness, claiming that
they had been friends for nearly fourteen years.[4]

Each petition contains tantalizing evidence of the social worlds
inhabited by slaves in colonial Mexico. The church required that couples
wishing to marry first had to apply for a marriage license. These applications include information about the status (free or enslaved) and calidad of
brides, grooms, and testigos—who were most likely close personal friends
or community leaders. This information allows us to chart at least three,
and as many as seven, important social relationships formed by bondsmen
and bondswomen.

That Africans and their descendents were marrying in New Spain
at all suggests that they were being integrated into Catholic society.
Every slave who appeared in these records had been baptized, had taken
a Hispanicized name, and had learned at least rudimentary Spanish
(there is no evidence that priests employed interpreters) and the basic elements of the Catholic faith necessary to petition to marry in the first
place.[5] Despite the powerful acculturative force of Christianity, however,

Afro-Mexicans proved more than able to manipulate Catholic institutions like marriage to define and maintain distinctive identities.

The creation of families was at once one of the most ordinary and most important processes in the lives of slaves in the New World. Understanding slave family, its form and function, is important because families served as the first line of defense against the dehumanizing effects of slavery. Furthermore, families were microcosms of the larger communities in which they were formed. The family was a "moral community" containing within its boundaries members who were emotionally involved and who shared, to some degree, a sense of common identity.[6] At the same time, however, the slave community provided a blueprint for family formation. Put another way, who slaves chose to cohabitate with or marry both defined and reflected their cultural and community identities. Marriage records provide a good way to explore the creation and evolution of slave communities because family formation via real and fictive kinship ties is evident within them in the form of the spouses and *testigos* that slaves selected.

The question that remains, however, is which marriage better reflects overall patterns for slaves in New Spain, the one that included four Angola bondspeople or the one that brought enslaved Africans and free and enslaved Mexican-born blacks together with Indians and Spaniards? And how might the answer to this question be affected by the transition from a predominantly African-born to Mexican-born slave population in the decades after the end of the regular slave trade in 1640? The answers to these questions provoke an examination of a series of assumptions about slavery and race relations and a reconsideration of the social and cultural histories of colonial Mexico.[7]

Spanish American slaves did have the right(s) to marry in the church, to select their potential spouses free from interference from their owners, and to cohabitate with their spouse one night per week.[8] Many scholars assert, however, that despite those theoretical protections, the overwhelming physical and psychological effects of enslavement in Africa, of the Middle Passage, and of colonial slavery isolated slaves from each other, preventing the formation of lasting family relationships among both Africans and Afro-Mexicans.[9] In addition, because slaves and their progeny were always a marked minority within colonial society, numerous historians contend that they were forced to turn to the indigenous majority and the growing mestizo population for marriage partners or to engage in concubinage with Spanish men.[10] The marriage of the Angola slave Lorenzo and his India bride María would seem to bear out that argument. Explorations of slave marriage patterns from Mexico City, however, suggest that Pedro and Mariana's marriage—celebrated by two African slaves—was more typical.[11] The goal of this chapter is to assess the implications of that trend and to explore how marriage patterns among Afro-Mexicans changed in the century following the close of the slave trade.

Race and Ethnicity in New Spain

Before assessing marriage patterns for slaves, we must first deal with the thorny issue of the meaning(s) of terms like "mulato" and "negra," employed to mark "race" in colonial records.[12] Our understanding of these words is shaped by concerns that derive from our own inability to completely escape late nineteenth- and early twentieth-century notions of race as biological and fixed. Our tendency to reify terms like "mulato" and "negro" as marking mutually exclusive groups also shapes our ability to assess the meaning of those terms.[13]

There is little debate that the Spanish crown attempted to create a racialized colonial social order. What has been hotly debated, however, is the success of that program. Initially, Spanish efforts to order society were personified by the ethnic dichotomy of the *república de españoles* and the *república de indios*, or the theoretically distinct judicial, ecclesiastical, and even physical worlds of Spaniards and natives.[14] The importation of African slaves and the growing casta population threatened the internal stability of the Spanish republic (where all non-Indians were theoretically housed).[15]

In response, the Spanish imposed the *sistema de castas* in the mid-seventeenth century.[16] The genre of casta paintings, which reflect imperial and elite frustration over the racial fluidity and the reality of racial mixture in New Spain in the eighteenth century, enumerated as many as thirty-two different racial categories based on the various mixtures of Spanish, African, and indigenous blood.[17] In practice, however, that number was reduced to five major categories: Spanish, Indian, black, mestizo (Indian-Spanish mix), and mulatto (African-Spanish mix).[18] Two other terms: *castizo* (three-quarters Spanish and one-quarter Indian) and *morisco* (three-quarters Spanish and one-quarter African) were used to a lesser extent. In the parish registers of Veracruz but not in those of Mexico City, Guanajuato, or San Luis Potosí, *pardo*—of mixed African and native descent—was another important category.[19] But, what were the differences among black, mestizo, mulatto, pardo, morisco, and castizo on the streets of the cities and towns of New Spain?

In practice, these ethnonyms were not exact indicators of parentage. For example, of the eighty-nine free mulatto babies that were baptized in 1705 in the main parish of the silver-mining city of Guanajuato, ten had one parent listed as Indian or mestizo. That pattern suggests that the term "mulatto" did not narrowly represent a person of Spanish-African heritage.[20] We are thus left to decipher the meanings of such terms in practice.

Scholars interested in "race" in novohispano society have proceeded along three interrelated lines. First, some have focused specifically on the role of race in ordering colonial society.[21] What these studies tend to ignore, however, is the potential meaning of race and racial identity independent of the social hierarchy. The centrality of *mestizaje*—the racial and cultural mixture of Indians and Spaniards—to general understanding of novohispano cultural history reinforces this emphasis on the connections between race and class. Much of the literature assumes that all lower-class colonial Mexicans, including those of African descent, with the exception of Indians, shared a mestizo culture regardless of race.[22] This picture generally ignores the significant portion of the population that claimed Afro-Mexican heritage throughout the colonial period.[23]

A second group of scholars have eschewed questions about race as a conceptual framework in order to understand the social order the Spanish *attempted* to create. They argue that the term "race" should be avoided because it imposes nineteenth- and twentieth-century connotations on premodern contexts.[24] Terms that emanate out of the documentary record like *raza* (lineage) and calidad are more appropriate, they contend, because they more adequately reflect colonial realities. Magali Carrera argues that "rather than being named as separate races . . . people are more often identified as being of separate *razas*, . . . which are demarcated by specific *calidades*" in colonial documents.[25] "Raza," the modern equivalent of "race," translated as "lineage" for the colonial period, was articulated in terms of *limpieza de sangre*, or "purity of blood." In the Old World, the Spanish began to make distinctions between Old Christians, marked by their purity of blood, and Jews, Moors (North

African Muslims), and New Christians (converted Jews or Moors) whose blood was impure on account of the religious infidelity of their ancestry.[26] Spaniards thus employed "raza" to connote a "generational association" with those groups and used it "to legitimize the discrimination and persecution of non-Christians (infidels) and their descendents."[27] Calidad, on the other hand, was typically expressed in racialized terms (e.g., Indian, mulatto) and was "an inclusive impression of one's reputation as a whole." It included reference to color (phenotype) as well ancestry and purity of blood (embodied in raza). Occupation, wealth, honor, integrity, and place of origin also potentially influenced calidad.[28]

These complicated definitions help us better understand the social hierarchy that the Spanish attempted to create. From their perspective, Indians were not associated with *mala raza*, or "bad or evil blood," because they were neophytes who had no exposure to Christianity prior to conquest and had willingly submitted to it afterward. As a result, they were free vassals and considered potentially redeemable. Moreover, they were defined by reference to a place, the Indies, rather than by reference to their phenotype. Similarly, the term used to designate a person of mixed Spanish-Indian descent, "mestizo," derives from the word *mezcla* (mixture). Afro-descendents, on the other hand, were named by reference to their skin color as "negros." The negative associations with the color black in the early modern Spanish mind as well as the fact that descendents of Africans were permanently stained by their mala raza, and were connected to slavery, thrust them into a distinctively socially alienated position. "Mulato," the term for a person of mixed African and Spanish descent, derives from the term *mulo* (mule), the sterile offspring of a horse and a donkey.

According to Carrera, the Spanish believed mestizos suffered from "diluted but not polluted blood," whereas they thought that African ancestry "permanently corrupted" Indian and Spanish blood.[29] The negative associations with African descent are sometimes evident in the famous casta paintings from Mexico. The violence depicted between a black woman and her Spanish husband in figure 4 is a common theme in these images. Similarly, figure 5 highlights the inability to overcome African heritage. In it, the child of an *albina* (one-eighth African and seven-eighths Spanish), whose depiction does not appear to reflect any Africanity, and a Spaniard is called a *negro torna atrás*, which could be translated as "regress or return to black," and is clearly represented in the

FIGURE 4. De español y negra, mulata. Andrés de Islas, *De español y negra, mulata, ca. 1785.* Courtesy of the Museo de América, Madrid.

FIGURE 5. De español y alvina, negro torna atrás. Anónimo, *De español y alvina, negro torna atrás, ca. 1785.* Courtesy of the Museo de América, Madrid.

painting as a black child. Contrarily, these series of paintings depicted the child of a Spaniard and a castizo as Spanish! The message is clear: indigenous heritage could be overcome, Africanity could not.

A key assumption that appears to underlie these discussions is that Afro-Mexicans internalized the negative judgments of their Africanity and blackness that emanated from official discourses. Herman Bennett argues those associations resulted in "racial ambivalence, if not outright contempt," among mixed-race persons of African descent "for their racial ancestry." Laura Lewis contends that the Spanish "thwarted blacks' claims to group identities" and excluded them from "membership in a proper community of persons" through their ideological construction of black and mulatto.[30] This, in turn, created an imperative for Afro-Mexicans to distance themselves as much as possible from the legacies of their racial heritage. The result was a strong impetus to "passing," or the attempt to escape the "negro/mulato" racial categories by securing indio, mestizo, or Spanish status.[31]

A third group of scholars focuses specifically on the experiences of Africans and their descendents in New Spain to present a more complicated view of the meanings of calidad. A consensus is emerging that Afro-Mexicans defined their group identities by way of reference to common African origins early on.[32] However, scholars suggest that as the colonial period progressed blacks and mulattoes tried to assimilate to a general casta or to Spanish culture. Some even place Afro-Mexicans at the heart of the creation of that casta or mestizo culture. Blacks and mulattoes, such historians argue, had more contact with the Spanish and Indian communities than the two had with each other. Some of these scholars theorize that Afro-descendents served as cultural intermediaries between the two, facilitating the creation of a mestizo culture.[33] Others explore Afro-Mexican attempts to navigate the complicated racial hierarchy and to assimilate after the mid-seventeenth century.[34]

Looking at marriage patterns as a function of self-defined racial identity provides a way to chart the community of Afro-Mexican slaves. The marriage patterns revealed in parish records provide the best test of these theories about mestizaje and assimilation, though we have to bear in mind that these records are not a means by which we can secure an objective understanding racial identities and race relations.[35] Exogamy (marriage outside one's social, racial, cultural or linguistic group) can be used to measure the assimilation of a particular group into society at large.[36] If slaves married Indians and other non-Afro-descendents, that would support the conclusion that they were a part of a larger multiracial, multiethnic, lower-class mestizo colonial culture.

To provide a broader perspective on slave community formation, I compare patterns in the selection of spouses with those in the selection of testigos/padrinos (wedding witnesses) from Mexico City (1640–1749) and the mining centers of Guanajuato (1669–1723) and San Luis Potosí (1665–1738). All available marriage applications for slaves from the Ramo de Matrimonios in the Archivo General de la Nación provide the primary evidence for the discussion of marriage patterns in Mexico City that follows. When apropos, I compare that data with marriages documented in the marriage registers of Sagrario Metropolitano parish that served the heart of Mexico City. Marriage patterns for the northern mining cities were similarly drawn from marriage registries of parish churches.

In order to proceed, a working definition of race is necessary that more explicitly considers the potential implications of distinctive racial identities. Race was a social construct in New Spain.[37] As a result, it was a prime locus of contestation among colonial subjects. In his study of plebian race relations in seventeenth-century Mexico City, R. Douglas Cope concludes that "a person's race might best be described as a shorthand summation of his social network" and that people of mixed ancestry "maintained strong ties with their parent population."[38] Cope's conclusions suggest that ethnic and racial identities were more than the definitions of calidad and raza might suggest. Reflecting current historical understandings, I approach race by treating phenotypical differences as a cue for the categorization of human beings that potentially reflects cultural differences.[39] Therefore, I employ the terms "race" and "racial identities" heuristically, despite all the inherent difficulties, because there appears to be a correlation between self-definitions using racialized terms and distinctive cultural communities in colonial Mexico.

Slave Marriage prior to 1650

The exploration of marriage patterns from Mexico City through the 1650s, when the slave population was predominantly African-born, suggests that Pedro and Mariana's marriage, the one that brought together four Angola slaves, reflected general patterns. Many studies of African marriages in Mexico City have argued that there were significant levels of endogamy, evidenced by the fact of high marriage rates between slaves who shared a common ethnic moniker (e.g., Angola).[40] This chapter proposes to go beyond those studies to illuminate how Africans constructed multiple new ethnic and community identities in Spanish America. I analyze selection patterns of testigos (wedding witnesses) alongside those of spouses in order to chart a web of slaves' social relations, which allows for a consideration of the potential meanings that slaves themselves associated with the ethnonyms they self-applied.

When one analyzes slave marriage patterns for Mexico City, three general trends representative of the pre-1650 period become evident. First, the majority of slaves who married prior to that date were *bozales* (African-born). Among the 185 slaves who petitioned for a marriage license between 1640 and 1649, approximately 72 percent were African-born and just over 25 percent were creole (Mexican-born blacks and mulattos). Second, only 11 of those 185 married someone not of African descent, greatly undermining the argument that Africans were forced to

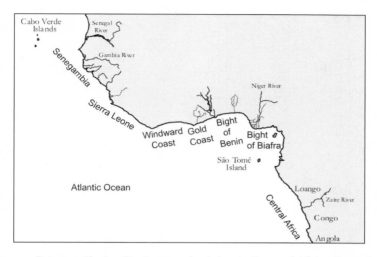

MAP 2. Primary Slaving Regions on the Atlantic Coast of Africa. By author

marry Indians and mestizos. And third, bozal and creole slaves exhibited very different spousal selection patterns. Whereas African-born slaves overwhelmingly married other bozales, creole slaves very rarely married Africans and were much more likely to select free spouses.[41]

The overwhelming majority of Africans in Mexico City hailed from Bantu-speaking West Central Africa, and rates of marriage with other slaves also from that region were high among them.[42] Over nine in ten listed their ethnicity as Angola, Congo, Banguela, Anchico, and Malemba (table 2.1 and map 3).[43] The terms listed in table 2.1 do not refer to specific precolonial African ethnicities.[44] Each term designates a general region of Africa from which slaves were recruited. Among West Central Africans, "Angolas" originated from what became the Portuguese colony of the same name in the region surrounding the slave port of Luanda. This included territories that had once been controlled by the Mbundu peoples (Kimbundu speakers) around the Kwanza River. The majority of slaves exported from Luanda, the primary Portuguese slave port in West Central Africa, were called Angolas by slave traders even if they were originally Mbundu, Ovimbundu, Imbangala, or Congo (which are subdivisions of the family of western Bantu languages).[45] Congo slaves were recruited in or near the areas controlled by the Kingdom of Kongo between the Kwanza River to the south and the Zaire River to the north.

TABLE 2.1. Ethnicity of African-Born Slaves (Brides, Grooms, and Testigos)
Listed in Marriage Applications of Slaves, Mexico City, 1640–49

Nomenclature in the Ramo de Matrimonios	No. of Slaves	%	Shipping Region (see map 1)
West Africa			
Caboverde	1		Senegambia
Mandinga	1		Senegambia
Nalu	2		Senegambia
Bran (Bram)	7		Senegambia
Arara	1		Bight of Benin
Carballi	1		Bight of Biafra
Subtotal	13	4.7%	
Central Africa (see map 2)			
Angola	218		Luanda and Its Hinterland
Congo	26		Between the Zaire and Kwanza Rivers
Malemba	9		East of Colony of Angola
Anchico	4		Interior, Zaire Estuary
Banguela	1		Banguela and Its Hinterland
Subtotal	258	92.4%	
Southeastern Africa			
Mozambique	3		Southeastern Africa
Xhosa	5		South Africa
Subtotal	8	2.9%	
TOTAL	279	100.0%	

Source: AGN, Matrimonios, vols. 1–229.

But the term "Congo" should not be equated with a former subject of
the Kingdom of Kongo, because not all slaves exported from the region
would have recognized themselves as such in Africa, nor would they have
all spoken the Kikongo language.[46] "Banguela" refers to slaves recruited
around the southernmost Portuguese slave port of the same name and
its hinterland. "Anchico" designates a grouping of peoples inhabiting the

interior of the region along the Zaire River who would eventually establish the Tio kingdom. "Malemba" (and "Matamba") refer to principalities formed along the eastern edge of the Portuguese colony of Angola in the interior (see map 3). Thus, these terms referred to fairly specific regions within West Central Africa from the perspective of slave traders and masters but not to specific African ethnicities.

According to specialists, precolonial West Central Africa was the most culturally and linguistically homogenous of the slave-exporting regions of Atlantic Africa. Jan Vansina, in his seminal *Paths in the Rainforests*, charts how the region came to be populated by a single linguistic family—western Bantu—over the final two millennia bc.[47] Subsequently, these peoples with a common ancestry developed distinct traditions and dialects over time that reflected local conditions. The region was not

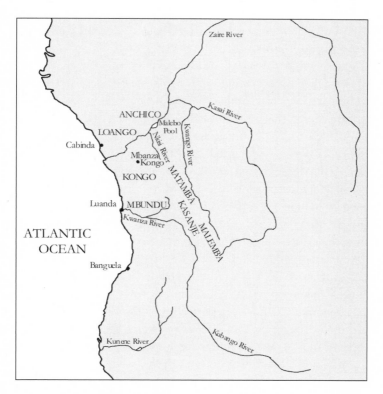

MAP 3. Major Ethnic Groups of Coastal Central Africa during
the Slave-Trade Era. By author

only linguistically homogenous but culturally as well. Precolonial West
Central Africans shared a single overarching cultural and political tradition *before* they arrived in the Americas. In other words, the cultures and
societies of the area constituted a single unit when compared to neighboring cultures even if western Bantu speakers failed to recognize that reality
in Africa.[48] Accordingly, people throughout West Central Africa would
not have identified themselves as sharing the same ethnic identity *in*
Africa. But the great majority of captives drawn from that region shared
common cultural and linguistic heritages that facilitated the generation
of new ethnicities within the diaspora.

Prior to 1650, the slaving frontier in West Central Africa extended at
most two hundred kilometers inland, largely encompassing the Kingdom
of Kongo and the region eventually encompassed by the Portuguese
colony of Angola. The great majority of captives were recruited from the
region south of the Kwanza River both because of Portuguese military
intrusions into the region from Luanda and the expansiveness of local
indigenous groups in the region. This supply of slaves was supplemented
by Portuguese and African slave-trading groups' raids on the Kongo border and the delivery of a limited number of slaves recruited in the interior.[49] These regions had a long history of interaction before the arrival of
the Portuguese, and the dominant languages spoken in each, Kikongo and
Kimbundu, were as linguistically similar as Spanish and Portuguese.[50]

Still, one might wonder what such terms meant to Africans in New
Spain and why they did not employ ethnic monikers that would have
better reflected their various localized ethnicities in Africa. According
to Douglas Chambers, despite the "bewildering variety" of ethnonyms
in Africa, the great majority of "named Africans" from a common slaving
region tended to group themselves into two or three major ethnicities
in the Americas, and, once established, the names of these groupings
remained quite stable.[51] Although not African in origin, these ethnonyms
took on their meanings within the diaspora; they came to represent spon-
taneously generated identities grounded in common languages, whatever
the dialectical differences that had to be overcome, and the shared cultural backgrounds of persons drawn from specific regions within Africa.[52]

Authorities in New Spain do not appear to have been as concerned
about the distinctions within the African population as they were about
distinctions between Indians and mestizos, or Indians and mulattoes, for
that matter.[53] For example, the marriage register for Sagrario parish in

Mexico City indicates that ecclesiastical authorities rarely recorded the ethnic differences among black (African and creole) slaves who married. For 1647–48, the marriage register lists 177 black slave brides or grooms but provides ethnicity for only 28 of them (16 percent). The rest are described simply as blacks. On the other hand, 82 percent of the 163 black slaves in extant marriage applications from the Ramo de Matrimonios for Mexico City during the 1640s listed their African ethnicity. Thirteen marriages involving at least one bozal from the extant marriage applications were cross-referenced to the marriages themselves, recorded in the Sagrario registry for 1647–48. Of the twenty-five slaves who claimed an African ethnicity in those applications only six (24 percent) also had their identity listed in the parish marriage book. This suggests, perhaps, that colonial authorities were not as responsible for policing the distinctions between ethnonyms and the ethnic communities they represented in colonial Mexico as we might have assumed. One might argue, then, that the impetus for ethnic naming came not from Spaniards but from Africans themselves.

Bozal slaves began to experience a new sense of self on their arrival in New Spain. Recently arrived Africans imported African cultural elements and therefore were central to maintaining ethnic divisions within slave populations. On the other hand, those new slaves, likely speaking little or no Spanish, were drawn to others pulled from similar regions in Africa with whom they could communicate. That gravitation likely resulted in their integration into a larger community of slaves whose cultural and linguistic heritages were similar enough to be mutually intelligible. An exploration of testigo selection speaks to the ongoing integration of African slaves into preexisting networks. Testigo testimonies suggest that Africans often spent considerable time in New Spain before marrying. Only 14 of 133 African brides and grooms from the 1640s presented a testigo who had known them for less than five years. Time in the colony allowed new slaves to familiarize themselves with other Africans and to better grasp the distinctions within the enslaved population. Through those interactions slaves learned of and continuously redefined new diasporic ethnic identities that were distinct from those they would have claimed in Africa and that became identified by terms like Angola or Congo. Slaves employed such terms to make distinctions between "us" and "them" that had resonance in their particular historical and geographic context.

To date, historians have treated only marriages between two Africans who shared the same ethnonym as endogamous. But is that approach potentially too narrow? Among the fifty-eight marriages uniting two Africans recorded in the Ramo de Matrimonios for the 1640s, forty-two were clearly endogamous marriages between West Central Africans of the same ethnicity (see table 2.2).[54] However, an important minority of West Central Africans married other West Central Africans who did not share the same ethnonym. For example, Bennett found that a good number of Congo slaves married Angolas. Of the sixty-seven Congo slaves who married from 1584 to 1640, twenty-eight married Congos and another twenty-eight married Angolas.[55] Given the cultural unity of West Central Africa, any marriage between two slaves originating from that region, regardless of their ethnic appellation, could be treated as endogamous. That twenty-eight of sixty-seven Congo slaves who married prior to 1650 selected Congo spouses highlights high levels of endogamy among a small population dominated by the Angolan majority. At the same time, however, the other twenty-eight Congos who married Angola slaves were also likely exhibiting cultural endogamy because the communities represented by those ethnonyms were not mutually exclusive. Thus, approximately 85 percent of West Central Africans who married in Mexico City prior to 1650 did so endogamously.[56]

Marriage patterns among the minority West African slaves also highlight their desire to secure spouses and friends from among slaves with similar origins, even though their small presence in the colony would seem to have militated against their adopting such a strategy. Although my sample is too small, Bennett supplies valuable information about the marriage patterns of slaves from West Africa. He found that among the forty-six slaves identified as Terra Nova (hailing from the Bight of Benin) some twenty-six found spouses who self-identified with the same ethnicity. Among the thirty-four Bran slaves (from Senegambia) included in his study, sixteen married another Bran, even though West Africans likely accounted for less than 10 percent of bondspeople in New Spain in the 1640s. Even when particular diasporic ethnicities represented clear minorities within the overall slave population, its members still sought endogamous marriages.[57] Thus, neither pan-Africanity nor race formed the basis of slave cultural identity in New Spain prior to 1650.

The simultaneous consideration of spouse and testigo choices highlights the significance of the overlap between the Angola and other West

TABLE 2.2. Marriage Patterns of Bozal Slaves, Sagrario Metropolitano, Mexico City, 1640–49

African Slave Grooms		African Slave Brides	
Grooms/Brides	No.	Brides/Grooms	No.
Central African Grooms		Central African Brides	
Angola/Angola	41	Angola/Angola	41
Angola/Banguela	1	Angola/Congo	6
Angola/Congo	1	Angola/Malemba	2
Congo/Angola	6	Banguela/Angola	1
Malemba/Angola	2	Congo/Angola	1
Malemba/Malemba	1	Malemba/Malemba	1
Subtotal	52	*Subtotal*	52
Angola/Negro	4	Angola/Arara	1
Angola/Mulatto	4	Angola/Caboverde	1
Angola/India	1	*Subtotal*	2
Angola/China	1	Angola/Negro	5
Subtotal	10	Congo/Negro	1
South African Grooms		*Subtotal*	6
Mozambique/Mozambique	1	South African Brides	
Xhosa[a]/Xhosa[a]	1	Mozambique/Mozambique	1
Congo/Xhosa[a]	1	Xhosa[a] /Xhosa[a]	1
Subtotal	3	Xhosa[a]/Congo	1
Other *Bozal* Grooms		*Subtotal*	3
Arara/Angola	1	Other *Bozal* Brides	
Bran/Nalu	1	Nalu/Bran	1
Caboverde/Angola	1	*Subtotal*	1
Nalu/Angola Libre	1		
Subtotal	4		
TOTAL	69	TOTAL	64

[a] Xhosa is a difficult ethnicity to pin down. Aguirre Beltrán places it within the Bantu language group originating in West Central Africa (*La población negra*, 241), while Palmer asserts that this ethnic group originated from Southeastern Africa (*Slaves of the White God*, 23).

Source: AGN, Matrimonios, vols. 1–229.

Central African diasporic ethnicities.[58] In the fifty-two marriages that
united two West Central Africans in the 1640s, nineteen included at
least two different West Central African ethnicities. Ten couples married
despite the fact that the bride and groom used different ethnonyms (the
most common example being an Angola groom taking a Congo bride).
The ethnicities listed by the testigos of these ten couples were also quite
variable. For example, on August 3, 1648, Manuel, a Malemba slave, and
Juana, an Angola slave, petitioned to marry. Among their testigos were
two Congo slaves named Manuel de Santiago and Domingo.[59] Another
nine ethnically endogamous unions included at least one testigo who
claimed a West Central African diasporic ethnicity different from that
shared by the bride and groom. For example, on April 2, 1644, Francisco
and Margarita, both Angola slaves, petitioned for the right to marry, with
Bartolomé, an Angola slave, and Juan Francisco, a Congo slave, as their
testigos.[60]

If the primary impetus for maintaining the different West Central
African diasporic ethnonyms came from within the African community
in New Spain, then we must assume that these Africans used them to
demarcate what they perceived to be important divisions within their
larger community, even if those divisions did not translate into mutually
exclusive ethnic communities. The sources considered here do not suggest
clear causes for these divisions. They might have been geographic, marking slaves from different regions within West Central Africa; they might
have been linguistic, in that Congos more than likely spoke Kikongo,
while Angolas predominantly spoke Kimbundu; or they might have been
an artifact of the longer historical association with Christianity in the
regions dominated by Kingdom of Kongo than in the region that became
the Portuguese colony of Angola.[61] Whatever the cause, however, it likely
emanated out of African and African diasporic, rather than Spanish imperial, concerns.

Creole slaves, on the other hand, present a very different case. They
rarely married Africans. Also, creoles, particularly men, often looked
to the free and the non-Afro-Mexican populations for spouses before
1650. Such patterns suggest that there was significant social distance
between Africans and creoles in the colony. Beyond the 1640s, however,
rates of racial endogamy by creole slaves increased, and that the relative
number who married Indians and mestizos decreased over time. This
trend emerged in the context of an increasingly creole-dominated slave

population, highlighting an important transition in the basis of the cultural identity of slaves from diasporic ethnicity to race.

Slaves constructed these overlapping ethnic communities across Mexico City's urban landscape. In only nine of the eighty-two marriages documented in the Ramo de Matrimonios that united two slaves in the 1640s were the bride and groom owned by the same person. In another eleven cases the bride or groom and at least one testigo were owned by a common master. But in only one case did the bride, groom, and all testigos share a common owner. These patterns suggest that slaves regularly looked outside the household or slaveholding unit for friends and potential spouses. These marriage petitions regularly brought together slave couples and testigos owned by at least three different masters from throughout the city.[62]

In the records, one can find a few rare cases of particular slaves who appear in more than one marriage party. On January 4, 1640, Mateo, an Angola slave owned by Joseph de Arauz, petitioned to marry Isabel, another Angola owned by Matías del Castillo. Their testigos, two more Angola bondsmen named Francisco and Marcos, testified that they had known Mateo for ten and eight years respectively. On the next day, Mateo again appeared before the ecclesiastical authorities, this time as a testigo for Francisco and Christina, two Angola slaves. Mateo testified that he had been friends with Francisco (a different Francisco from Mateo's testigo of the same name) for eight years and that he had known the bride for over twenty years. Francisco, the second groom, and Mateo's fiancée, Isabel, were owned by the same person. Combining these two marriages we can chart five different long-term friendships established by Mateo with Angola slaves owned by four different masters. Doing so highlights how Africans sought out social relations with people of common ethnic backgrounds throughout the city.[63]

In addition, testigo testimonies suggest that the process of community formation based on diasporic ethnic identity began, in many cases, in Africa or during the Middle Passage before slaves reached the Americas. On December 15, 1646, Pedro, an Angola slave owned by Francisca Navarro, and Christina de la Cruz, an Angola slave of Antonio Langes, petitioned for the right to marry. Francisco, a thirty-year-old Angola slave belonging to Luís de Vergaza, testified that he had met the bride and groom in Angola. The language of his testimony suggests that they became acquainted after their capture, either while waiting to be placed on board ship or once aboard. Despite the fact that all three had different masters in Mexico City, they maintained the bonds they forged during the Middle Passage.[64] The importance of such shipmates as the pillars of nascent Afro-American slave communities cannot be overstated.[65] Ties forged on board slave ships among slaves from a common cultural region of Africa provided the initial relationships on which African diasporic communities were built throughout the Americas even though in Africa these slaves would have identified themselves as members of more specific communities. Those bonds were based on common cultural backgrounds, not just common experiences as chattel aboard ship.

Although the slave trade destroyed the family and kinship ties that were central to identity in precolonial African societies and so African ethnicities rarely survived the ordeal intact, it did not destroy language, memory, belief, experience, and expertise.[66] The survival of those cultural elements made it entirely possible that a slave originating from any West Central African subregion (see map 2) could have recognized cultural traits in common with other slaves from the same region and would have been able to build communities based on those commonalities, despite the fact that they might have come from different ethnicities within it. Thus, as old identities—articulated in terms of lineage or village—were destroyed, new ones—diasporic ethnicities—were created. In that sense, terms like Angola, Congo and the like were more than shorthand for geographic origin. They also had meaning in the lives of slaves, serving as cultural markers. Africans appropriated ethnonyms imposed by their enslavers to describe the new identities they were creating in the Atlantic world, identities that moved beyond localized African ethnicity even as they built on the cultural and ideological commonalities shared by societies within Africa.

Gender and Marriage Selection

An important trend within novohispano slave marriages after 1650 was the increasing divergence between the number of bondsmen and the number of bondswomen who married. In Mexico City in the 1640s men and women married in comparable numbers (1.2 men to 1 woman). After 1650, however, enslaved men married in significantly higher numbers than did women. As a result, an increasing majority of slaves, including women, married nonslaves. In Mexico City after the 1660s, a majority of bondsmen married free women, and over time more and more did so. The same was true for slave men in Guanajuato and San Luis Potosí, where less than one in five slave men married other slaves. Slave women, on the other hand, continued to marry slaves through the 1720s and 1730s in Mexico City. Only then did a majority of bondswomen begin to marry free men. In both Guanajuato and San Luis Potosí slave women married free men more often than they did slaves (see table 2.3).

Rates of illegitimate births among slave mothers indicate that the relatively low number of bondswomen who married compared to men after 1660 was not created by a shortage of women. Between 80 and 90 percent of slave mothers who baptized children in San Luis Potosí and Guanajuato were unwed.[67] Consensual unions and families composed of women and children were, therefore, the dominant family groups for slave women. These units, due to their very nature, are not documented in the marriage records.

Slaves faced very different social pressures depending on their gender. Patterns of family and community formation indicate how slaves responded to those pressures. Women may have avoided marriage owing to the additional burdens that it created. Slave women already shouldered a double burden as slaves (producers) and women (reproducers and sexual objects) in a patriarchal and hierarchical society.[68] Each slave woman would have had to weigh the advantages and disadvantages of marriage that, it could be argued, represented a third type of burden, legal subservience to her husband. In a society where divorce was not an option, choosing not to marry may have given slave women the ability to leave one relationship and initiate another in ways not possible for married women. Legitimacy and limpieza de sangre, so important to the novohispano elite, were largely irrelevant for slaves.[69] Not marrying had little or no negative repercussions for children of slave women and allowed these women to form relationships free from interference by the church.

Some have suggested that marriage may have been attractive to slaves, particularly women, because of the theoretical protections afforded slave families by the church.[70] If marriage provided slave women more room to maneuver in their relations with their masters, they did not seize on that opportunity in great numbers. Importantly, in New Spain the protection that was supposed to prevent the dividing of married slaves was afforded only to couples consisting of two slaves. Priests warned every free person who sought to marry a slave that he or she was obligated to follow his

TABLE 2.3. Sex Ratio and Marriage Choice by Status of Spouse for Slaves

Ramo de Matrimonios	Sex Ratio of Slaves Who Married	Slave Grooms		Slave Brides	
		No.	% with Slave Brides	No.	% with Slave Grooms
Mexico City					
1640–49	1.2	102	79.4%	86	94.2%
1660–1749	2.0	230	34.3%	114	69.3%
Sagrario Metropolitano, Mexico City					
1647–48	1.1	110	79.1%	99	89.6%
1691–92	1.9	68	47.1%	35	88.6%
1736–37	2.8	39	15.4%	14	42.9%
San Luis Potosí					
1655–1738	2.2	168	18.5%	78	39.7%
Guanajuato					
1669–1723	4.3	139	7.9%	31	35.5%

Sources: Mexico City: AGN, Matrimonios, vols. 1–229; AGN, AGH, Sagrario Metropolitano, Cuidad de México, libros de matrimonios de castas, 1647–48, 1691–92, and 1736–37; San Luis Potosí: AGN, AGH, Sagrario, San Luis Potosí, libros de matrimonios de castas, 1655–98, 1698–1704, 1687–97, 1703–22, and vol. 7, 1722–39; Guanajuato: ABCG, libros de matrimonios de todas calidades, vol. 1, 1669–83, vol. 2, 1683–96, vol. 3, 1705–26, vol. 4, 1716–23.

or her enslaved spouse wherever he or she might be sent or sold. In fact, priests often conducted a separate interview of the free person to determine if he or she fully understood the extra obligations that marrying a slave entailed.[71] Many slave women likely decided that consensual unions or concubinage were more advantageous, or at least less disadvantageous, than marriage.[72]

Another reason that novohispano bondswomen did not marry was that they were overwhelmingly creole after 1660. In other New World contexts, African-born slaves married at much higher rates than did creole slaves. Marriage provided an excellent mechanism through which Africans could forge support networks. Creole women, on the other hand, relied on real kinship ties (siblings, parents, etc.) and fictive kin (godparents), to create and extend their community, making marriage less necessary.[73] When, after 1650, the slave population became increasingly creole, the relative numbers of slave women who married in New Spain declined sharply.[74] That trend reflects the changing characteristics of the slave population and perhaps a change in the importance of marriage to slaves.

Lastly, it should be noted that male masters of female slaves may have resisted slave marriages even though they had no formal authority to do so. Concubinage could have advantages relative to marriage for both master and slave. Several authors have argued that in some cases slave women were able to reduce the burden that slavery placed on them and their children by submitting to concubinage.[75] If nothing else, it is important to recognize that forces outside the control of slave women may have impacted marriage rates to some degree.

The idea that slave women secured unfettered agency by engaging in sexual relations with their masters is, however, potentially problematic in light of the skewed power differences between the two. For at least one slave girl, the advances of her master were unwelcome, and when she resisted them he took matters into his own hands. On July 14, 1761, Justa Rita de Villaseñor, a mulatta slave, accused her master, Francisco Hernández, of having raped her when she was thirteen years old. Rita charged that Francisco "had forcefully taken her virginity against her will with little fear of God."[76] Francisco admitted that he had had sex with his slave and that he had taken her virginity but denied the rape charge, arguing it was consensual sex.

Exploring who male slaves married sheds a slightly different light on female marriage patterns. Slave men tended to marry free women, particularly in San Luis Potosí and Guanajuato, where over 80 percent choose free brides. In Mexico City's Sagrario parish, there was a clear transition in male slave spouse selection from slave to free brides after the end of the slave trade. In the 1640s, almost 80 percent of male slaves married slaves. By the 1690s, only 47 percent of male slaves married slave women.[77]

Some scholars argue that the fact that slave men choose free women as their brides might reflect the value that bondsmen placed on freedom. Slave men, following that logic, chose free women because the status of their children was solely dependent on the legal status of the mother. Thus, a male slave who married a free woman insured that his children would be born free.[78] It should be noted, however, that such children were also born free without the formality of marriage. The suggestion that slave men actively pursued free wives so that their children would not be subject to slavery might be an imposition of a modern prizing of liberty on a premodern population, an issue explored in depth in chapter 6.

One possibility is that marriage for men in colonial Latin America, even slave men, was a means of social mobility. A slave man who married a free woman was marrying above his social position. Therefore, in their decision to marry slave men may have been institutionalizing relationships that provided upward social mobility. When social mobility was less of an issue, slave men may have continued to maintain consensual unions. That theory also speaks to the low numbers of female slaves who married. If marriage was a means of upward social mobility, then slave women, ranking near the bottom of the social hierarchy, had little to offer as prospective spouses.

Slave Marriage after 1650

Three important demographic changes occurred within the population of African descent following the middle of the seventeenth century, changes that significantly affected the contours of the cultural community to which slaves belonged. First, the African presence in New Spain waned and creoles achieved majority status following the end of the regular slave trade. Secondly, free Afro-Mexicans achieved numerical superiority over slaves, although the exact timing of that transition is not entirely clear.[79] Third, by the last decades of the seventeenth century mulattoes had become a majority within the Afro-Mexican population, slave and free. If diasporic ethnicity as highlighted by marriage patterns in Mexico City prior to 1650 was important to the evolving slave cultural community in the colony, what happened to that community after the end of the slave trade?

Slave marriage patterns became very complex in Mexico City after 1650 and would become even more complicated over time.[80] That complexity can make interpreting slave marriage patterns confusing. For example, marriage applications from the Ramo de Matrimonios between 1660 and 1749 suggest that black slave men married mulatta women more often than any other racial group. The Ramo de Matrimonios contains thirty applications from black slave men seeking to marry mulatta women; by contrast, there are only fourteen applications from black slave men seeking to marry black women. Black female slaves exhibited similar tendencies, as the eleven who married mulattoes were second only to the thirteen who chose black men during the same time period. (For a breakdown of slave marriages by race and status between 1660 and 1749, see tables 2.1A–2.4A in the appendix.) If exogamy can be used to measure the assimilation of a group into society at large and if endogamy serves as an indicator of the strength of ethnic or racial identity and community, how should these slave marriage patterns be interpreted? Was union of a black and a mulatto endogamous or exogamous? Cope found that connections between blacks and mulattoes were an enduring feature in Mexico City's marriage market, suggesting that those two groups shared a common social network.[81] The connections between different Afro-Mexican racial categories are particularly clear in the case of slaves. The relations between these two groups (blacks and mulattoes) might suggest the need to move beyond the treatment of official racial categories as distinct cultural groups.

This is not to argue that black and mulatto represented exactly the same thing in New Spain. The differences between the two could be very significant, reflecting in part the power of the racialized social hierarchy that the Spanish imposed. The differences between blacks and mulattoes (and perhaps those between blacks and pardos and moriscos as well) were contextual and could have been related, in one way or another, to occupation and/or phenotype. But they did not necessarily demarcate mutually exclusive racial identities. The marriage patterns bear that out. Identity was based, in large part, in one's heritage, and terms like "black" and "mulatto" reflected differences (as the Spanish intended) while referring to a larger cultural community at the same time.[82] For this reason, treating a marriage between a black and a mulatto as exogamous appears flawed. To date, discussions of racial interaction in colonial Mexico have not recognized that the difference between black and mulatto was one of degree rather than kind; such accounts use racial labels to designate distinct categories and argue that black men were particularly exogamous because of their tendency to marry mulatta women. That argument is problematic because it masks the strength of the distinct social networks grounded in racial identities in New Spain.

In Mexico City, male slave marriages were heavily racially endogamous through the end of the seventeenth century. In Sagrario parish, these marriages were endogamous in nearly nine in ten cases in the 1690s and in nearly seven in ten as late as the 1730s. That high level of endogamy is also evident in patterns from the Ramo de Matrimonios. Over 70 percent of male slaves married Afro-Mexican women between 1660 and 1749. Although female slaves did not marry in great numbers, those that did exhibited even higher rates of endogamy, and for longer, than did men. Over 85 percent of bondswomen who married in Mexico City selected other Afro-Mexicans through the middle of the eighteenth century.[83] Male and female slaves rarely, if ever, married Indians and mestizos, again undercutting the assumption that they were forced to turn to those populations for spouses and lovers.[84] If marriage patterns can be regarded as a shorthand summation of social networks, then slaves were clearly immersed in a community that included both blacks and mulattoes.

In the face of this data, it is easy to forget that each of these marriages was not only about creating community but also about creating families and that each one involved slaves and free people who were at times willing to try to overcome the significant obstacles to marriages between free and enslaved. The story of Manuel Serrano de la Cruz, a mulatto slave, and Rosa Rodríguez, his free mulatta bride, drives home the point that each wedding was a special moment for those involved. In 1703, Manuel petitioned to wed Rosa, but in the course of her testimony, she stated that she no longer wished to proceed. Three years later, Manuel renewed his petition and Rosa now affirmed her wish to marry him. According to Rosa, she had been forced to reject Manuel's initial proposal, most likely by her parents, because there had been threats that his master would send him to work in an obraje if they married. On July 20, 1706, only three days after Rosa testified that she truly wished to marry him, they celebrated their wedding in the main cathedral in Mexico City.[85]

Similarly, Miguel de Plaza, a bozal slave, petitioned to marry Paula Francisca de Rermeo, a free mulatta, in Mexico City in 1735. According to Miguel, they wished to wed because they had been having an "illicit relationship" over the preceding four years that had resulted in the birth of four young children. Miguel feared that his master would object to his marriage, and send him to an obraje to prevent it. Miguel turned to the church to intervene, as was his right under imperial and church law, so that he might "put himself in God's grace by the means of the Holy Sacrament of marriage." On July 18, 1735, one day after his initial petition, Miguel and Paula received their marriage license and likely married soon thereafter.[86]

In the northern mining zone of New Spain, slaves were less endogamous than in Mexico City. Approximately three in five slave men married Afro-Mexican women in Guanajuato and San Luis Potosí. Slave women, on the other hand, married Afro-Mexican men in nearly three in four marriages recorded in those two cities.[87] The apparently reduced levels of endogamy in these two mining centers are most likely due to the smaller relative size of the Afro-Mexican populations found there. Mexico City had the largest population of both enslaved and free Afro-Mexicans throughout the colonial period and the high rates of racial endogamy there reflect that. As a rough estimate, 18 percent of people who married in Guanajuato over the course of the seventeenth century were Afro-Mexican, compared with 26 percent of those who married in Mexico City's Sagrario Metropolitano parish between 1694 and 1696.[88] Guanajuato and San Luis Potosí were also located in the Bajío region, which is often associated with the highest levels of racial and cultural mixing throughout the colonial period. In those instances higher percentages of exogamy do not necessarily suggest a total breakdown of racialized cultural communities; population size must be considered when assessing endogamy or exogamy.[89]

Padrino and testigo selection patterns further illustrate the changing contours of the Afro-Mexican community throughout the colonial period.[90] They suggest that spouse selection patterns may not provide a complete picture of the community to which slaves belonged.[91] Slaves in Guanajuato exhibited relatively low levels of endogamy when compared to Mexico City. Yet both bondsmen and bondswomen selected Afro-Mexicans as padrinos at much higher rates than they did as spouses in that city. Male slaves married endogamously in 60 percent of recorded marriages, but 73 percent of their padrinos were Afro-Mexican. Similarly, while 70 percent of slave women married blacks or mulattoes, 83 percent of their padrinos were Afro-Mexican.[92] That comparison suggests that the levels of endogamous marriage in that city masks the importance of the Afro-Mexican community to slaves there.

As but one example, Santiago de la Cruz, a mulatto slave owned by Doña Luisa de Rivas, married a mestiza named María in the main cathedral in Guanajuato in 1683. Two mulatto slaves, Francisco and María de la Concepción, served as their padrinos.[93] Santiago's mestiza bride might suggest that race was unimportant to him. But his padrinos potentially highlight how central his own racial identity may have been to his larger cultural community. Comparing padrino/testigo selections with spouse selection provides evidence of the importance of other slaves to slave grooms even as they married outside that slave community. These patterns reinforce the possibility a modicum of social mobility may have been an important consideration for slave men who married.[94]

Subtle differences between padrino/testigo selection patterns based on race and legal status when compared to spouse selection patterns provide a fuller, more nuanced picture of the social universe inhabited by slaves. They highlight the importance of other blacks and mulattoes, slave and free, to the slaves of colonial Mexico. Following the close of the slave trade the Afro-Mexican community transitioned from one grounded in diasporic ethnic identities to one based largely in a racialized identity not fully captured by labels like mulatto or black.

Final Considerations

The argument to this point has been that slaves became an important part of racialized social networks dominated by free people of African descent in the second half of the seventeenth century. To better assess that conclusion we must reconsider the overall marriage market in New Spain. The selection patterns in table 2.4 suggest that the endogamy rates for slaves I have outlined do reflect general trends within the overall Afro-Mexican

TABLE 2.4. Slave Marriage Patterns, Sagrario Metropolitano, Mexico City, 1694–96

| | Women | | | | | | |
	Spanish	Castiza	Mestizo	Indian	Mulatta	Black	TOTAL
Men							
Spanish	483	5	8	1	15	0	512
Castizo	1	3	6	1	3	0	14
Mestizo	6	4	90	13	18	1	132
Indian	0	1	10	27	1	0	39
Mulatto	6	5	47	10	132	7	207
Black	0	0	8	1	28	25	62
TOTAL	496	18	169	53	197	33	966

Source: Cope, *The Limits of Racial Domination*, 79.

population.[95] If we look more closely look at table 2.4, however, we run into some of the same problems in determining the extent of endogamy among Afro-Mexicans we have already encountered. More black men married mulatta women than married blacks. Does that mean that they were largely exogamous?

Numerous scholars contend that calculating marriage rates as percentages does not provide the best measure of endogamous or exogamous behavior. Percentages are misleading precisely because they do not take into account the different sizes of, or the sex ratios within, particular racial groups within the total population. To address those concerns, Cope suggests calculating conditional kappas (Ki), as recommended by Philip F. Rust and Patricia Seed, which allows one to measure the endogamy of different racial groups within the larger population.[96] This particular measurement is attractive because it calculates relative endogamy by both sex and racial moniker. A conditional kappa of "1" suggests complete endogamy, while a kappa of "0" indicates random mixing, and thus a higher conditional kappa suggests greater endogamy. The first six rows in table 2.5 represent the conditional kappas for the marriages listed in table 2.4 by race and sex as presented by Cope. In his discussion of endogamy, measured through the conditional kappa, Cope found that Spaniards were particularly endogamous (owing to the high value of the neutral conditional kappa, which measures the endogamy of the entire racial group), while other racial groups had "fairly high" endogamy.

What happens, however, if the terms "black" and "mulatto" are not reified as distinct, mutually exclusive categories but instead are treated as differences in degree and are combined? The final row in table 2.5 presents a recalculation of kappa as a measure of endogamy but treats the blacks and mulattos in table 2.4 as parts of a larger Afro-Mexican cultural community. It is very important to note that combining blacks and mulattos had no impact on the relative endogamy of other racial groups. When treated as a whole, Afro-Mexicans became the second most endogamous group within the sample, exhibiting significantly higher relative endogamy rates than Indians and mestizos.[97] Put simply, when marriages between blacks and mulattos are defined as *interracial* rather than *intraracial* the conditional kappas undermeasure racial endogamy and thereby mask the strength of Afro-Mexican social networks.

Data from other regions of New Spain suggest that Afro-Mexicans were highly endogamous when their numbers within the population made

TABLE 2.5. Conditional Kappas by Racial Group, Sagrario Metropolitano, Mexico City, 1694–96

Racial Category	K_i for Men	K_i for Women	"Neutral" K_i (Nonsex Specific)
Spanish	.884	.944	.913
Castizo	.199	.154	.174
Mestizo	.614	.459	.525
Indian	.674	.489	.567
Mulatto	.545	.580	.562
Black	.382	.741	.504
Afro-Mexican	.624	.771	.690

Source: Calculated from table 2.4. Also see Cope, *The Limits of Racial Domination*, 80.

it possible. For example, Patrick Carroll's data from Jalapa, Veracruz, suggests that although blacks, mulattoes, and pardos represented a smaller portion of those who married (Indians followed by Spaniards were the largest racial groups in Jalapa), they proved to be very endogamous, more so than their counterparts in Mexico City. Combining his data on various Afro-Mexicans (blacks, pardos, and mulattoes) and treating them as a single group for 1711–20, Carroll found that the intramarriage rates among Afro-Mexican men and women in Jalapa were 75 percent and 88 percent respectively. Again, because simple percentages do not take into account population size and sex ratios, I present the conditional kappas for Carroll's data on Jalapa as a fuller measure endogamy in table 2.6. Two patterns are immediately evident: 1) all groups, especially Spaniards and Indians, exhibited extremely high rates of endogamy; and 2) Afro-Mexicans, particularly women, were highly endogamous as well. Considering the comparatively small number of blacks, mulattoes, and pardos who married in Jalapa, the evidence suggests that racial identity was of primary importance in spousal selections.

All of this discussion leads to the following conclusion: the vision of the lower orders of novohispano society as a large, unidentifiable mass of castas is misplaced. In population centers like Mexico City, Guanajuato, San Luis Potosí, and Jalapa, racial identity played a key role in determining social networks for persons of African descent. In other words, the

TABLE 2.6. Conditional Kappas by Racial Group, Sagrado Corazón, Jalapa, Veracruz, 1711–20

Racial Category	K$_i$ for Men (N)	K$_i$ for Women (N)	"Neutral" K$_i$ (Nonsex Specific)
Spanish	.935 (373)	.960 (366)	.947
Mestizo	.922 (113)	.753 (136)	.829
Indian	.955 (736)	.919 (750)	.937
Afro-Mexican	.731 (228)	.862 (198)	.791

Source: Calculated from table 5 in Carroll, "Los mexicanos negros, el mestizaje y los fundamentos olvidados de la 'raza cósmica,'" viii.

terms used to mark calidad, those moments of racial self-identification, did mean something; they served as social markers of cultural identity. This suggests that the notion of a single process of mestizaje in New Spain is too simple.

The argument is not, however, that Afro-Mexicans developed a "racial consciousness" that might have served as a foundation for collective resistance. Blacks and mulattoes were drawn to each other for reasons that they may not have fully understood and may not have been able to articulate themselves, but they were drawn together nonetheless. This resulted in a shared cultural community and/or a shared racial identity. Slaves were at the core of those communities even as they underwent significant change across the colonial period. There is no indication that those identities became articulated in the overtly political way that phrases like "class consciousness" or "racial consciousness" might imply. Chapter 3 picks up this line of argument and hypothesizes that cultural difference underwrote the social networks based in racial identity evident in marriage patterns.

CHAPTER 3

Black and White Magic

Curanderismo, Race, and Culture

✣ ON DECEMBER 16, 1741, ANTONIO DEL CASTILLO WROTE TO THE
Holy Office of the Inquisition of New Spain regarding the illness of
María Joseph de Guzmán. This letter prompted inquisitors to investigate
Juan Pavón, a mulatto soldier, for being a *curandero supersticioso* (superstitious curer) who employed witchcraft. According to this letter and the
testimonies that followed, María had developed a tumor in her chest. She
and her husband, a free mulatto named Pedro Guzmán, made numerous
attempts to find a cure without success, even seeking the assistance of a
French surgeon. Finally, Juan Pavón, Pedro's friend, informed them that
María had been bewitched. Micaela de Peralta, he charged, caused María's
illness by serving her tainted *atole* (a corn drink) and a biscuit. Pavón then
offered to cure María, which involved him sucking fish bones, hair, and
hairy worms from her chest.[1]

This single case and the eighty-six other denunciations of curanderismo, or curing magic, found in the files of the Inquisition from the
eighteenth century provide an excellent way to explore the articulation of
both elite and popular culture in New Spain. The exploration of this specific form of witchcraft provides a window into how the average colonial
in New Spain conceptualized the connections between illness and health,

medicine and magic, and the natural and supernatural worlds. Those issues were inextricably linked in the colonial mind, but that linkage is difficult to comprehend from the modern perspective. This chapter examines the constructions of elite and popular culture through the prism of racial identities while concentrating on the specific genre of curing magic.

Traditionally, magic and curing in eighteenth-century Mexico have been treated as a mestizo cultural form that represented a mixture of Indian and European religious, magical, and medicinal beliefs and practices.[2] Recognizing the importance of mulattoes and blacks among those accused of practicing witchcraft in New Spain, some scholars are willing to assert that such informal religious practices, still understood as a mestizo cultural form, were a combination of European, indigenous, and African traditions.[3] These scholars, with the exception of Joan Bristol, stop short, however, of interrogating the practices of witchcraft for differences based on the self-applied racial identities of practitioners.[4]

Laura Lewis proposes a different conception of novohispano witchcraft as a particularly indigenous cultural product. She argues that colonial Mexican society is best understood in terms of a dichotomy between the "sanctioned" Spanish domains of imposed legal and ideological institutional structures such as the courts and the sistema de castas and the "unsanctioned" world of witchcraft, where an alternative power emanated from the Indian majority. On this account, mulattoes, blacks, and mestizos were basically intermediaries between those two domains and, at times, consumers of Indian witchcraft.[5]

Discussing magic and curanderismo as a mestizo or Indian phenomenon, however, masks some of the subtle differences in practice and belief that can be classified by their culture of origin (European, Amerindian, or African). Spaniards (including Europeans and creoles), mestizos, and Afro-Mexicans performed what could be very different cures based on the practices within their communities and, more importantly, the cultural foundation from which those practices were derived. The high levels of cultural contact among mulattoes, blacks, and even mestizos with both Indians and Spaniards and the shared rituals, materials, and symbols, which resulted from cultural similarities and exchange, should not obfuscate those differences. A comparison between Afro-Mexican curers and their Spanish and mestizo counterparts brings those distinctions into clear focus.[6] A critical analysis of witchcraft and curing brings into clearer focus the variations within colonial Mexican popular culture that reflect and refract the social networks grounded in racial identity discussed in chapter 2.[7]

Mexicans could and did call on curanderos of different racial backgrounds to assist them with a variety of maladies and grievances. Colonial Mexicans could believe in the efficacy of the magic employed by members of different racial groups because the elements (materials, practices, rituals, and symbols) of which it was made came from European, indigenous, and African systems and therefore were familiar. Mexican inquisitors likewise regarded magic as a practice common to different racial groups; as far as they were concerned, all curing and witchcraft reflected the popular culture of the racially mixed, ignorant underclass. They either failed to recognize differences within these practices that were associated race or they regarded them as insignificant.

Black versus White Magic

Colonial Mexicans understood magic as taking two forms: white and black. White magic was used for benevolent, protective, or curative purposes, while black magic was used specifically for malicious ends. Regardless of whether it was used for good or evil, magic conflicted and competed with the teachings of the Catholic Church and therefore was subject to repression by the Inquisition, "which enforced church-defined religious and gender norms for acceptable behavior."[8] Bristol argues that this was especially so in the case of Afro-Mexican practitioners. She writes that "when blacks and mulattoes transgressed the boundaries of calidad by seeming to claim too much authority of their own, Spaniards defined their activities as witchcraft and denounced them."[9]

This dichotomous understanding of magic reflected a mixture of indigenous, European, and African cultural beliefs. In precolonial Nahua medicine, the supernatural and the natural were inextricably linked, as were the positive and negative forms of witchcraft.[10] All ancestors, spirits, and deities that inhabited the supernatural realms within Nahua cosmology could have both harmful and beneficial effects in the natural world. They could cause or cure disease in individuals and communities. All the gods in the pantheon played positive and negative roles and were associated with specific and generic diseases as well as with their remedies. The diagnosis of disease and the determination of proper treatments entailed linking specific symptoms to the responsible god. Once the responsible god was ascertained, specific medicines considered to be the embodiment of that god were prescribed.[11] In practice, however, not only gods but also individuals and their hostile, anticommunity desires could be the cause of sickness, understood as occupying a continuum from personal illness to community suffering through famine, epidemic, or low fecundity.[12] In the precolonial period there was both a medical profession and a substratum of nonprofessional practitioners—magicians, diviners, and curers—all of whom shared similar understandings of illness, curing, and medicinal materials.

Europeans, unlike their Nahua counterparts, largely divorced magic from official political structures and religion. In theory, Spaniards considered magic to take two distinct forms—*hechicería* and *brujería*. Brujería was believed to be a supernatural, psychic power commonly obtained through an explicit pact with the devil.[13] The *bruja* or *brujo* (witch or warlock) was generally thought to have renounced Christianity and to have bartered his or her soul in exchange for certain malicious powers that could be used at whim. Hechicería, on the other hand, was associated with the use of materials and incantations but did not necessarily constitute a negative or evil act. It could be employed for good or evil depending on the desires of the practitioner.[14] Curanderismo and divination were potentially white forms of hechicería.[15] Black magic was brujería or hechicería enacted with bad intentions.[16] In practice, however, colonial Mexicans did not make clear distinctions between brujería and hechicería. While illness could be caused by supernatural forces, including the devil and/or God, it was not necessarily as closely associated with religious belief as it was in indigenous and African cultural systems.

The eighteenth century marks an important transitional period in European understandings of illness and medicine. Prior to that period medicine was based on the theories of Hippocrates and Galen. Health was understood to be a balance of four humors (yellow bile, black bile, blood, and phlegm) and two sets of contraries (hot/cold and moist/dry). Illness resulted from humoral imbalance, and curing was the attempt to reestablish that balance through medication, bloodletting, and the like.[17] The transition to clinical medicine in the eighteenth century that was inspired by the Enlightenment, however, was a slow and uneven process. The impact of scientific and clinical innovations on popular colonial Mexican understandings of health and illness was minimal at best.[18]

Catholicism, on the other hand, offered a remedial system comprehensible to lay Catholics. Ecclesiastical medicines included orthodox remedies such as holy water, clerical blessings, pilgrimages, and exorcisms. Also, miraculous curative powers were associated with particular relics and images.[19] Furthermore, it was a common belief that some holy people were born with the grace of God to heal.

The predominantly West Central African origins of slaves in New Spain allows for a relatively uncomplicated comparison of Afro-Mexican witchcraft with Kongolese and Angolan magical traditions. Such a comparison leads to a greater appreciation of African influences in Afro-Mexican culture. Magic and curing were central to West Central African cultural life and could take both professional (community-oriented) and nonprofessional (individual-oriented) forms. Priests represented the community, while magicians (healers) and witches attended to individuals. Priests and magicians healed, witches harmed.[20] In both West Central African and Nahua cultures illness was generally understood as the result of witchcraft practiced by individuals (witches) and supernatural forces such as gods or spirits.[21]

Although this is specifically an inquiry into the racial and cultural differences found within novohispano curing magic, it is important to take a step back and realize how prominent these specialists were within the daily lives of most colonials. Sickness was everywhere and life expectancy was short, and when people fell ill they both turned to the medical profession—barbers, doctors, surgeons—and to nonprofessional curers. Owing to the general shortage of university-trained physicians and surgeons, empirics (licensed practitioners apprenticed to physicians) handled tasks like setting broken bones and pulling teeth.[22] But, as we will see, members of all levels of society, from black slaves to the social and economic elites of Mexico City, turned to curanderos to help them with a variety of issues ranging from mundane ailments such as earaches to deadly illnesses. In many cases, sick colonials sought out the advice of both, highlighting how highly esteemed curanderos were in novohispano society.

Whites' Magic

In New Spain, the folk medicine practiced by Spanish and mestizo curanderos represented a mixture of appropriated ecclesiastical medicines, pre-Enlightenment medical theories, and borrowed indigenous herbal and medicinal knowledge. Such borrowings of symbols, materials, and rites were not necessarily accompanied by an understanding of the cultural framework from which they originated. On the contrary, Serge Gruzinski eloquently argues that Spaniards, mulattoes, blacks, and mestizos who appropriated indigenous practices did so without penetrating the social reality from which they were derived. For Gruzinski, non-Indian curanderos were simply capitalizing on recipes that functioned as expedients to health.[23] In the process these symbols and materials became divorced from their cultural context.

Close examination and comparison of white, mestizo, and Afro-Mexican curanderos, however, indicates that such cultural borrowing could involve the assimilation of the appropriated element(s) into the practitioner's cultural system. When a Spanish curandero used an indigenous herb, the symbolic meaning was defined by European, not indigenous, cultural understandings of healing and illness. Similarly, when a black or mulatto prescribed peyote it was potentially incorporated into an Afro-Mexican belief system.[24] The integration of those elements produced changes within each culture that resulted in a process of convergence, which makes it possible to speak of variants of colonial Mexican culture by the eighteenth century. The high levels of cultural exchange between Indians, Afro-Mexicans, and Europeans is precisely what allowed for that convergence, but it did not result in a single cultural system in the colonial period.

Keeping this integration of practices in mind, we can identify at least three types of white/mestizo curanderos. The first were healers who claimed divine providence to cure. Borrowed indigenous materials were not important elements in their cures. The second is the type described by Gruzinski. These healers divorced medical knowledge from the supernatural altogether, employing Nahua herbal remedies and/or pre-Enlightenment medicinal theories but ignoring the cosmological vision that underwrote them. For such curers, medicine was nothing more than an expedient to health.[25] The third form represented a marriage of the first two. Elements appropriated from Nahua and European systems were incorporated into a Catholic cultural system in which God was the primary power in the healing process. Herbs did not heal because of their place within larger Nahua cosmological systems nor because of their rational properties but rather because God made them do so.

Healers of the first type often testified that God, Jesus, or the Virgin Mary had chosen them and granted them the grace to cure. For example, Francisca de Avilés, a Spaniard, claimed to cure with God's "benediction" and without the use of "superstitious herbs." Similarly, Petra de Torres, a Spaniard, asserted that she possessed the grace, blessing, and power of the Virgin Mary to cure. Petra maintained that she fell ill during the *matlazáhuatl* (typhus?) epidemic of 1772 and ascended into heaven. The Virgin Mary then instructed her to return to the world of the living because only she had the power to cure the sick and assist women in childbirth.[26] Marian apparitions were not uncommon in colonial Mexico, the most famous, of course, being that of the Virgin of Guadalupe.[27] Numerous curanderos claimed that Mary had appeared and given them her grace to cure.[28] However, claims of holy grace to conduct magical cures competed with the church, unfairly in its eyes. Curers who ascribed holy grace to themselves put Christian devices to unapproved uses and thus left themselves open to persecution by the Inquisition.[29]

If Petra de Torres and Francisca de Avilés represented prototypical Spanish practitioners who cured with divine grace, then Juan Manuel Sánchez typifies the second type—those who appropriated indigenous and European materials and practices as mere expedients to health. Juan Manuel stood accused of superstitious curing with a root called *siyuquieguna* or *hierba de mujer* (woman's herb) and of using brujería to cure an Indian named Alberto Martín. Juan Manuel admitted prescribing the root as a medicine. He also confessed to curing Esteban Vicente's infected ear by draining it with a tube made from castor bean leaves and prescribing a salve made from the castor leaves fried in almond oil. However, although he begrudgingly admitted that he was known as "el brujo" (the warlock), he denied using witchcraft in any of his cures. Esteban Vicente and Simona María, both Indians, likewise testified that although Juan Manuel was known as "el brujo" he did not use witchcraft to cure them.[30]

Juan Manuel Sánchez may be the personification of the European curandero who appropriated indigenous medicinal knowledge without an understanding of its cultural meanings. Clearly, references to siyuquieguna, which in indigenous cultures may have been understood as the embodiment of a particular deity (whose identity remains unknown), could have had important religious connotations within the indigenous community and for Sánchez's indigenous patients. However, when employed by a Spaniard it lost any religious importance and retained only its rational value. Sánchez was clearly a knowledgeable curandero. Yet most of his actions as described in inquisitorial documents, unlike those of his counterparts, do not appear to have supernatural undertones.[31]

The influence of elements of pre-Enlightenment European medical theories is also apparent in the cases brought against Spanish and mestizo curers in religious courts. Juana de la Pampa y Palacios diagnosed Manuel Duarte as suffering from "burnt yellow bile" and prescribed water of barley and other medicines to restore his humoral balance.[32] Similarly, María Tiburcia Reinantes, a mestiza, prescribed a drink made of *tlacopatl* (a root with properties similar to sarsaparilla) and *contrayerba* in order to reestablish the balance of yellow and black biles in one of her patients.[33]

The most common form of Spanish and mestizo curanderismo, however, represented a marriage of the first two. According to these healers, medicines worked because God made them do so, not because of their rational properties or their symbolic meanings in a Nahua cosmology.[34] The cases in the Inquisition files are full of examples of curers who married pre-Enlightenment medicine with popular Mexican Catholicism. For example, María Tiburcia Reinantes described the healing process as a battle against the devil, the cause of illnesses. Therefore, she would invoke the names of Jesus, the Holy Trinity, and the Virgin Mary and make her patients pray while preparing her medicines to combat the devil. She called on God to insure that her cures were successful and would utter "Where Jesus is mentioned, all evil is destroyed" to insure victory over illness. Likewise, Juana de la Pompa y Palacios had "deposited herself in Christ" in order to serve the sick. She would invoke the name of the Father, the Son, and the Holy Spirit and those of the sainted apostles Peter, Paul, and Michael while making the sign of the cross over her patients' wounds or afflicted areas.[35]

In similar fashion, José Antonio Hernández practiced what appears to be an appropriation of transubstantiation in some of his cures. He would fill a cup with water mixed with salt and make the sign of the cross over the cup saying, "God the Father, God the Son, the Holy Spirit, the Virgin, Holy Mary come to us and assist us."[36] José Antonio would then tell those attending his cures that if they looked into the cup they would see images of Jesus or the Virgin Mary. He then gave to cup to his patient, proclaiming that it contained the sacramental body of Christ and would cure his/her illness. A number of witnesses claimed to have in fact seen the images.

This is not the only one of José Antonio's healing practices that was closely related to the Catholic faith. He also employed powders and herbs that he purchased at local *boticas* (pharmacies) or collected in the countryside, which he then consecrated in the Sanctuary of the Virgin of Guadalupe.[37] José argued that he possessed the knowledge of illnesses and herbs by the grace and wisdom of God and the Virgin Mary.[38] According to his wife, he used the sign of the cross and recited the Pater Noster, Ave María, and the prayer to the Virgin of Guadalupe in his cures. He was also reported to have cured twelve lepers and one cripple with his touch. These reports were clearly meant to suggest connections between José Antonio and Christ.

Numerous witnesses testified that José claimed to have a crucifix on the roof of his mouth visible only on Fridays and to have cried in the womb three times and have been born on Holy Friday.[39] Such claims resonated in colonial Mexico, as people believed that a child who cried in the womb would have extraordinary curative powers.[40] These signs legitimated José Antonio's claims that he was a *saludador* (healer) who cured with the grace of the Virgin Mary.

Similarly, María Tiburcia Reinantes claimed to possess the mark of the cross on the top of her head and a bronze cross on her chest, which she described as symbols of her grace to cure. Inquisitors saw the cross on her head but concluded that María had scarred herself with a knife. Medical doctors and inquisitors may have felt these curers were dangerous and potentially heretical, but the public did not generally share those sentiments. Many of José Antonio's patients appeared to hold him in the highest regard. Likewise, one of María's patients, a Spaniard named María Gorenza Vigueras, testified that she believed María was a saludador given the grace to cure witchcraft by God.[41]

José Antonio and María Tiburcia are excellent examples of practitioners of Spanish and mestizo curanderismo as understood in eighteenth-century Mexico. In their minds, herbs and medicines were mediums through which the power of God, Jesus, and the Virgin Mary operated. José's claims that he transformed salt water into the body of Christ and that God had granted him ability to heal (signaled by the cross on his palate, his birth on Good Friday, and his crying in his mother's womb) strongly suggest that Spanish curing magic was a marriage of popular Catholicism and general medicinal knowledge.

Blacks' Magic

Uncovering a distinctly Afro-Mexican cultural variant of curanderismo is a more difficult task. Europeans, Indians, and Africans interacted and exchanged cultural elements throughout the history of colonial New Spain. European and indigenous knowledge had been diffused throughout the different systems of curanderismo to the point that Indians used Catholic saints in their cures and Spaniards used indigenous herbs. Nearly all of the practices, materials, and symbols employed by black and mulatto healers can be traced to indigenous or European origins. But these materials were often integrated into and employed within a distinctive vision of illness and healing, and it is that system, not the materials and symbols, that must be brought into focus.

If African cultural systems continued to play an important role within the Afro-Mexican community during the eighteenth century, then such influences should be manifested in Afro-Mexican curanderismo. The ethnic endogamy experienced by West Central Africans in the sixteenth and seventeenth centuries provided the underpinning of Afro-Mexican cultural patterns. Blacks and mulattoes incorporated materials and practices into a belief system derived from West Central African traditions. The many similarities among Afro-Mexican, Spanish, and mestizo practices are obvious, but they do not override the significant differences among the belief systems that those practices emanated out of.

As in the case of Nahua cosmology, West Central African conceptions of magic and witchcraft and healing and illness were intricately connected with the supernatural forces that surrounded them. According to Willy de Craemer, Jan Vansina, and Renée Fox, all West Central African cultures shared a core cultural constellation defined as the "fortune/misfortune complex." The central focus of this constellation was the prevention of bad fortune and maximization of good fortune—defined as health, psychic security, fecundity, harmony, power, status, and wealth.[42] That complex was based on the assumption that order, harmony, and goodness are the natural state and that illness, disharmony, and evil are the result of imbalance and impurity caused by witchcraft. The complex provided a system of symbols, rites, beliefs, and ceremonies that served to establish and maintain social, and therefore supernatural, harmony. Healing, within that system, was a ritualistic and symbolic process of purification through which balance was reestablished.

The fortune/misfortune complex remained a core feature of West Central African cultural systems, even as they countenanced frequent changes in symbols, beliefs, and rituals. In New Spain this flexibility allowed Christian or indigenous symbols, practices, and beliefs to be incorporated without alteration of the basic cultural constellation. To put it another way, ritual only has meaning within its cultural foundation, and symbols only have meaning in relation to other symbols within a single ritual. In West Central African cultural systems, in both Africa and the New World, rituals, symbols, and beliefs were variable, but the cultural foundation remained essentially unchanged.[43] Therefore, when Catholic and indigenous elements were appropriated by Afro-Mexicans they assumed new meanings defined by the cosmological visions of that community. Within that cultural complex, both in Africa and the New World, the reestablishment of social and supernatural balance was achieved through ceremony. Afro-Mexican curing ceremonies had much in common with West Central African practices.

In 1772, a free mulatto named José Quinerio Cisneros was denounced to the Holy Office of the Inquisition for practicing curanderismo.[44] The three cures carried out by José that are described in his trial followed the same general pattern. Therefore I treat only significant differences here. A Spaniard named Juan Marino de Inquiza was deathly ill with an unnamed ailment when José came to cure him. Upon his arrival José built an altar to various images of the Virgin Mary ("Our Lady of Solitude," "Our Lady of Suffering"), Jesus ("Our Most Excellent Lord"), and Saint Anthony. After José built the altar, he played the guitar and sang "well-known" prayers to "Our Holy Lord" and "Our Lady of Pilar." As he sang, he cut a cross in the floor with his knife and placed lit candles at the head, feet, and arms of the cross as well as on the altar. José then drove his knife into the floor and placed a lit candle next to it. He asked the sick man to lie down on the cross and proceeded to rub his entire body. Then he used a little pot that held three lit wicks to suck the illness out of Juan's navel.[45] After he completed the massage he mixed a salve made from the powders of tobacco, tlacopatl, and *salvia de Nuestra Señora de San Juan de Lagos* (sage), which he rubbed on Juan's body.[46] Lastly, he gave Juan a decoction of the heart of *guisache* (acacia), the heart of maguey, *mamana*, and *estafiate* (mugwort). He spent the rest of the night with Juan, playing the guitar and singing. The following evening he performed the same cure, only this time he offered Juan holy water to drink. Then, using branches of estafiate drenched in holy water, José beat Juan about the head, shoulders, and chest.[47]

This curing ceremony was clearly a complicated combination of symbols, practices, and medicines. Sticking the knife in the floor was a symbolic action that served to cleanse and protect the curandero, his patient, the witnesses, and the room from witchcraft.[48] Similarly, the massage, the symbolic act of sucking out the illness, and the beating with the branches all fell under the rubric of ritual purification. These actions highlight the interconnectedness of the physical and supernatural worlds within Afro-Mexican curing magic. Such was not the case in the cures performed by Spaniards and mestizos that I have already described.

All three of the cures attributed to José Quinerio took the same form. The only significant difference among them was the images employed in each cure. For example, in his cure of Gregorio García he used images of Our Lady of the Rosary and Saint Joseph, as well as a crucifix, in building his altar, which were very different from the images he employed in his cure of Juan de Inquiza. This variability of images between cures proves to be an important element in Afro-Mexican curanderismo. In all of the cures attributed to him, altars to the saints, ritualistic cleansing actions, and music were as important to the ceremony as the medicines used.

Saints' images also played an important role in the curing ceremonies performed by María de la Concepción, a forty-six-year-old mulatta. On November 15, 1732, Francisco Fraile, a Spaniard, denounced María for curanderismo. Francisco had been suffering from *mal de aire* (a general term for respiratory issues) for months. After the advice and services of numerous doctors and surgeons had failed to cure him, he asked a friend, Juana Venzes, if she knew of any curanderos that might be able to help him. Juana then introduced Francisco to María.

At their first meeting, María informed Francisco that the source of his illness was *maleficio* (demonic witchcraft) but that she could cure him. To initiate her cure, María rubbed an ointment that contained tlacopatl over Francisco's entire body and then left. When she returned, she applied the ointment again and proceeded to massage Francisco's head. María asked for some water, took a mouthful, and then sucked a nopal needle and a small stick from Francisco's head.[49] At this point María informed Francisco and Juana that she would need to purchase more herbs in order to cure him. Juana gave María two *reales* (one real = $1/8$ peso) to purchase *ululuque* (*ololiuhqui*), peyote, and Santa Rosa.[50]

After she procured the herbs she had Francisco ingest them on at least three occasions. The nature of the testimony makes it difficult to determine the exact order of her administerings. Therefore, we will deal with the more significant ones. The first time María prescribed the herbs she again rubbed the tlacopatl ointment over Francisco's body and sucked numerous objects from his head. Then she served him the herbs on a sugar cube and left him to sleep for the night. The next day María asked Francisco how he passed the night. He replied that he had not slept at all because he had a vision that made him very afraid. María asked if he had left a candle burning that night. Francisco said no, and María concluded that was why he had experienced the hallucination. Another witness testified that María would generally leave a candle burning through the night while performing her cures. When questioned about the candle, María responded that she lit the candle to Our Lady of the Rosary to secure her assistance in her cures. Afro-Mexicans treated saints, personified by images or candles present during the cure, as active participants in the curing action. Thus, María may have concluded that the cure went awry because the idol or image of the Virgin Mary was missing, and perhaps she felt that without this ingredient, she could not ensure the cure's success.

The next time that María saw Francisco she again gave him the herbs and told him not to be afraid. She had Francisco lie down on a sheet in the middle of the floor where she again commenced to rub his entire body with the tlacopatl ointment and blew *copal* (resin from the plant genus *Copaifera*) smoke over his body.[51] Then María lightly beat his entire body with wet willow branches. It is not clear whether or not Francisco experienced another vision on this occasion.

The final time María attempted to cure Francisco she gave him a bundle of maguey, estafiate, a piece of *ocote* (*ocotl*, or pine), two pieces of *ololuihque*, and some peyote wrapped in a piece of cloth. She testified that she gave him this bundle of herbs because they were most effective against maleficio. It is not clear if Francisco was to ingest the herbs or if they were to serve as a talisman against witchcraft. At this point, María informed Francisco that she could not cure him because she was only one person and two were attacking him. Earlier, she had explained that Polonia, an Indian with whom Francisco had had a love affair, had bewitched him with the assistance of a powerful witch named Miguel

Playa. She promised to return with another curandero to complete the cure, but the Inquisition apprehended her before she could do so.

In the early 1720s, Antonio de Alvarado, a mulatto, was denounced before the Inquisition for curanderismo supersticioso.[52] Like José Quinerio Cisneros, Antonio employed basically the same cure for all of his patients. First he would inform them that they were bewitched. Then he would place a ball of cotton with some salt in his mouth and suck his patients' bodies where they felt pain. When Antonio sucked a patient he would remove various foreign objects like nopal and maguey needles (cacti), mesquite slivers, bones of fish or birds, and in one case the teeth from a porcelain comb. These objects were not the cause of the illness but rather physical manifestations of witchcraft. On a few occasions his cures were more elaborate. In one such cure, Antonio treated a woman's rash by washing the afflicted areas with an herbal mixture that included Rosa de Santa María (a feminine form of peyote) and administering an unnamed purgative.[53]

Like José Antonio Hernández, Antonio de Alvarado claimed that he had cried in his mother's womb and had a cross on the roof of his mouth visible only on Fridays. Again, both were meant to serve as evidence that he possessed the grace of the Virgin Mary to cure. Indeed, Antonio told one his patients that the Virgin Mary had appeared to him under a palm tree and told him to build a temple in her honor in an unknown location.[54] All three claims were common enough to have cultural currency among average colonial Mexicans even if the inquisitors doubted their validity. Of all the Afro-Mexicans examined in this chapter, Antonio could most easily be described as practicing magic that conformed to the white/mestizo form of curanderismo. His claiming to have divine grace and to have had Marian apparitions place him within that framework. However, "sucking" the illness from his patients was a symbolic purification and cleansing that likely falls under the rubric of the West Central African "fortune/misfortune" complex.[55] That said, Antonio de Alvarado provides evidence of how closely related the different forms of Mexican curanderismo actually were.

When Juan de Acosta was suffering from pains in his legs, arms, and stomach he called upon Sebastián Hernández, a black slave owned by the Hospital of San Juan de Dios in Zacatecas. Sebastián informed Juan that he was bewitched but that he would cure him. Sebastián built an altar to an image of Our Lady of Solitude in Juan's room. On that altar he placed two candles, *romero* (rosemary), copal, Rosa María, a little wine, some tobacco, and some paper. Once he completed the altar he left for the night.

The next night Sebastián began his cure by burning the copal and romero and bathing his makeshift altar in smoke and then playing the guitar and singing. He had Juan lie down on a clean sheet on the floor and gave him the Rosa María to eat. Sebastián proceeded to rub Juan's body in all the areas that were causing him pain. Then, using the paper from the altar, he washed Juan's entire body. After that he asked Juan stand up on the sheet and shake his arms and legs before allowing him to return to bed. Sebastián collected dirt, small pebbles, hair, small sticks, and tinsel on the sheet from Juan's body. He wrapped them in the paper he used to wash Juan and disposed of the bundle in the fire. Like Antonio de Alvarado and María de la Concepción, Sebastián represented the foreign objects as the physical manifestations of witchcraft, not as the cause of the illness. Finally, once he was finished he gave all those present a cigar that they smoked together.

While Sebastián was conducting his cure he was drinking mescal (liquor distilled from agave cactus) and singing. Remarkably, Juan de Acosta, Sebastián, and the other witnesses were able to recall what he sang. The song, constructed from the testimony of Sebastián and the witnesses, follows. The first, second, and ninth verses, marked by brackets, were not included in Sebastián' testimony but come from the testimony of another witnesses.

> [Señor Estafiate, already arriving at the door]
> [Rosa María, already arriving at the door]
> Come to me, Virgin of Solitude
> Help me, Mother [and] Saint Nicolás Tolentino
> with my need
> Virgin, Lady of my soul
> Favor me, Lady
> Virgin of the Candelaria
> [With your permission I can cure]
> To this rosary that God gave to me
> In order to pray to the Conception
> Come my little brothers, perfume with smoke
> The pure Virgin that is in the altar.[56]

The connections between the herbs that were prescribed, the image on the altar, and the song need to be explored in greater detail. The central idol in the altar was Our Lady of Solitude, referenced in the third line, and the primary medical agent in the cure was Rosa María, named in the second line. In invoking the Virgin Mary four times, in different forms, he appears to be calling on her to actively assist him in the cure, to empower the herb/drug Rosa María to combat Juan's illness. Similarly, Saint Nicolás Tolentino was associated with the masculine from of peyote.[57] "My little brothers," referenced in the second-to-last line, refers to the romero and copal that Sebastián used to perfume the altar and the patient with. In essence the song served as a blueprint for the cure, putting voice to the symbolic actions that separate a failed cure from a potentially successful one.[58]

Sebastian's trial includes testimony regarding two other cures he conducted. In each he carried out a ceremony similar to the one he conducted for Juan. For example, Nicolás de Rojas was suffering from a large cut on his arm. Sebastián built the altar to an image of the crucified Christ and other images and covered the wound with an herb called *yoloache* (*yolloxochitl* or *flor de corazón*), and carried out a cleansing ceremony. That ceremony also included the use of copal and rosemary smoke, the removal of foreign objects from Nicolás' body, and the prescription of peyote and Rosa María. This time when Sebastián sang, he sang in a what witnesses called "*mexicano*" that appears to be a mixture of Spanish and Nahuatl:

Axo pegua lino suchi clavellina	Now begin, little flower, carnation
Que digo, querer decir cuál esta rosa	that I say, [I] wish to say this rose

Deciphering these verses is difficult because the first line appears to be Nahuatl, but only *axo* and *suchi* are clearly of Nahua origin. *Axo* is a corrupted spelling of *axa* or *axcan* which means "now." In Spanish *pegar* means to stick or glue, therefore *pegua* could be a misspelling of *pegue*, *pegué* or *pega*. On the other hand, *pegua* could be a misspelling of *pehua* which is Nahuatl for "begin." Similarly, *lino* is difficult. In Spanish it refers to flax or linen, but in this case it probably means "little." *Suchi* was a commonly used corrupted spelling of the Nahuatl term *xochitl*, which corresponds to flower. *Clavellina* could refer to little flower or carnation.[59]

Despite these difficulties, the first line is clearly a call on the *yollox-ochitl* applied to Nicolás' arm to awaken and begin the curing process. This connection can be made because *suchi* is a corrupted spelling of *xochitl*, and *yolloxochitl* was the herb used to cover Nicolás's wound. Once again the song played a central role in the ceremony. The medicine was just material without song. Song symbolically transformed this material into an element with curative purposes. The trial transcript does not include the verses Sebastián employed in his third cure. We do know that he prescribed peyote, built an altar to the images of Saint Nicolás, Saint Anthony, and Saint Michael, and sang "to the saints." In this cure it appears that peyote, the masculine equivalent of Rosa María, was associated with one or more of these male saints.[60]

A mulatto curer named Julián, who operated in the same general vicinity as Sebastián, conducted very similar cures. He, like Sebastián, initiated his cures by building altars to the saints. For example, he built altars to Jesus of Nazareth and Our Lady of Solitude. He also had his patients lay on a cloth in the middle of the floor and administered massages and washings. Julián would show his patients the cloth he had used to wash them, and it would be covered in a silver or gold dust. He also claimed to remove other foreign bodies from his patients. It is entirely possible that these two men knew each other and shared medicinal knowledge, as Ángela de León claimed that both men had cured her on separate occasions.[61]

Afro-Mexican *Curanderismo*

Examining these cases makes the central questions clearer. Could the practices of these various Afro-Mexican curers reflect beliefs that were different from those found in indigenous, mestizo, or Spanish culture? And, if so, how are those differences related to West Central African belief systems? There is no single element common to all of these cures that can be traced to precolonial Africa in the way that peyote and the Virgin Mary can be traced to their cultures of origin. Recall, however, that the basis of West Central African cultures was the "fortune/misfortune complex" and within that system illness was the result of impurity and imbalance. Thus, medicinal practices were rife with symbolic elements that infused the rational materials and that were aimed at reestablishing harmony, balance, and health.

At least four core elements can be identified that reflect West Central African cultural influences and serve to differentiate Afro-Mexican curanderismo from its Spanish/mestizo counterparts. They are: 1) ceremonial cleansing and purification; 2) the repeated use of certain medicinal materials; 3) a distinct understanding and use of Christian elements; 4) and the use of song and/or music. The combination of these elements yields a specific variant of Mexican curanderismo similar to, but still distinct from, that practiced by non-Afro-Mexicans.

Ritual cleansing and purification played a major role in cures enacted by the Afro-Mexican curanderos. Sucking the illness out of the patient's body, giving ritual washings and massages, lightly beating patients with branches, and covering patients with smoke are all manifestations of ritualistic cleansing. In fact in only two of the ten cases of Afro-Mexican curanderos at the heart of this chapter was there no mention of some form of ritual purification.[62] José Quinerio Cisneros used a little pot with lit wicks to suck the illness from his patients' bodies. Similarly, Juan Pavón, whose story opened this chapter, Antonio de Alvarado, and María de la Concepción all claimed to have sucked foreign objects—cactus needles, bones, slivers of wood, hair, and worms—from their patients with their mouths. The act of sucking out illness was one of the most widespread therapeutic features of Bantu (i.e. West Central African) healing practices in Africa. In the Americas, the practice continued and was tied to the idea of restoring purity, fortune, and health.[63]

Even in those cases where sucking was not employed, many Afro-Mexican curanderos removed foreign objects from their patients. Sebastián Hernández and Julián each collected such objects from their patients' bodies in the process of ritual washing or massage. For example, Julián removed a cricket, some worms, and two sticks, one white and one black, from a patient.[64] As I have noted, those materials extracted from the body were the symbolic markers of impurity, illness, and witchcraft but not cause of illness itself. María de la Concepción underscored the symbolic power of removing such objects from a patient when she admitted to faking it in order to impress upon her patient the severity of his illness.[65]

The ritual of burning of copal, romero, and tobacco were equally important to the process of cleansing and purifying persons and objects. María de la Concepción, Sebastián Hernández, and Julián burned some mixture of all three to cover their patients and the ritual elements of the cure in smoke. Similarly, María and José Quinerio Cisneros used tobacco- and tlacopatl-based ointments to cover their patients' bodies. Tobacco and copal served both prophylactic and cleansing purposes in precolonial Nahua religious practices, warding against witchcraft and disease.[66] If similar practices did not exist in West Central African cultures, then Afro-Mexicans no doubt integrated them into their own culture of curanderismo because the function fit their larger conceptions of the healing process. Gonzalo Aguirre Beltrán argues that the practice of sticking a knife in the ground symbolically protected those participating in the cure against witchcraft.[67] The ritual beating with branches of willow or estafiate served similar ends. Craemer, Vansina, and Fox argue that ritual is a symbolic action that embodies the goals and values of the practitioner and the culture from which he/she emerged.[68] These symbolic rituals of cleansing and purification can be seen as emanating from a cultural system in which purity and balance were the equivalents of health and in which healing constituted the symbolic action of restoring them.

The second feature that distinguishes these practitioners was the common body of medicines used to cure a variety of ailments. Peyote, Rosa María (under various names), tobacco, tlacopatl, copal, estafiate, and romero were common medicines used by Afro-Mexicans. Importantly, few if any Spanish or mestizo curanderos used tobacco, copal, peyote, or Rosa María in any of their cures. Even more significant, however, was the fact that particular Afro-Mexican curers used the same medicinal materials in cures for different problems. For example, Sebastián Hernández used peyote and Santa Rosa for a cut arm and eye problems, among other ailments. Nearly all of the materials used were indigenous in origin. This does not mean that indigenous understandings of particular substances were completely lost during the process of integration. That process of borrowing and incorporation resulted in new, but not revolutionary, understandings and uses of indigenous and European elements. What we witnessing here is a process of creation in which elements of all three constituent cultures are combined, exchanged, altered, and reinterpreted in the genesis of distinct variants of Mexican popular culture.

In precolonial Nahua medicine, particular medicinal materials were used for specific maladies. Those materials could be prescribed for a number of different illnesses, but the primary function of the curer was to ascertain the cause of the illness and to recommend the appropriate herb. In West Central African medicine, however, the symbolic meaning of medicines was not constant from one cure to the next. In fact, practitioners tended to employ the same ingredients in a variety of cures and charms (preventative medicine). The alleged specificity and potency of a particular ingredient was defined within the context of the cure. Though many medicines have specific pharmacological values, the lists of recipes for Afro-Mexicans show that particular ingredients were used over and over again. Experience with particular ingredients convinced individual practitioners of their efficacy.[69] These medicines did not have one symbolic meaning; rather their meaning changed depending on their use.[70] Therefore, when Afro-Mexicans incorporated indigenous and European medicinal materials into their own cultural understanding of curing, they may have adopted the practice of making generalized use of preferred materials from West Central African curing traditions.

West Central African medicines were not limited to herbs and drugs. Material objects such as idols, shrines, and musical instruments served as symbolic medicines. The images of the saints and candles employed in the curing ceremonies filled similar roles and were just as important as music and pharmaceutical substances. While Afro-Mexican curers often used the same pharmaceutical materials from one cure to the next, they did not use the same saints' images. Compared to Spanish and mestizo curers, Afro-Mexicans utilized a much greater variety of holy images. While many Spanish or mestizo curers credited divine providence for their ability to cure, they did not, as a group, use holy images as central elements in their healing processes, although Joan Bristol did find an example of a Bohemian Jesuit physician in eighteenth-century New Spain who associated particular saints with specific maladies.[71]

Afro-Mexicans used various representations of the Virgin Mary (Our Lady of the Rosary, Our Lady of Sorrows, Our Lady of Solitude, Our Lady of Pilar) and Jesus (the crucified Christ, Jesus of Nazareth) as well as representations of Saint Nicolas, Saint Anthony, Saint Michael, and Saint Joseph, among other images. Even more striking is the variation among images used by particular curanderos. José Quinerio Cisneros, in his treatment of Juan Marino de Inquiza, built an altar to Our Lady of Solitude, Our Lady of Suffering, Our Most Excellent Lord, and Saint Anthony. For the cure of Gregorio García he employed images of Our Lady of the Rosary, Saint Joseph, and a crucifix. Sebastián Hernández and Julián likewise used various images in their cures. This may suggest either that particular images were associated with particular disorders or that image choice was highly discretional and determined by the context in which the cure was being carried out. Furthermore, Afro-Mexicans viewed the saints as active participants in the curing process, in contrast to Spanish and mestizo curers, who claimed that God, Jesus, or the Virgin Mary empowered them with the grace to cure. For black and mulatto healers, the saints or whatever superpower they represented, not the curers themselves, empowered the medicinal element to cure.

Other scholars have recognized the importance of saints and their images in Afro-Mexican curanderismo. Aguirre Beltrán, for example, attributes that importance to a syncretic worship of African *orishas* or *vodús*. In other words, the saints served as masks behind which Afro-Mexicans hid the West African gods they worshipped.[72] But there is no evidence from the eighteenth century that the importance of saints was linked to ancestral West African gods. At the same time, however, the saints were not worshipped by Afro-Mexicans in the same manner as by Europeans. Rather, they represented Christian elements successfully appropriated and incorporated into West Central African cultural understandings. They were not Old World manifestations in either the African or European sense but new understandings of Old World concepts formed through cultural contact and exchange in the Atlantic world in general and New Spain in particular. Thus, they retained many of their Catholic meanings while acquiring new significance in Afro-Mexican cosmological visions.[73]

Perhaps a comparison with Catholicism in precolonial West Central Africa will clarify how Afro-Mexicans may have envisioned Christian holy objects such as images of the saints, rosaries, candles, and crosses. Catholicism has a long history in West Central Africa. In 1491, the king of Kongo and much of the Kongolese nobility converted to Christianity and created an official Christian cult as a means of further legitimating their power. By the early seventeenth century, and perhaps earlier, most of the people of Kongo identified themselves as Christians and were usually accepted as such by outsiders.[74] Furthermore, the Portuguese spread Christianity throughout what became the colony of Angola and the neighboring regions.[75]

The majority of slaves imported to New Spain came from West Central Africa and thus many may have already been familiar with Catholicism. Exploring how those West Central Africans understood Christian elements in Africa might help illustrate how those who were not familiar with Catholicism may have understood these elements once they were exposed to them in the Americas. Catholicism in West Central Africa took a distinctively African form.[76] Conversion did not result in the destruction of local indigenous beliefs; rather Catholicism was integrated into a larger cultural system.

One area of sixteenth- and seventeenth-century West Central African Catholic ritual that is relevant for our discussion of New Spain is the centrality of charms or fetishes known as *nkisi* (pl. *minkisi*). In the precolonial period the Kongo thought a *nkisi* was a personalized supernatural force that had chosen, or been induced, to submit itself to some degree of human control effected through ritual performance. *Nkisi* also referred to the physical charm or fetish that housed the supernatural force. The *nkisi* was the physical embodiment of that force, which could only be activated or empowered by knowledgeable practitioners. The *nkisi* object was thought of as the container for the *nkisi* force. The centrality of fetishes or charms seems to have been universal along the Atlantic coast of West Central Africa.[77] *Minkisi* were not, however, conceived of as deities like the orishas or vodús of West Africa.

The widespread use of charms in West Central African religion was encouraged by the Christian practice of using iconographic material and distributing religious medals. John Thornton argues that Catholic priests handed out individual charms or fetishes in the form of religious medals by the thousands in Kongo. These items were accepted and treated as objects with power because they were regarded as Christian *minkisi*, that is, as new forms of older religious symbols. Christian holy items became very powerful religious objects reflecting African, not European, belief systems. West Central Africans eagerly accepted and wore medals and crosses, carried rosaries and relics, and protected themselves from witchcraft by repeating the sign of the cross.[78]

Even if slaves imported to New Spain had not experienced Christianity in West Central Africa, they and their descendents would have, most likely, approached images of the saints and other religious items as *nkisi* in much the same way as they would have in Africa. Images of the saints thus may have been central to Afro-Mexican curing ceremonies because practitioners believed they were the containers that housed the supernatural forces that would make a cure successful. For the Kongo, in particular, the art of healing was, in part, concerned with the manipulation of particular *nkisi* to combat witchcraft and/or illness. And there were as many *minkisi* as there were diseases, which suggests a high level of variability.[79]

This might help explain the centrality and variability of saints' images to cures performed by Afro-Mexicans. What is very clear, however, is that Afro-Mexicans employed images in very different ways from their Spanish and mestizo counterparts.

Medicines were not just prescribed for ingestion but were also symbols employed during the curing ceremony. In West Central African curing ceremonies those symbols were given specific meaning through song. This leads to the final ceremonial element of Afro-Mexican curanderismo that separates it from that practiced by Spaniards and mestizos. For black and mulatto healers, music cured. It communicated with powers above and beyond the visible world. Songs articulated the medical significance of materials within a given curing ceremony.[80] No Spanish or mestizo curer whose cases in the Inquisition records I examined employed music in his or her cures.

The ceremony attributed to Sebastián Hernández and the testimony of Nicolás Candelario highlight the central role music played in Afro-Mexican curanderismo. For Sebastián, the song was a blueprint of the cure, linking the medicines and images of saints together into a single ceremonial action. Nicolás, a mulatto curer, also sang when he prescribed peyote and Rosa María in the form of a drink. During one cure he sang, "San Antonio Bendito / Cure this man / Virgin of Guadalupe, give him health / Cure this man." The song represents, as it did for Sebastián Hernández, an outline of the curing action in which the practitioner called on specific saints to empower the herbs. Furthermore, when inquisitors asked Nicolás if he believed that music had the power to heal he replied, "I believe that music can heal the sick because for thirty years I have been using music combined with the peyote/Rosa María drink to cure." Later in his testimony Nicolás clarified his point when he said that "the peyote and Rosa María together with the music have the power to heal."[81]

Clearly, for both Antonio and Nicolás the music was a core unifying element of their curing ceremonies. There are also clear associations between the medical materials used, the saints, and the song. Sebastián Hernández called on four different manifestations of the Virgin, embodied in the herb Santa Rosa, on Saint Nicolás, personified by the peyote, and on the tobacco and copal to help him effect his cure. Likewise, Nicolás called on the Virgin of Guadalupe and Saint Anthony, embodied in the same herbs, to heal his patient. He also testified that song was a central ingredient in his curing ceremonies. For Afro-Mexicans like Sebastián

Hernández, José Quinerio Cisneros, Nicolás Candelario, and Diego Barajas song and music were as important to the cure as the herbs they prescribed and the ritual cleansing they performed.

Not every Afro-Mexican curandero employed all of the elements I have described—purification, repeated use of the same medicines (including nonpharmaceutical materials), song, and holy images, many of which were absent in other non-Afro-Mexican forms of curanderismo—but they were widespread enough in Afro-Mexican curing ceremonies to evidence West Central African cultural influences in Mexico.[82]

The difficulties in extrapolating the cultural currency of magic and curing for the Afro-Mexican community from a limited number of case studies are obvious. However, the documents created by the Inquisition provide at least two other methods to measure the importance of magic, both positive and negative, within that community. One method is to measure the proportion of denunciations for all forms of witchcraft brought against Afro-Mexicans in the eighteenth century. The second method is to calculate the relative frequency of accusers by race. If magic and witchcraft were central to Afro-Mexican cultural life one might expect blacks and mulattoes to be overrepresented as defendants and underrepresented as accusers when compared to Spanish and mestizos.

A survey of the race of those accused of witchcraft in New Spain across the eighteenth century reveals some striking patterns. Recall that Indians were not subject to the Inquisition. More mulattoes stood accused of practicing witchcraft than any other racial group, and, more specifically, they dominated the categories of divination, curanderismo, and hechicería. Brujería was the only category not dominated by mulattoes. When all persons with African heritage are treated as a single group they represent a majority, approximately 51 percent, of all persons accused of practicing witchcraft and curing in eighteenth-century Mexico.[83] Only when Spaniards (17 percent) and mestizos (25 percent) are combined do they rival the number of Afro-Mexicans accused of similar crimes.

These figures take on greater significance when they are compared to the relative population of people of African descent in New Spain during the eighteenth century. If magic and witchcraft did not play a more significant role in the community and cosmology of any single racial group, then one would expect that accusation rates would be similar to population ratios. Accusation rates substantially higher than population ratios could indicate the increased importance of witchcraft for that particular group. Aguirre Beltrán's pioneering work provides two population esti-mates for the eighteenth century. Since Indians were not theoretically subject to the Inquisition, we can, therefore, focus on the population ratios of blacks and mulattoes within the non-Indian population. In 1742, blacks and mulattoes represented 30.5 percent of the non-Indian population. By 1793, Afro-Mexicans accounted for only 25.4 percent of the non-Indian population. Based on those population percentages Afro-Mexicans were accused of and tried for witchcraft 1.5 to 1.8 times more often than would be expected if accusations were random.

Many scholars would argue that the high level of Afro-Mexican defen-dants is an indication Afro-Mexicans were feared by the rest of colonial society and that the Inquisition served as a powerful tool of accultura-tion. Accusing a person of brujería and hechicería not only stigmatized him or her but also made an example of him or her for the community and thus served as a method of controlling individuals and cultural forms. Diana Luz Ceballos Gómez contends, for example, that only blacks were accused of brujería in Nueva Granada because it was an effective way for the state and church to control and acculturate what they considered to be a dangerous segment of the population. Joan Bristol argues that Spaniards deployed the Inquisition to "reassert authority," using it to denounce blacks and mulattoes who gained too much power through their healing abilities.[84] Such conclusions could be correct from the point of view of the powerful and a policy of domination through assimilation. However, we cannot forget the power of belief. Magic and witchcraft were real, constant, and vibrant elements in popular novohispano culture. The curanderos examined in this chapter believed in magic and in their own ability to cure. The overwhelming majority of their clients believed in them as well. Afro-Mexicans were accused of practicing witchcraft and curing because they practiced them—not because the state and church invented a crime by which to acculturate them.

A second method of measuring the acceptance of witchcraft and curing by particular racial communities in Mexico is to compare the racial iden-tity of accusers. While the cases I looked at do not permit a comprehensive study of this particular question, they do offer up some interesting com-parisons. The eighteen curanderos examined in depth herein generated at least thirty-one denunciations before the Inquisition. For example, five different people in four Mexican cities denounced Antonio de Alvarado. Of those thirty-one accusers only four (13 percent) were Afro-Mexicans.

Spaniards, however, made nineteen (61 percent) of those denunciations. If those ratios reflect larger patterns within accusations they could indicate that witchcraft and magic were established and understood elements of the Afro-Mexican community. Furthermore, these ratios may suggest that the Afro-Mexican community possessed internal mechanisms other than the Inquisition to define and uphold community morality.

Conclusions

Let us take a step back and consider chapters 2 and 3 in combination. Slaves were not part of the indistinguishable casta middle. Spouse selection patterns among slaves indicate that they were a core element in the social networks that drew free and enslaved blacks and mulattoes to each other and served to distinguish them from non-Afro-Mexicans. A close scrutiny of curanderismo trial transcripts indicates that differences in racial identity played a central role in the understanding of and uses to which witchcraft and magic were put in Mexico. This suggests that the social networks described in chapter 2 were based on more than the power of the sistema de castas in ordering society or the shared socioeconomic status of colonials potentially marked by casta categories. They were grounded, in part, in shared cultural visions that served to demarcate mulatto and black from mestizo and Spanish and probably from Indian as well. Those social networks seem to point to distinctive but clearly not exclusive cultural communities. The terms used to identify calidad and raza, therefore, were about more than a complicated calculus of phenotype, heritage, occupation, wealth, and honor. Cultural identity must be added to that list for Afro-Mexicans as it would be for Spaniards and Indians. Still, it bears repeating that although it appears that shared cultural understandings drew Afro-Mexicans together, there is nothing to indicate that those potentially unrecognized similarities were transformed into some form of "racial consciousness" that led blacks and mulattoes to challenge their subordinate positions in the social hierarchy in any collective, race-based manner.

The discourses of magic and witchcraft did not fill the same role in the European, mestizo, and Afro-Mexican communities. The differences in the function of these discourses allow for discussions of both cultural continuity and cultural mestizaje in colonial Mexico. Magic and witchcraft in New Spain were informed by an overarching cultural perspective generated by contact and interaction among European, indigenous, and African groups, yielding a conception of sorcery that was significantly different from earlier European conceptions but that was not homogeneous. Rather than viewing the cultural history of the colonial period as a single process of mestizaje it would be more fruitful to conceive of this history in terms of multiple, parallel, and, at times, overlapping processes of cultural formation. The result was not completely distinct cultural communities but variations on a larger common culture recognizable to most members of society, even if they were not aware of the cultural foundations on which it was built.

Importantly, the cultural community created and maintained by Afro-Mexicans was shared by slaves and their free counterparts. As the population of African descent transitioned from a heavily enslaved, African population to one dominated by creoles and free people of color, slaves were not completely isolated because of their social position. Historians have long recognized that identity is multiple and layered. For slaves, the racial identity they shared with free persons was important to their lived experiences. Thus, even as slavery imposed distinctive constraints on slaves and placed them in subject positions particular to their social status, their experiences were not solely defined by their enslavement. Yet they were slaves, and the very particularities of their enslaved status, explored in the following three chapters, prove as essential to understanding the lived experience of slavery in New Spain as their racialized identities.

CHAPTER 4

"I Renounce the Virgin Mary"
Mastery, Violence, and Power

✣ ON EASTER SUNDAY IN 1696, "FOUR STRONG BLACK SLAVES" dragged Ignacio de Armijo from his cell and pinned him to the ground while Juan de la Cruz, another bondsman, whipped him. Armijo, a sugar plantation slave, was being punished on orders from the mayordomo for having run away. Each of the slaves charged with holding Armijo grabbed an arm or a leg while de la Cruz began to beat him. After approximately ten lashes, Armijo blasphemed, saying "I renounce the Virgin Mary and the Holy Sacrament." At this point the mayordomo removed the bit from his horse's mouth and jammed it into Armijo's mouth to gag him and thus prevent him from blaspheming again. The overseer then ordered Juan de la Cruz to complete the beating. Armijo testified that he had originally begged, in the name of the Virgin Mary and the sacraments, to be released from his punishment and that he blasphemed only when it became clear that his overseer was intent on carrying through with the beating.[1]

Armijo's flogging and his blasphemous outburst is a very representative scenario in the over one hundred existent blasphemy cases against slaves heard by the Inquisition in New Spain. In a great majority of those cases, bondspeople committed blasphemy during, or immediately preceding, physical punishment for running away, stealing, or failing to complete their duties. The involvement of other slaves as the instruments of the punishment was also common in such cases. Masters regularly employed bondsmen to punish other slaves and in some cases even empowered slaves to impose such beatings on other enslaved persons without specific orders to do so. The progression from begging for mercy to renouncing God, the Virgin Mary, Jesus, the saints, and the holy sacraments in some combination was also routinely described in such cases. Lastly, the intensification of violence suffered by slaves after the religious breach was also a regular occurrence. These patterns speak volumes about mastery, slavery as an institution, and the lives of bondspeople in New Spain.

These public displays of power and violence would have certainly served to reinforce slaves' awareness of their denigrated social position and highlighted the extent of the power that masters enjoyed over them. The accounts surrounding slave blasphemies provide stark evidence of the violence that was fundamental to the experience of bondage. The extent of that violence is brought into clear focus when one considers that blasphemies committed by nonslaves, even other blacks and mulattoes, rarely if ever occurred in the context of physical punishment. That brutality underscores the significant power differential between the enslaved and those that claimed ownership over them.

Case files for slaves accused of blasphemy or witchcraft against their owners as well as those for slaves suing their masters over *maltratamiento* (mistreatment) considered in this chapter not only remind us of the inherent violence in master-slave relations. They also draw attention to the ongoing social definition of what constituted acceptable behavior for both masters and slaves and to the fundamental role that slaves played in that construction. Bondspeople were not powerless or cowed into submission in the face of violence. They constantly contested and/or accommodated mastery as they fought to make their lives as livable as possible.

Equally important, these cases bring into clear focus the degree to which slaves were integrated into colonial society. The bondsmen and bondswomen who testified in them clearly understood the religious, institutional, and cultural context in which they operated. Their actions constantly betray their immersion in the colonial social milieu. They suggest that slaves were often aware of the institutional and legalistic avenues open to them. Slaves also proved themselves to be "good Christians" in the eyes of the Inquisition through their ability to recite important Catholic prayers like the Nicene Creed and the Hail Mary as well as the

Ten Commandments and the confessional prayer. At the same time, slaves had also learned to curse from their Spanish oppressors. They picked up dangerous utterances and exclamations employed by their enslavers that defied social norms and expectations.[2]

In the face of the violence inflicted on bondsmen like Ignacio de Armijo, it is tempting to treat their blasphemy as a resistive act, an assertion of slaves' humanity in the face of insufferable treatment. Some have ascribed even greater political weight to these blasphemous acts by arguing that they represent "attempt[s] to challenge the way that society was structured, and the ways that power and authority were allocated."[3] That slavery was harsh and that the enslaved bitterly contested that reality is well established, but treating blasphemy as a "socially patterned verbal act of resistance" potentially aimed at undermining the social hierarchy presupposes a level of intent on the part of slaves that we cannot presume to know in a majority of cases.[4] Slaves did occasionally testify that they had a more immediate goal when they blasphemed: to end the violence they suffered. But such actions were not necessarily aimed at a redistribution of power.[5] In only a very small minority of cases did slaves consciously and purposefully commit a religious crime, usually blasphemy, in order to gain an audience before the Inquisition to denounce an abusive master. We must resist the temptation to universalize the experiences of those few and constantly remind ourselves of the circumscribed set of potential punishments for masters and potential rewards for the enslaved on the rare occasions when abuse was established in the eye of the courts.

Definitions of slave resistance also make the term unwieldy. Numerous scholars attempt to distinguish between types of slave resistance but often conclude that only "political" resistance—defined as collective, antisystemic action, overtly aimed at the destruction of slavery—counts as bona fide resistance. Blasphemy, following this reasoning, would be defined as token resistance—characterized by individual, unorganized, self-serving action not necessarily in the best interests of slaves as a group and devoid of revolutionary implications and therefore representing bondspeople's capitulation to their own domination.[6] Conversely, the tendency to treat any act, like a blasphemous outburst, that forced slaveholders to recognize the humanity of their bondspeople as a form of resistance oversimplifies master power and slave reactions to it.[7]

Lastly, treating blasphemy as resistance does little to help our understanding of the other slaves who appear in these cases, particularly those

who administered and in some cases ordered the punishment that led
to the outbursts in the first place. The recent emphasis on the resistive
capabilities of dominated groups, especially slaves, has left many of us
reluctant or ill equipped to discuss subordinate action that appears to lack
resistive intentionality, such as slaves' holding down, informing on, or
beating other slaves.[8]

Blasphemy, maltratamiento, and witchcraft cases involving slaves
serve as a window into ordinary master-slave relations even as the crimes
discussed in them appear, on the surface, to be extraordinary. We should
not only focus on the crimes themselves or speculate about intentionality
on the part of slaves or masters; rather, our approach to these acts must
be more subtle. In slave blasphemy and witchcraft cases, the religious
breach was but one in a series of events described in these trial transcripts, and the cases only offer mere snippets of the constant conflict and
negotiation between masters and slaves also evident in maltratamiento
cases. Recognizing that will allow us to expand our inquiry beyond the
blaspheming slave to consider the experiences of other bondspeople
as well as their free counterparts. Masters, overseers, the slave being
punished, slaves who administered the beating, and witnesses (both slave
and free) all provided testimony on the circumstances that led to the religious breach, often presenting contradictory versions of events. We must
also recognize the state's intervention into master-slave relations in these
blasphemy and maltratamiento cases as a singular event in ongoing negotiations between masters and slaves rather than as a defining feature of
bondage in Spanish America. Master-slave relations emerge, then, as a
hegemonic process, as the conflictive negotiation of acceptable behavior
through the interaction of the distinctive and often contradictory ideas of
what constituted legitimate social behavior, or the private transcripts, of
the enslaved, their enslavers, and other free members of society.

Slave Blasphemers

Slave blasphemy fell into two general categories. Most commonplace were
cases in which it was uttered in reaction to physical punishment. What
may have normally been cries of pain and anger or pleas for mercy were
transformed into blasphemous outbursts. Those instances in which slaves

consciously employed blasphemy preemptively to avoid or end punishment were similar in nature but were much less common. In both cases, the blasphemy occurred in the context of an extremely violent and painful punishment but not one that was necessarily seen as illegitimate or unjust in the eyes of slaves, particularly the slave being castigated.

The second type of blasphemy case is distinct because it occurred in a context in which the punishment had breached some line of propriety from the slave's perspective and often from that of other witnesses as well. In these cases, testimonies highlight disagreements over whether or not the punishment was deserved, whether the offense warranted the punishment inflicted, and/or whether the form of punishment was socially acceptable. Still, in most cases the slave's intent was not to draw attention to excesses. In rare cases slaves appear to have purposely and consciously committed blasphemy in order to gain an audience before the Inquisition and air grievances against their masters. Treating blasphemous outbursts as part of a larger hegemonic process highlights the negotiated nature of mastery and slavery. These blasphemous outbursts were but one moment in ongoing conflicts over legitimate and humane punishment and acceptable workloads.

On September 25, 1660, two soldiers captured Antonio, the fifteen-year-old slave of Licenciado Jerónimo Morón, a lawyer for the Real Audiencia, on the streets of Mexico City and returned him to the home of his master. According to Morón, his son Joseph de Morón, and their fifty-year-old slave Agustina, Antonio was notorious for running away for short periods of time.[9] On this occasion, upon his return, Morón ordered Antonio to be tied to the stairs and flogged. Don Jerónimo, Don Joseph, and Agustina all testified that Antonio blasphemed on receiving the first lash. Joseph added that his father became incensed and struck Antonio again while asking "What did you say?"[10] Antonio responded that he had renounced the devil. At that point Don Jerónimo stopped beating Antonio, placed a wooden gag in his slave's mouth, and left Antonio bound to the stairs while he went to alert the Inquisition of what had transpired. After his father left, Joseph punched a still-gagged Antonio in the mouth, drawing blood, after he heard the slave blaspheme a second time. Antonio, whose testimony was not taken until two years after this incident, asserted that he first begged them, for the love of God, to stop beating him. Then, when that plea fell on deaf ears, "due to the pain and fear of his punishment," he reneged. But, he added, his blasphemy was not "heartfelt"; rather it was motivated by fear and the pain of the beatings he suffered.[11]

Neither Antonio nor Agustina indicated that the punishment was unjustified or particularly cruel within the confines of slavery. Rather, both slaves understood that the Morones were entitled to punish a truant slave and that being tied to the stairs and beaten was within the bounds of socially acceptable punishment.[12] Antonio reacted to the pain of the punishment, understandably, but we cannot infer from that reaction that his intent was to threaten or undermine his masters' authority symbolically or otherwise.

In a similar case, Juanillo de la Cruz, the black slave of Alonso Ramírez, ran away from his master's *panadería* (bakery) in Mexico City after a domestic dispute. Juanillo fled after he struck Nicolasa, also Ramírez's slave, in the head following what appears to have been a lovers' quarrel. Juanillo went to a nearby panadería where he hid out and worked for about ten days. When the *panadero* (baker) discovered that Juanillo was a slave he quickly returned him to Ramírez. Juanillo was also tied to a staircase to be punished. Ramírez also ordered one of his slaves, Francisco, to administer the punishment. Francisco testified that he beat Juanillo, as ordered, and the blows were "moderate" in his eyes.[13] According to multiple witnesses, Juanillo blasphemed after seven lashes. After approximately seven more lashes, he begged for forgiveness for his blasphemy. His master put a stop to the beating and turned Juanillo over to the Inquisition. The slaves who participated in the punishment gave no indication that it was unjustified or overzealous.[14] Both Juanillo's and Antonio's blasphemy appears not to have been an overt resistive act but a reaction to the pain caused by their beatings.

Slaves often blasphemed, or threatened to blaspheme, to preempt or avoid eminent punishment. In 1693, on a hacienda called Parandian in Pinzándaro, Michoacán, Felipe de la Cruz blasphemed when other slaves grabbed him on orders from their master to punish him for some unnamed offense. Felipe was subsequently beaten for his blasphemy and then begged to be released in the names of the Virgin Mary and Our Lord God. He did not, however, blaspheme again while being punished. The witnesses in the case, all slaves, testified that they believed Felipe blasphemed out of fear of his impending punishment. Many added that Felipe was a good Christian. The Inquisition, in its decision not to pursue the case, agreed with that assessment and concluded that his outburst was distinct from true, heartfelt blasphemy.[15]

The case of Jerónima de San Miguel, the black slave of Doña Mariana de Salas Valles, again highlights the use of blasphemy in the face of imminent punishment. Doña Mariana believed Jerónima to be a thief. As a result, she moved to sell Jerónima to Licenciado Salvador de Suasnaba, who planned to send the slave to his ingenio. Jerónima pleaded with her mistress to allow her to search for a new master in Mexico City. More than likely, ingenios, like obrajes, had a terrible reputation among slaves. Jerónima also likely feared losing the freedom of movement afforded her in the urban environment of Mexico City. Doña Mariana refused to help Jerónima unless she returned the stolen goods. At that point, Jerónima blasphemed. Throughout her trial Jerónima vehemently maintained her innocence with regard to the stolen items, but she admitted blaspheming out of her fear of being sent to the ingenio. The Inquisition sentenced her to one hundred lashes. However, the trial proceedings do not make clear if she was sent to a sugar plantation or not.[16]

That none of these bondspeople appear to have viewed the beatings they received or witnessed as illegitimate does not mean that slaves were resigned to the fact that masters had unlimited access to physical violence. Nor does it suggest that they were incapable of publicly objecting to excessive violence. In other contexts, slave blasphemy, usually unconsciously but at times very consciously, drew attention to actions by masters that were perceived as unwarranted, illegitimate, and/or cruel. Thus, blasphemy trials allow the historian to tap into ongoing colonial discourses regarding acceptable and nonacceptable treatment. Numerous examples from New Spain highlight the reality that slaves did not simply accept that masters had an unlimited rein in punishing them. Rather, these slaves point out that some line had been crossed, that some socially constructed understanding of what constituted acceptable punishment had been breached.[17] Blasphemy may or may not have been employed consciously by slaves to mark that breach, but in either case they initiated a discourse on what degree of physical coercion on the part of slave owners was acceptable.

Juan López Páez de la Baña, an obraje owner from Puebla, appeared before the Inquisition on April 30, 1686, to denounce Pascual for blasphemy. Pascual, a slave owned by Juan Godínez, worked in Páez's obraje. Páez and his overseer, Onofre de Arteaga, were inspecting the workers' progress the previous day when they discovered that Pascual was missing some of the wool he had been given to process. Arteaga, the overseer, then ordered that Pascual be beaten "because he habitually wasted or stole wool." Four slaves from the obraje, including Diego Vaquero, held Pascual to the ground while a free mulatto convict flogged him.[18]

There is little agreement as to what exactly transpired next. According to Páez, the overseer ordered that Pascual receive twenty-five to thirty lashes, which the overseer himself saw executed. Slightly contradicting his employer, Arteaga testified that he didn't count the number of lashes Pascual received, but that he was sure that it was fewer than fifty. Importantly, neither Páez nor Arteaga actually heard Pascual blaspheme. The slave Diego Vaquero presented a very different version of events. He asserted that Arteaga had ordered that Pascual "be beaten until he returned the wool" and that he received a total of 136 lashes before Arteaga relented. Vaquero, who was holding Pascual down during the beating, also said that he heard Pascual blaspheme under his breath, renouncing God and his saints, about midway through his punishment. Antonio de la Cruz, another slave, corroborated Vaquero's testimony. Once the beating was over, and Pascual had been placed in shackles, Vaquero confronted him, asking if he had, in fact, renounced God. Pascual angrily responded "Well, would I have to blaspheme if they didn't treat me in this manner?" Vaquero pressed, "Was your blasphemy heartfelt?" to which Pascual answered in the affirmative. Vaquero then informed Arteaga and Páez what he overheard, and they then turned the case over to the Inquisition.[19]

There is much of interest in this case. While some might be tempted to treat Pasqual's blasphemy as a resistive act, the fact that he did so under his breath suggests it was not. That another bondsman felt compelled to report that blasphemy, even in an instance that appeared to border on abuse, is also quite suggestive of the power dynamics that animated slavery. This also marks one of the few cases in which mention was made of the specific number of blows a slave was to receive. What is difficult to determine, however, is what number of blows was socially acceptable. It is apparent from their testimony that Páez felt that twenty-five to thirty blows was within the realm of reason, whereas Arteaga believed fifty lashes to be socially acceptable. Based on Vaquero's testimony Pasqual blasphemed after some sixty or seventy lashes. The discrepancies in this case speak to a lack of consensus as to what counted as unacceptable treatment of slaves.

In a similar case, a mulatto named Padilla also blasphemed while being beaten in an obraje. Padilla, who had been sent to the obraje by his owner for attacking a man, testified that he had been punished for not completing his daily quota. The workload for enslaved workers had recently been increased from ten to fifteen libras per day per slave, and on the day in question he and two companions had failed to card five of the forty-five libras they had been given to process. Rafael de Bustamante, the mayordomo, ordered that all three be beaten. A black slave named Lucas de Vivero testified that he heard Padilla receive approximately ten to twelve blows from Bustamante. Padilla was visibly angry after that beating, cursing about how Bustamante had treated him.

After being punished, Padilla apparently planned to seek out the owner of the obraje to complain that the slaves did not have enough time to complete the extra work they had been given. Upon learning of Padilla's intent, Bustamante began to flog him again, delivering a "very cruel blow, very different from those he received from his owner."[20] Witnesses, enslaved and free alike, testified that they overheard Padilla cursing at Bustamante and that after receiving four lashes he renounced God, the Virgin Mary, and the saints, as many as six times. Padilla testified that he first threatened to blaspheme if the second beating didn't stop and that Bustamante's response was to flog him even harder. Padilla subsequently blasphemed. Antonio de Silva, the obraje owner, became enraged over the blasphemous outburst and ordered that Padilla receive ten to twelve more lashes and then be placed in leg irons. Apparently, the next morning before being taken to the Inquisition, Padilla blasphemed again, enraging the mayordomo's assistant who smacked Padilla in the mouth, knocking out two teeth.[21]

Padilla and Pascual both received a beating for not completing their assigned daily tasks. Padilla, feeling that the workload was unfairly increased, decided to complain but was punished again, this time even more cruelly, and in his mind illegitimately. In blaspheming, Padilla and Pascual neither rejected the right of masters or overseers to punish them for not finishing their work nor questioned the legitimacy of whippings as punishment. Rather their blasphemies were reactions to perceived excesses. Padilla's actions suggest that he, at least, felt it was reasonable for a slave to openly complain to owners and overseers about what he perceived to be unacceptable punishment and workloads.

Numerous other bondspeople blasphemed during what may have originally been perceived as legitimate punishment that crossed a line into excessive or brutal treatment. For example, Nicolás de la Cruz—an enslaved worker in the crushing mill of Capitán Agustín Gutiérrez, a silver miner in Pachuca—blasphemed while being beaten on orders from the mayordomo. Nicolás had begged to be released from his punishment, as might be expected, but renounced God when he was struck in the genitalia.[22] Similarly, on a sugar hacienda near Cuernavaca numerous slave witnesses testified that Coquis, another slave, blasphemed owing to the particular cruelty of his punishment. According to them, Coquis was beaten across his belly, "received blows in an irregular and very sensitive area," and had been whipped on parts of his body that were already covered in wounds from previous floggings.[23] These two cases suggest that there was an unspecified consensus as to what was appropriate when it came to floggings. Blows delivered to the back and or the buttocks were acceptable. But beating slaves on their stomachs, striking their genitalia, or whipping a slave on the open wounds from a previous beating seemed to be unacceptable.

Ramón González, a mulatto slave whom his mistress, Doña Ana de González de Godoy, had rented to the obraje of Melchor Díaz de Posadas, testified that he lost consciousness while being flogged behind his knees. His buttocks were apparently so badly damaged from being beaten and burnt with boiling sugar that he could no longer be flogged there. The use of boiling sugar or hot oil/grease on slaves, particularly in regions where they had been recently beaten, was not an uncommon practice. It was, however, a matter of bitter contention between masters and their slaves, who often described it as abusive. Although González claimed to have passed out from the pain, which was corroborated by multiple witnesses, he stood accused of blaspheming during this particular punishment. González apparently first begged an image of Christ to save him from his punishment and later blasphemed as he was beaten by two men, at the same time, for over an hour.[24]

Mateo de Andrade, another slave, was ordered to pour a jar of urine over Ramón's wounds, perhaps to sanitize them but more likely to inflict more physical and psychological suffering. Mateo told Ramón that "Fernando Díaz [the overseer and Melchor's son] is wrong for beating you so cruelly, because you are not his slave."[25] Another slave testified that the beating was so violent and cruel that it "scandalized" the other bondspeople in the obraje.[26] The language employed by these slaves to describe the cruelty and ferocity of the flogging highlight the existence of a fuzzy line between acceptable and unacceptable treatment that Fernando had breached.

The Díaz de Posadas obraje appears to have been a particularly cruel place for the enslaved. During the inspection of the obraje in 1660, numerous bondspeople testified about the mistreatment they received there. The slave Nicolás Bazán testified that he had received over fourteen thousand lashes in a four-month period for stealing and selling wool.[27] In the context of his trial, he and Geronimo de Vergara, another slave, claimed that as many as six slaves, including Bazán and Ramón González, had blasphemed while being flogged in the obraje. In the course of his trial, Bazán described life in the obraje as follows:

> One of the more prominent punishments they employ in the obraje is to place [us] in a *gargantón*—a combination of a collar and handcuffs that totally immobilizes the victim. It is so harsh that any Christian would be in great danger of renouncing God and his just Faith. Although [I] was tormented for many days in the gargantón, God gave me the strength to endure.

Bazán would contend that the abuses these "Christian slaves" suffered at the hands of their "Christian master" were far worse than those endured by Christians martyred at the hands of Turks and Moors.[28] Ramón González added that Fernando Díaz had instituted a series of "cruel" punishments after becoming the mayordomo of the obraje. He would regularly order fifty lashes with a handful of switches and order that to be followed by as many as two hundred blows from a whip. In the documents from the 1660 inspection of this obraje and the blasphemy trials of González and Bazán, testimony surfaced that at least two other slaves had been beaten to death by Melchor and Fernando Díaz de Posadas. One of these slaves, Nicolás de Urresti, had died after receiving an "infinite number of lashes" that caused him to faint numerous times. When he lost consciousness, cold water was poured over his body until he awoke, and then he was beaten once more.[29]

Compare the experiences of these obraje slaves with the description of life in the obraje of Antonio Álvarez, in Mexico City, given by Juan Pablo, an Angola bondsman who worked there in 1651. When asked to address the causes of a blasphemy committed by another slave, Juan Pablo testified that although the workload imposed by his master was not excessive, any slave who failed to finish his daily quota could expect, and was resigned to, a beating. In describing those punishments, Juan Pablo testified that a slave would generally receive between six to twelve lashes that would be delivered "in a noncruel manner."[30] This description seems consistent with Padilla's testimony that he received ten to twelve lashes for not finishing his daily quota in the de Silva obraje.[31] Juan Pablo understood that not meeting imposed workloads would result in punishment, but he also conveyed the sentiment that in his view this punishment was not to be excessively harsh.

That slaves recognized that punishment was the expected response for not completing the labor they were assigned is made obvious by the case of Francisco de la Cruz, a slave who labored on the Santa Bárbara ingenio, near Cuernavaca. One morning in 1664 the mayordomo, Juan Alonso, also a slave, noticed that Francisco had disappeared from the field where he had been assigned to work. Juan Alonso found Francisco in a neighboring field apparently sleeping off the effects of the previous night's drinking. Juan Alonso then ordered that Francisco be beaten for not completing his duties. After six or seven lashes, Francisco blasphemed.[32]

The fact that slaves could and did physically reprimand other slaves further illuminates the point made by Juan Pablo: slaves could expect to be beaten for not completing their work. That slaves recognized the right of masters and mayordomos to punish them is made apparent by the fact that in none of these cases is there any evidence of a slave refusing an order to assist in punishing another slave. Yet slaves could and did question the justness, method, and severity of certain physical punishments. In many cases bondspeople made those concerns known and thereby pushed back against master power. At the same time, being forced to participate in, or even witness, such regular acts of violence impressed upon slaves the authority and power that their masters possessed.

Whether or not slaves blasphemed purposely to draw attention to these perceived excesses in these instances is largely beside the point. From the historian's perspective, their blasphemy led to the creation of sources that highlight the negotiated character of master-slave relations by underlining the fact that masters did not have complete power over their bodies. Such power was limited by social convention. By marking perceived abuses slaves were constantly contesting what counted as acceptable treatment at the level of personal relationships, the combined weight of which determined acceptable levels of treatment in society at large.

A case very similar to that of Pascual further illustrates this point. On June 30, 1666, on San Antonio Atlacomulco, a sugar plantation near Cuernavaca, a slave named Juan Congo blasphemed while being flogged by his overseer, Juan González. According to witnesses, free and slave alike, González ordered Juan Congo to be beaten because he was not performing his duties correctly. Many of those same witnesses, including slaves, also testified that Juan Congo was simply not completing the work he was assigned. Yet after being beaten, unfairly in his eyes, Juan Congo complained to Manuel de Lima, the owner of the ingenio. Lima, seeing the wounds on Juan's body, gave him a little tobacco and sent him back to the boiling house with orders for González not to beat him anymore. On learning this, González became enraged and began to beat the slave again. Juan Congo begged González, in God's name, to stop beating him, and only when he wouldn't did Juan Congo renounce God three times.[33]

The slaves, the overseer, the free workers, and the master involved in this particular case all had different ideas about what constituted just and legitimate punishment. Congo, the slave being beaten, felt that the original punishment was unwarranted. On the other hand, his coworkers—both slave and free—indicated that he was not fulfilling his duties and therefore was legitimately punished. Yet they all expressed the sentiment that the second beating, in direct defiance of their owner's order, was questionable. The owner, through his actions, seems to indicate that the first beating was excessive and perhaps unwarranted. Or perhaps he was just trying to placate Juan Congo with the order not to beat him again and the small gift of tobacco. The overseer responded to Congo's circumvention of his authority with more violence.

Those familiar with discussions of slavery in British North America and Iberoamérica might suggest that Spanish and Catholic law provided protections for slaves in New Spain that included limits on violence. Thus, such historians might argue, when slaves voiced their discontent, when they spoke out against abusive treatment, they did so with a preestablished, codified definition of what constituted acceptable punishment in mind.[34] But Spanish law did not establish strict measures of treatment and did not define what was abusive. The *Siete Partidas* of Alfonso "the Wise," codified between 1263 and 1265, provided the basis of Spanish colonial jurisprudence and slave law through the nineteenth century. That code of laws loosely defined the nature of the master-slave relationship. The laws stipulated that masters had complete control over their slaves and could dispose of them as they pleased. At the same time, however, masters were restricted from killing, starving, or mutilating their slaves, except in special circumstances. Further, masters were prohibited from striking their slaves in a manner contrary to natural reason or causing wounds or injury so serious that they could not be endured.[35] A 1545 set of royal ordinances largely restated these restrictions. They urged masters to treat their slaves well, not to punish them without cause, and not be overly cruel in those punishments, and they forbid masters from castrating or crippling their slaves.[36] What constituted reasonable, endurable, or cruel punishment, however, remained undefined.

Yet the *Siete Partidas* did provide slaves theoretical access to civil and religious courts where they could accuse their masters of maltratamiento. At the same time, the *Siete Partidas* severely limited the punishment for such an offense. The law did not allow slaves to press for emancipation in cases of cruelty. Rather, the normal consequence for maltratamiento was a warning by the court to the master to treat his or her slaves better. In extreme cases, a judge could compel the offending slave owner to sell the abused slave to someone who might treat him or her better, thereby allowing slaves to escape abuse but not their status as slaves. That a slave could escape abuse but not slavery itself reinforced the social system of slavery by forcing slaves to accept the legitimacy of their bondage, no matter how cruel it appeared. In practice, however, the courts rarely ordered "abusive" masters to sell their slaves.

The *Siete Partidas* therefore can be said to have provided a loose framework within which mastery and slavery were negotiated, as is evident in the blasphemy cases we've looked at. For example, Juan Pablo testified that slaves could expect to receive six to twelve lashes for not finishing their work in the Álvarez obraje. Pascual, on the other hand, had received well over a hundred lashes. According to witnesses, Ramón González was beaten continuously by two men, who alternated blows, for over an hour. González himself described the implementation of a new "cruel" punishment regime that included as many as two hundred lashes for not completing daily quotas.

But at what point did those beatings move from socially acceptable to abusive? The Inquisition itself regularly imposed punishments of fifty, one hundred, or two hundred blows on slaves for religious offenses. However, in these instances the punishment was intended to serve as a deterrent and so was purposely harsh. The Carolingian Instructions on Slavery, issued in 1789 with the intention of providing a more specific set of legal boundaries on the master-slave relationship, did define acceptable punishment. Masters were empowered to employ imprisonment, shackles, stocks, or beatings. But, those beatings were not to exceed twenty-five lashes and were to be administered with a "gentle instrument" that would not cause serious bruising or bleeding.[37] Importantly, however, these restrictions were issued *after* the period under consideration here and were, in fact, retracted in 1795 under increasing opposition from slave owners throughout the empire.[38] Slaves generally blasphemed within the first fifteen blows, perhaps suggesting that acceptable levels of physical coercion were far below those normally meted out by the Inquisition and were more in line with levels that the Carolingian Instructions attempted to impose.

In addition, masters often recognized moments when they had breached acceptable levels of punishment. That Páez de la Baña and his mayordomo underreported the number of blows that Pascual had received by nearly one hundred suggests as much. Again, however, Melchor and Fernando Díaz de Posadas provide the most extreme example. According to Nicolás Bazán, they attempted to bribe Ramón González, promising him his freedom and 500 pesos if he would not reveal what had actually transpired in their obraje. González, in fact, kept up the ruse that nothing extraordinary had occurred during his punishment and denied the bribe offer, until the Inquisition threatened him with torture. At that point he corroborated the cruelty and bribery charges. Melchor and Fernando clearly feared the repercussions of their actions, even if they were not necessarily restrained in their treatment of their bondspeople.[39]

Slaves did not only contest the number of blows they received. Whether or not the chastisement was deserved and whether it was delivered in an acceptable manner was also hotly negotiated. Slaves also bitterly resisted beatings delivered to sensitive parts of their bodies and regarded the practice of dripping boiling/burning liquids on their wounds as beyond unacceptable, although masters acted and spoke as if the latter was clearly within their rights of dominion over their slaves.[40]

Maltratamiento

The few extant cases in which slaves brought their masters before ecclesiastical or judicial authorities for maltratamiento, and the limited number of bondspeople who blasphemed in order to gain an audience before the Inquisition to denounce the treatment they received at the hands of their owner, further highlight the negotiated nature of slavery. The judicial structures of colonial New Spain were unsettled, and there was no one court that had full jurisdiction over masters and slaves. At least four, perhaps five, different courts operated simultaneously in the colony with potentially overlapping jurisdictions.[41] The viceroy served as the president of the *audiencia* (royal high court), which served as the court of last resort for both the civil and criminal courts for non-Indians as well as for criminal cases against Indians. The ecclesiastical court, also subject to viceregal authority, heard cases related to family law, church doctrine, and the clergy.[42] The Inquisition, founded in 1571, fell outside both viceregal and episcopal authority and was responsible for maintaining moral and religious orthodoxy throughout the colony.[43] Adding another layer to this complexity was the fact that the ecclesiastical courts had jurisdiction over civil and criminal cases brought by, or against, member of the clergy. Similarly, the Inquisition adjudicated cases brought by or against officers and staff of the Holy Office. Ecclesiastical and inquisitorial courts regularly heard cases involving slaves owned by members of society that fell under their jurisdiction. Thus, for example, when Joseph Martínez, a black slave, found himself accused of attacking his wife and her lover in bed with a knife, resulting in the lover's death, his criminal case was heard by the Inquisition because his owner, Don Diego Martínez Hidalgo, was an accountant and *alguacil mayor* for the Holy Office.[44]

Slaves proved capable of negotiating these complicated structures. In the process, they interjected superior patriarchal authorities into the master-slave relationship and used those authorities to mediate the conditions of their enslavement.[45] The temptation to argue that the ability of slaves to interject the state into master-slave relations was a defining characteristic of novohispano and by extension Spanish American slavery is a powerful one. But the ongoing conflicts and negotiations between masters and slaves were quite variable in their form and were not limited to those instances of state intervention.[46] And in fact such interventions, although exceptional, bring into view the ongoing but routine contestations, the normal social dynamics, of master-slave relations.[47]

Maltratamiento cases were a rarity in New Spain. After 1640, there were as few as eight cases initiated by slaves against their masters for abuse. The number of such cases was significantly fewer than the number of slaves accused of blasphemy, for example. The suit brought by Joseph de Leyba, a mulatto slave, in March 1706, against Don Alonzo de Guevara y Saman represents an interesting dispute between master and slave within the context of a maltratamiento case. The case opens with a petition that Joseph and his enslaved wife Jacinta de los Reyes be allowed to search for a new owner owing to the abuse they suffered at the Guevara's hands. Joseph charged that in two separate instances Guevara had attacked and wounded him in a manner that was outside the norm of master-slave relations. On one occasion, Guevara had thrown Joseph against a wall and hit him "so terribly hard in the head with a key" that his head split open. On another occasion, Guevara inflicted a severe knife wound on Joseph's hand. This type of violence is very different from that in the majority of abuse and blasphemy cases documented in the records.[48] Based on these initial testimonies, the inquisitor ordered Guevara to sell his two slaves.

Guevara's response is interesting and puzzling. First, he argued that Joseph's claims of abuse were lies and that he was well within his rights when he punished his slaves. Guevara also provided the court a copy of a criminal case against Joseph in which he stood accused of robbing another man outside a local tavern. Perhaps he hoped to use this case to convince the court that extraordinary measures were required to discipline Joseph. Or, his goal may have been to simply to undermine Joseph's credibility. In addition, Guevara included a copy of a *carta de libertad* (manumission deed) dated June 5, 1706, after the initial petition, which would free Jacinta upon his death and that also stipulated that any future children she might have in the interim were to be born free.[49] The case ends before we learn if the order to sell Joseph and Jacinta was upheld or not. Still, the conflict between the slave, the master, and representatives of the state suggest that conflict and accommodation were central to master-slave relations.

The conditions described in the case against Martín de Ortega for abusing his slaves sound very similar to those found in the trial transcripts of slave blasphemers. In May 1642, Juan Pérez de Escobar, a local official, charged Ortega with abusing his slave Agustín by "tying him to a pillar, flogging him with a rough rope, and then applying hot pitch and copal to his buttocks, thereby putting his life in danger."[50] Subsequent testimonies given by two of Ortega's slaves, María Magdalena and Domingo de la Cruz, corroborated this version of events. A doctor who examined Agustín described two large scabs on the slave's buttocks that appeared to be burns. In the end, Ortega admitted chastising Agustín as described but asserted that this was the first time he employed that particular punishment. He went on to argue that he was well within his rights to punish his slaves as a master but still begged mercy from the Inquisition. Ortega was ordered to sell Agustín and to pay a fine of 100 pesos plus an additional 12 pesos to cover the costs of the case. Why Ortega's treatment rose to the level of abuse in the eyes of the court, despite the similarity to descriptions in other cases that were not defined as abusive, is not made clear in the documentation.

In July of the following year, Martín de Ortega again stood accused of abusing his bondspeople. In this case, María Magdalena charged that although Ortega had been twice warned not to abuse his slaves, he had visited so many "extraordinary malicious torments" on her that she had lost count. In addition to claiming to have suffered floggings and burnings like those described in Agustín's case, María also asserted that Martín refused to allow her to cohabitate with her husband once per week, as was customary. Lucas Ruiz, a Spaniard who had known Ortega for over thirty years, confirmed María's testimony, swearing that he witnessed Ortega beat her severely and then pour boiling sugar or hot bacon fat on her wounds. He went on to testify that he "felt sorrow" for all of Ortega's slaves because of the abuses they suffered but particularly for María, "who was a good slave and undeserving of such mistreatment."[51] Although Ortega was ordered to sell María she was eventually returned to him. She was still in his custody when she died in 1647.

The proceedings against Ortega provide interesting insights into the mindset of slave owners in colonial Mexico. After the second case, when María Magdalena was returned to Ortega, he was warned that he would not be permitted to punish or molest her in any way, under penalty of excommunication and a fine of 500 pesos. Ortega, in a petition to the Inquisition requesting that the restrictions be removed, argued that such an order turned the master-slave relationship on its ear, rendering it "as if [he] were subject to the slave and not her to [him]."[52] Throughout his cases, Ortega, like Guevara, asserted that he did not chastise his slaves excessively or without reason and that his actions fell within his rights as a slaveholder. He insisted that he was rightfully punishing his slaves for their thievery, drunkenness, roguery, and general untrustworthiness. He was clear that he viewed the Inquisition's actions as undermining his authority as a master.[53]

A limited number of other slaves committed religious offenses, often either blasphemy or threatening suicide, in the hopes of appearing before the Inquisition to air grievances about what they perceived as brutal and unjustified treatment. For example, Juan de Morga claimed to have made a pact with the devil, a religious offense more egregious than simple blasphemy, in order to secure an appearance before the Inquisition to complain of years of mistreatment at the hands of his master. Juan claimed to have suffered tremendously over a three-year period at the hands of Diego de Arratia, whose cruelty extended beyond numerous severe beatings that "ripped skin from his back" and on one occasion left him unable to speak for days. In his desperation, Morga asserted, he called out to the devil to help him escape his sufferings.

Arratia began tormenting Juan as soon as he purchased the slave. Almost immediately, Arratia had Juan placed in chains and branded on the face. The brand consisted of an *s* and a nail (*clavo*), which in Spanish form *esclavo*, or slave. Later, Arratia had Juan branded a second time, this time with a mark that extended from ear to ear. Once the second brand healed, Arratia had a barber enlarge the initial mark because he didn't think it was large enough. Arratia also stood accused of dragging Juan behind a horse over rocks and cacti, crippling one of Juan's legs with a hammer blow, and knocking out the slave's tooth, also with a hammer.

Morga testified that he repeatedly ran away to escape Arratia's abuses. He also suggested that he had often contemplated committing suicide either by placing his head in a stamp mill (for crushing silver ore), throwing himself down a mineshaft, or poisoning himself with a mixture of wine and salt. After being captured following one unsuccessful escape, his captors tied him up to prevent him from fleeing as he was dragged back to Zacatecas. He testified that in that moment he renounced God and offered his soul to the devil in return for assistance. Almost at once, he testified, his bonds broke. He apparently tried to hang himself with the rope but was prevented from doing so by his captors and was subsequently severely beaten. At some point after returning to Zacatecas, where his suffering persisted unabated, Juan again called out to the devil to assist him. At that moment, he testified, an Indian man appeared and offered him an herb that would prevent Arratia from abusing him only if he would promise to cease attending mass and praying to the saints. Soon thereafter, Morga successfully escaped Arratia's control and eventually was able to denounce himself before the Inquisition.[54]

Slaves like Juan de Morga who committed religious offenses to appear before the Inquisition in hopes of ameliorating perceived mistreatment were the exception, not the norm. It was risky since it exposed the slave to further punishment from the Inquisition. The best that bondspeople could hope for in adopting such a strategy was that their owner would be admonished not to abuse them or that they would be sold to a new master who might treat them better. The Holy Office was not in the business of taking slaves away from their masters, even abusive ones.[55] Still, inquisitors did take some pity on Morga. They did not punish him severely for his heretical activities, and they ordered that he be sold to a new master. After over a year in the Inquisition jail, he was released into the custody of Mateo Díaz de la Madrid, who had apparently purchased him from Arratia. His descriptions of his master's cruelty are truly exceptional, and his willingness to throw himself on the mercy of the Inquisition as a heretic underscores his desperation.[56]

What all of these cases suggest is that slaves were aware of the particular demands their social position placed on them. As Juan Pablo explained, slaves recognized that their primary function was to labor and that failing to meet the expectations with respect to quality and quantity of work would result in punishment. However, slaves had their own expectations, such as that punishment should be administered in a socially acceptable manner. Ramón Gutiérrez, for example, distinguished between the humane treatment of a previous overseer and the particular cruelty of the new one in the obraje where he worked. Masters and overseers did not, from the perspective of slaves, have unfettered control over their human property. Slaves marked potential violations (at times by blasphemy) in order to resituate the norm, to flag the breach.

Masters and Blasphemy by Slaves

The responses of slave owners to slave blasphemy also highlight the negotiation over what level of physical coercion was acceptable. A common thread throughout these cases is the intensification of physical violence that masters, or overseers, brought to bear against slaves following the religious breach. That escalation of violence following a blasphemous outburst may suggest that masters and overseers were in fact restrained in their initial punishments. Slaves, by blaspheming, eliminated any pretense of restraint. Thus, blasphemy provided masters the opportunity to punish or, better, to abuse their bondspeople to a degree that would have been unacceptable in other circumstances.

On May 7, 1658, Don Bartolomé Rey y Alarcón, rector general of the Holy Office, brought Nicolás, his eighteen-year-old slave, to the secret jail of the Inquisition on charges of blasphemy. Nicolás's jailers testified that he was so badly beaten about the face, neck, and backside between his kidneys and knees that he was unable to stand, causing them to fear for his life. Nicolás and another slave named Antonio de la Havana testified that Don Bartolomé had brought all of his slaves together that night to inquire about the whereabouts of yet another bondsman, Sebastián, who had run away to marry a free mulatta. When Nicolás denied having any knowledge of Sebastián's whereabouts his master ordered Juan, another slave, to strip, bind, and beat Nicolás.

This particular case is striking because of the very different descriptions given by the master and his slaves regarding what transpired next. According to Don Bartolomé, he became so enraged when Nicolás, after two or three lashes, blasphemed that he smashed Nicolás in the face with a stick approximately fifteen to twenty times before carting the slave off to the Inquisition for trial. The slaves, however, gave a much different account. According to Antonio, Nicolás was flogged for so long that he began to make up stories about Sebastián's whereabouts in hopes of ending his suffering. When that did not work, he began to plead in the name of the Virgin and the holy sacraments for the beating to stop. Doña Isabel de la Rosa, Don Bartolomé's wife, ordered Juan to continue beating Nicolás. At this point, "the cruelty" of the beating compelled Nicolás to threaten to blaspheme if it continued. His masters did not relent, and Nicolás, "owing to his suffering," blasphemed approximately ten times.[57]

At that point, according to Antonio, his masters ordered that Nicolás continue to be beaten, relenting only when "he appeared near death." Juan also testified that he beat Nicolás so severely that the young slave fainted away and nearly died. Meanwhile, Don Bartolomé began to beat Nicolás about the head with the stick, while Doña Isabel stood on his throat and kicked him in the face numerous times with a heavy shoe. Then they bound his arms and legs and took him to the Inquisition.

Antonio's and Juan's accounts are significant because in describing the ferocity of the violence and the suffering Nicolás endured, they both use terminology that is rarely seen in these cases. All of the slaves, Nicolás included, conveyed the sense that the beating descended into the realm of abuse fairly quickly. Antonio clearly stated that he believed the punishment was too cruel (*azotaban tan cruelmente*), while Juan testified that Nicolás suffered too much (*tan afligido*). The Inquisition, interestingly enough, agreed with the slaves Juan and Antonio, and ordered Don Bartolomé to sell Nicolás to a good person without abusing him in the interim. This was one of the few cases in which the Holy Office, or any other court for that matter, interceded in a master-slave relationship and ordered a master to sell his or her slave. The case of Juan de Morga was one of the few others suggesting that the threshold of abuse at which inquisitors would intervene and force a master to sell an abused slave was quite high. Importantly, however, Nicolás did not request to be sold, nor did he blaspheme with the intention of asking the Inquisition to force his master to sell him. In this case, not only did the reason for the beating seem questionable in the eyes of the slaves; the treatment Nicolás received also clearly violated some socially constructed norm regarding the acceptable levels of physical coercion that could be used against a slave.

One last case highlights numerous threads woven together throughout this chapter. It includes the intensification of violence following blasphemous utterances by slaves and conflicting testimonies presented by slaves and their masters that reflect the competing visions each had of slavery. In it, Juana Gertrudis, a black slave owned by Martín de Santibáñez and his wife Juana Marques Coronel, accused her mistress of cruelty when brought before the Inquisition for blasphemy in 1666. Juana Gertrudis had run away from her masters' home after being accused of stealing some silver. After nine days, two male slaves owned by her masters captured her and returned her to their home. Santibáñez testified that on her return Juana Gertrudis was tied up and that his wife ordered one of the slaves to beat her. She blasphemed, he claimed, after the first blow, which enraged him so much that he began to hit her in the mouth with a stick until she fainted. At that point he stopped, picked Juana up, and carried her to bed.

Juana Gertrudis presented a very different description of events. She admitted running away but defended herself by asserting that her mistress, Juana Marques, constantly mistreated her. She insisted that the

source of Marques's abuse stemmed from her belief that Juana was having an affair with Santibáñez. Juana denied the affair as well as the theft
of the silverware. She said that while she was being beaten under the
supervision of her mistress, she pleaded with Doña Juana to "forgive as
God forgives."[58] In response, her mistress ordered that she should be
beaten until she was near dead. The slaves complied and testified that
because Juana was so "terribly afflicted" she eventually blasphemed. That,
however, did not end the beating and eventually she blasphemed two or
three more times.

The two slave men who captured and beat Juana provide a slightly different version of events from that of Juana and her owners. Juan Asencio, a
black slave, testified Juana blasphemed on the third or fourth blow, which
enraged their owner so much that he beat her in the head with a stick,
saying "Shut your mouth, dog."[59] Those blows incited Juana to blaspheme
again, further infuriating her owners. Santibáñez then left the room but
Doña Juana, according to both Juan Asencio and Domingo, demanded
that they keep beating her. Juan testified that he and Domingo alternated
dealing blows for nearly one and a half hours before Doña Juana ordered
them to stop. At some point during the beating, Juana recanted her blasphemy, proclaiming her belief in God.

Although Juana's testimony regarding the cause of her mistress's
abuse was not verified by her fellow slaves, there was a clear discrepancy
between the description of events given by Santibáñez and Marques and
that given by their slaves. Slave-owning women's jealousy over real or
perceived sexual relationships between female slaves and masters could
obviously affect the treatment of these bondservants.[60] Juana's blasphemy
may have created a pretense for Marques to take out her frustrations,
unrestrained, on her slave's body.

These cases suggest that blasphemy often resulted in the intensification of aggression aimed at slaves rather than prompting masters to cease
their punishments. Javier Villa-Flores found that in 80 percent of blasphemy cases against slaves, the punishment continued or was intensified
following the religious breach before the bondsperson was turned over to
the Inquisition for official punishment.[61] Rather than protecting slaves,
blasphemy gave masters a pretense to brutally punish their slaves. It gave
masters almost unfettered access to violence, something that they may
have longed for, or even believed was their prerogative, but that under normal circumstances they were denied. If slaves used blasphemy as a socially

patterned form of resistance, they had to do so with the clear knowledge that they would likely face unrestrained violence from their masters.

The actions and testimony of slaves who administered or witnessed these beatings also shed light on the negotiated nature of master-slave relations and on the immense power of slave owners at the same time. There is no evidence in these documents that slaves ever refused an order to beat another slave. By their actions—holding fellow slaves while they were being flogged, informing on each other, and actually beating another slave, even to the point of death—slaves marked the significant power differential they faced. They recognized that their masters had authority to use physical coercion against them in ways that they could not against free workers. They also recognized that particular actions or inactions on the part of a slave could result in violence against his or her person. Their reactions to perceived excessive treatment reflect their understanding that violence was not to be used capriciously and that there were unspecified limits to the level of coercion masters could employ.

It was not only blasphemy that led to the amplification of violence against a slave during a beating. Slaves also testified, on occasion, that simply begging for assistance from Mary, Jesus, or the saints would enrage their masters and overseers and could often result in taunting and the intensification of the severity of their suffering. Baltasar de los Reyes, a Congo slave, testified that his master gagged him with a rope during a beating to prevent him from continuing to beg the Virgin Mary for assistance.[62] According to numerous witnesses Fernando Díaz de Posadas would often mock slaves who cried out for assistance from Jesus, Virgin Mary, or the saints while being flogged. Don Fernando ridiculed Ramón González when he reportedly begged an image of Jesus to free him from a flogging. Juan "el Noble," a free mulatto, testified that Don Fernando responded angrily to Ramón's pleas for help from Jesus, saying, "There is no one more powerful in my home than me, and only I can free you" while continuing to beat Ramón. Juan added that Fernando often became very angry and indignant when slaves begged for the assistance of God or the Virgin Mary while being whipped.[63]

The strong likelihood that a slave would be subjected to unrestrained violence following blasphemy when combined with the possibility of even more physical punishment at the hands of the Inquisition, which could impose an additional fifty, one hundred, or even two hundred lashes on slaves found guilty of blasphemy, militates against the possibility that slaves were consciously employing blasphemy as resistance.[64] The experiences and testimonies of slaves highlight the presence of an unfixed, socially negotiated level of acceptable treatment by masters. They illuminate the existence of differing opinions between and among masters and slaves as to what exactly constituted excessive, illegitimate, or cruel punishment. Rather than being codified in law, such levels were determined in large part by the lived experience of individual slaves and masters. The very ability of slaves to communicate a sense of violation put a subtle drag on master agency, and the combined weight of these contests between masters and slaves determined what was acceptable or not. In many of these cases, slave testimonies highlight that what slaves perceived as egregious treatment was defined by a lifetime of experience. What slaves objected to was the intensification of physical coercion or increased workloads to degrees beyond what they normally experienced on a daily basis. Slaves, therefore, recognized elements of their own oppression and worked to alleviate them as best they could. In imposing themselves, as much as was possible, on the ongoing negotiation of the social statuses of mastery and slavery in New Spain, they altered the nature of rule there.

This is particularly true of creole—American-born—slaves who had been raised within the context of colonial Mexican slavery and therefore had no other social reality that they could compare their experiences to. African-born slaves generally reacted very differently to the rigors of slavery in the Americas. For example, Africans were, for the most part, more likely to rebel or run away than were their American-born counterparts.[65] Perhaps in part they reacted that way because New World slavery did not meet their expectations based on their experiences with the institution in Africa.[66] Also, the fact that African-born slaves were less likely to become integrated into the social fabric and community into which they were imported may have made them more likely to rebel or flee.

Being raised and socialized in the milieu of New World slavery had important effects on creoles' reactions to their oppression.[67] The levels of brutality and the social distance between master and slave that may have seemed so foreign to most Africans were part of the lived experiences of creole slaves. While the point is relatively simple, the implications are profound. Mexican-born slaves had been raised and socialized in an environment in which their social status made it possible that they would be subject to increased workloads and increased levels of physical coercion not acceptable for nonslaves. The examples of slaves who questioned the legitimacy of the exercise of master power, however, clearly high-light that creole slaves in New Spain were capable of actively working to improve their social position, of empowering themselves at the expense of their masters.

Slave Witchcraft

The agency exercised by slaves in the conflicts within blasphemy cases becomes even more obvious in the trials of slaves who stood accused of bewitching their owners. Masters proved to be very fearful of the power of slave witchcraft. Their testimonies emphasize how slaveholders treated their slaves differently as a result of that fear. These cases highlight the reality that slaves influenced how their masters treated them and there-fore did play a role in defining acceptable and unacceptable behaviors on the part of their owners. As such, it is important to pay specific attention to the expressed goals of slaves who employed magic against their masters.

In 1695, Doña Sebastiána Martínez de Castrejon appeared before the Inquisition to denounce Dorotea, previously her slave, for witchcraft. Doña Sebastiána testified that about five years earlier she had fought with Dorotea in the kitchen and in the process had struck her. At that moment Dorotea captured an ant running across the floor and crushed it between her fingers. Immediately, Doña Sebastiána felt a great burning sensa-tion throughout her entire body that caused her tremendous pain and left her bruised all over. Two or three months later, just before Doña Sebastiána was going to flog Dorotea, she went outside to urinate and was again assailed by pains throughout her entire body. Her genitalia and legs swelled up so badly that she could not make it back to her room. She consulted two curers, who informed her that Dorotea had bewitched her in some manner. Sebastiána testified that she was sure Dorotea was the cause of both attacks and that her powers were diabolical.[68]

Sebastiána also claimed that Dorotea had bewitched her husband, Diego Gómez de Padilla. Don Diego went to bed in perfect health after severely beating Dorotea, only to awake with a terrible pain in his eyes, causing him to cry profusely. Diego lost sight in one eye and was slowly losing sight in the other. He went to see an Indian curandero who likewise associated his physical ailment with Dorotea's powerful magic. Don Diego and Doña Sebastiána attributed all of the maladies that they suffered to witchcraft used by Dorotea to prevent physical punishment or retaliate against it. They clearly feared their slave's magical powers. Sebastiána suspected Dorotea's powers were derived from a pact with the devil and eventually convinced her husband to sell her.[69]

Similarly, a slave named Joseph de Francisco accused Ana, the mulatta slave of Don Nicolás de Peralta, of using witchcraft to tame her owners. According to Joseph's testimony, he had given Ana a skull that he had removed from an altar dedicated to the Virgin Mary in the Convent of San Agustín in San Luis Potosí. Ana planned to crush the skull into a powder and serve it to her mistress and master in hot chocolate or a soup in order to prevent them from abusing her. Ana also fed her mistress powders from a ground-up roasted toad that she captured at a nearby lake to alleviate the abuses she suffered at her mistress's hand.[70]

The power of slave magic, and the fear that it inspired in slave owners, is made clear in the story of Fray Diego Núñez, prior of the monastery of Our Lady of the Assumption in Amecameca, outside Mexico City, and his slave Manuela de Bocanegra. Padre Núñez wrote a long letter to the Inquisition in 1733 in which he charged that Manuela had bewitched him with the help of the devil after he caught her having sex with a young painter. Fray Diego described in great detail the afflictions he suffered at the hands of Manuela's powerful magic. He wrote that he endured the worst pains "in the most humid" and sensitive "parts of the body" for over eight months, during which time it was excruciating to urinate and defecate. Moreover, he began passing foreign bodies in his urine and excrement, including more than two hundred stones in a fortnight, hair (both human, but not his own, and that of various animals), pieces of wool, and a paintbrush. All of these things expelled from his body were, in his mind, signs that Manuela had bewitched him. Most incredibly, the cleric claimed that "in the course of his illness a wound had suddenly appeared along the length of his bottom, in the form of piles that had 'transmuted the lower posterior to look like that of the female sex.'"[71] In other words, she had regendered him as a woman. Magic was such a powerful weapon because people like Fray Diego perceived its power to be real.

The connections between sex magic and slave magic used against masters are also made obvious by the case of Mariana. In 1650, Mariana de Rueda and her husband, Alonso Díaz Barriga, accused their slave, also named Mariana, of witchcraft. Mariana had a reputation as a powerful witch who would provide other women with powders of ground-up baked bats, dried mule brain, grave dirt, and ground-up human bones in order to attract men. As was the common practice, she advised women to serve men these items in a drink such as atole (a corn drink) or chocolate. Similarly, she advised one woman to serve her husband her menstrual fluids and the water she used to wash her genitalia with in order to stop his abusive behavior.

Her masters also accused her of secreting ground-up roasted bats and grave dirt in their food and drink in order to "tame" them, to prevent them from mistreating her. On another occasion, Doña Mariana thwarted her slave's plan to serve her half a vulture brain in order to make her "stupid." In fact, she testified that she suspected that Mariana had been giving them such powders for over sixteen years. But she did not confront or punish her slave because she dreaded Mariana's witchcraft.[72]

A priest named Tomás de Cárdenas also denounced Juana, another black slave, accusing her of witchcraft in 1678. While serving in an obraje, Juana had apparently confessed to Cárdenas that she had successfully robbed her master using a magical powder to unlock the door to the room where he kept his valuables. Cárdenas added that Rufina, another bondswoman, confided in him that she had witnessed Juana give her owner, Antonio Calderón, chocolate mixed with the aforementioned powder, the hair of some mulatta, and the nails of an unnamed animal to bewitch him. Father Tomás went on to say that her witchcraft had prevented Calderón from punishing his slave after he discovered the thefts. Priests and slave owners alike were very concerned that the enslaved could employ witchcraft to control masters, to limit and restrict their power over their bondspeople.[73]

The testimony of another Spanish cleric, Antonio Escudero de Rosas, against his father's black slave Cristóbal again highlights masters' real fear of slave witchcraft. Shortly after purchasing the slave in 1655, Father Antonio's father's household came under attack from a *duende* (spirit) or *trasgo* (goblin) summoned by Cristóbal. The ghost began assailing the house with stones throughout the night, keeping everyone up. Moreover, various valuables, including a number of silver objects, went missing. Despite the efforts of Antonio's father, who eventually commissioned a priest to conduct an exorcism to drive out the evil spirit, the house became nearly uninhabitable. Cristóbal's fellow slaves attributed the attacks to his desire for revenge against Ageda, a young slave woman, for refusing his sexual advances and against his master for an undeserved beating. They also accused Cristóbal of bewitching Ageda, causing her to fall ill, after she rebuked him. According to Luis, another slave, the disturbances stopped only after Cristóbal stepped outside the house while it was being pounded with rocks one night and spoke something in a language that he and other witnesses could not understand. Months later, the attacks on the house resumed again after Cristóbal had been sent to an obraje. In fact, they became even more dangerous, as small fires began to break out in locked rooms throughout the house, which witnesses attributed to Cristóbal's goblin. Cristóbal, however, denied that he was responsible for the attacks, and the Inquisition eventually dismissed the charges against him.[74]

Slave magic appears to have had an important gendered element to it. In the majority of cases in which slaves stood accused of employing magic against their owners the defendants were women. Magic was a powerful weapon that women in colonial Mexico employed to tame, weaken, attract, or otherwise influence men. Men believed in magic and feared being bewitched by women. Thus, power derived from magic by women was not simply symbolic but real. Slaves, particularly slave women, employed magic in a similar fashion to weaken or attack their owners, often putting powders in their owners' food, which, importantly, they typically prepared or had access to.[75] Like slave women, slave men employed sex magic to attract or keep lovers, and it is conceivable that they employed similar magic against their owners.

Conclusions

The various accounts related in the blasphemy, maltratamiento, and witchcraft cases highlight how slaves actively accommodated and challenged owners' authority in the daily, ongoing contests that defined master-slave relations. What actions slaves might take were determined by a larger structure of power relations—structures that they helped maintain and, more importantly, that they altered through their daily contestations with their masters. The articulation of the master-slave relations, and any relationship of power in colonial society for that matter, was fraught with inconsistencies, unknowns, and conflict. Just as men and women struggled over the meanings of patriarchy and the definitions of women's roles within colonial society, so too slaves contested their servitude on a daily basis within the social spaces and with the cultural language at their disposal. Thus they largely recognized their social position *but* actively sought to improve their lot in their daily contestations with their masters (which might even include actions that appear to be accommodative). But they did not necessarily translate that into a sense that the social order, which determined their denigrated social status, was illegitimate.

These conflicts over treatment and the social and cultural understandings that informed them were key components of a distinctive Afro-Mexican slave identity under construction in New Spain. The ability of bondspeople to influence, however slightly, the articulation of mastery and slavery in practice also speaks to their ability to create and maintain distinctive cultural communities in New Spain. At the same time, the experience of slavery fundamentally contributed to the creation of a sense of self and community that served to differentiate Afro-Mexican slaves from mestizos, Indians, and Spaniards. Perhaps more importantly it also functioned to distance slaves from their free Afro-Mexican counterparts with whom they constructed social networks and cultural communities.

Slaves did not, however, develop a "slave consciousness" that would allow them to challenge slavery collectively, just as they did not develop a "racial consciousness" to combat the racist structures of colonial society. In fact, the sense of being both Afro-Mexican and enslaved, the subtle variances between being mulatto or black, the different experiences within enslavement based on gender, among myriad other issues, all worked simultaneously to undermine the development of any such consciousness. The following chapter picks up this thread to explore how even flight and collective slave resistance draw attention to the negotiated nature of master-slave relations in the colony. These conflicts illuminate the limited ability of slaves to develop a consciousness that could have been the foundation of a fundamental challenge to slavery as an institution in New Spain prior to the 1770s.

CHAPTER 5

"The Great Escape?"
Slave Flight and Rebellion

✢ ON JUNE 6, 1769, COLONIAL AUTHORITIES FINALLY REACHED AN
extraordinary peace accord with a group of runaway slaves who had
been terrorizing the sugar- and tobacco-producing region of Córdoba,
to the east of the Mexico City, for decades. Colonial negotiators and
local planters begrudgingly accepted an official treaty that granted the
runaways their freedom and the right to establish a free town eventually
named Nuestra Señora de Guadalupe de los Morenos de Amapa (herein-
after Amapa) after over forty years of armed conflict and intrigue.[1] This
chapter explores the daily conflictive negotiations of mastery and slavery
in New Spain introduced in the other chapters as manifested in more
overtly "political" and potentially collective forms of slave actions, such
as flight, armed rebellion, and the creation of runaway communities, or
palenques, which had a long and interesting history in the colony.[2]

The founding of Amapa occurred amid a major outbreak of collective
slave resistance in eighteenth-century Córdoba. In this instance, during
the course of a series of armed slave rebellions between 1725 and 1769,
a group of runaways, a majority of whom had fled during a 1735 slave
rebellion, established six palenques in the mountains within the district
of Teutila, in what is now Oaxaca. The occupants of one of these strong-
holds, Palacios de Mandinga, would eventually receive their freedom and

the right to establish and populate the free pueblo of Amapa following a long series of armed clashes and subsequent negotiations with Spanish authorities that were concluded in 1769.[3]

In 1725, a group of slaves who had fled during a slave rebellion in Córdoba joined forces with other cimarrones and established the palenque called Mandinga. In 1734, the group consisted of twenty-three runaways, a large number of whom had escaped in 1725. This group promised to lay down their arms in return for the right to establish a free pueblo, an offer apparently rejected. Instead Spanish authorities sent numerous armed expeditions in against the cimarrones. Those attempts to destroy the palenques failed owing to rough terrain, the runaways' expertise at avoiding capture, and a network of informants who kept the cimarrones abreast of Spanish plans.[4]

Following the failed attempt by the cimarrones to negotiate peace in 1734, a major slave rebellion erupted in Córdoba. Apparently, a rumor that the king of Spain had freed the slaves around Córdoba began to spread throughout the region.[5] Planters charged that the cimarrones, frustrated over the collapse of negotiations with colonial authorities, had created the rumor and were "pouring their damned notions of liberty" into the slave quarters in order to foment rebellion.[6] The origins of the rumor are not evident from the sources. It may be that news of the failed negotiations, which had they succeeded might have included the possibility of liberation for the runaways involved in them, became transformed into a general rumor that planters were refusing to recognize a royal order of emancipation. In June 1735, as many as five hundred slaves, representing as much as one-quarter of all slaves in the region, gathered at the ingenio of Omealca near Córdoba and demanded that local authorities obey the king's rumored order to free them.[7]

The Spanish response was swift and forceful. By early July, they had sent six hundred militiamen in the region to crush the uprising. In a letter dated July 7, 1735, viceregal authorities impressed on subordinates in Córdoba their desire for a rapid resolution of the problem. They recommended that the slaves who had fled their masters be given ten days to return. Once that amnesty period passed, however, punishment for those captured and for those implicated in the rebellion was to be swift, severe, and public. In addition, the viceroy pressed local priests to do all that they could to convince the rebels that the "liberty" supposedly granted by the king was a hoax. Although planters lamented that it took nearly five months, the Spanish force did finally squash the rebellion. They captured many of the insurgents, including two mulatto slaves named José Pérez and José Tadeo (aka "the Carpenter"), who they then executed in 1737 as the principal leaders of the uprising. Significant numbers of the 1735 rebels successfully escaped, however, and joined or formed numerous palenques, including Mandinga, in the region.

The rebellion of 1735 clearly shook the Spanish population in and around Córdoba. Over thirty years later, in the context of the negotiations that eventually resulted in the foundation of Amapa in 1769, planters described the 1735 rebellion as having had crippling effect on regional sugar and tobacco production. Perhaps most frightening to the local planters, a sentiment they clearly expressed in 1769, was the contact between the rebels and slaves on local ingenios. Planters feared that those ties would result in a persistent state of unrest and potential rebellion.[8]

Following the violence of 1735, the Spanish authorities in Córdoba attempted numerous unsuccessful expeditions to subdue the palenques. Conditions remained unsettled—rebellions broke out again in 1741 and 1749—until 1762, when the cimarrones once again petitioned for their freedom. This time they appealed directly to the viceroy, tying their desire for freedom to his call for men to assist the Spanish army in defending the coast against potential British naval attack following the loss of Havana. The viceroy agreed. But once the pressing need for their assistance had passed, and the cimarrones had returned home, planters refused to recognize their liberty and again tried to reduce them to their former slave status.[9]

As time passed, the cimarrón group experienced internal divisions, owing, in part, to the arrival of new runaways. In 1767, when the cimarrones began their final negotiations with Spanish authorities, the total population of Mandinga was sixty-nine persons, triple the size it was in 1734.[10] Many of the older runaways and their families continued to favor a peaceful solution. A minority of newer runaways rejected accommodation with the Spanish. In 1767, the older cimarrones, led by Fernando Manuel, renewed their petition for freedom. Tensions within the group resulted in armed conflict between the followers of Fernando Manuel and a radical group led by an ex-slave named Macute, who apparently was the leader (*capitán*) of the entire group. In the end Fernando Manuel and his group defeated Macute's followers and took seventeen "captives" to Córdoba to be returned to their masters.[11]

This was a striking turn of events. It was not uncommon for runaways to agree to become slave catchers in the wake of negotiations to secure their own personal freedom. In this instance, however, the cimarrones led by Fernando Manuel actually returned seventeen of their compatriots to their masters, perhaps as a show of good faith, during ongoing negotiations. In addition, by 1771 Fernando Manuel's men had captured as many as twenty-seven other runaways and were pursuing some eight more near Orizaba.[12]

Finally in 1769, the cimarrones were granted their freedom and given permission to build a new pueblo on a site chosen on the Amapa River. For their part, the recently freed ex-slaves swore allegiance to the king, vowed to obey the local authorities, pledged to serve in the colonial militia, agreed to capture and return future runaway slaves for a fee, and promised to pay the tribute that the crown imposed on free blacks.[13] They also agreed not to visit the slave quarters of any ingenio without written permission from the owner or a crown official. This final restriction did not apply to those runaways who still had family members living in slavery. According to the introduction to the baptismal book of Amapa, Fernando Manuel named the town Nuestra Señora de Guadalupe de los Negros de Amapa, in honor of Our Lady of Guadalupe for her assistance in defeating Macute and his supporters (see fig. 6).[14]

That these runaway slaves were able to negotiate their liberation from their enslavement is truly remarkable. But did the fact that they could mark a significant change in slavery and slaves' perceptions of their servitude in New Spain? Although slavery persisted longer in central New Spain than most historians have recognized, well into the eighteenth century, by the 1760s the institution had begun to slide into economic unimportance. The overall numbers of slaves began to decrease rapidly by the middle of the eighteenth century. That general decline raises the question: did slaves recognize an institution in decline and increasingly seek to escape their servitude via flight or other means? This was certainly the case in nineteenth-century Brazil and Peru after the end of the slave trade, when abolition loomed on the horizon, but in the case, for example, of the Córdoba rebellions, the sources do not include any testimony from slaves regarding the causes of their initial rebellion and flight, and so we don't know why they fled their enslavement in the first place.[15]

There is significant debate on how best characterize the political nature of long-term flight and rebellion by slaves.[16] This is particularly true when it comes to distinguishing them from day-to-day forms of resistance.[17] Whether or not such actions were motivated by "attempts to secure freedom from slavery" or "attempts to overthrow slavery" *our* interpretations of them are framed by our understanding of liberty as the antithesis of slavery.[18] Historians continue to approach them in terms of slaves' "desire for freedom" and their "desire to destroy slavery," which underwrote their relations with slaveholders.[19]

Were rebellions and individual acts of flight moments when the "radicalism" of slaves came to the fore? Did slaves hold back in the daily conflicts between masters and the enslaved evident in blasphemy and witchcraft trials, rendering the moments of revolt an exclamation of "truer" hidden transcripts?[20] With those questions in mind, this chapter situates the novel form of collective rebellion that resulted in the foundation of Amapa within a broader exploration of the experiences of slave

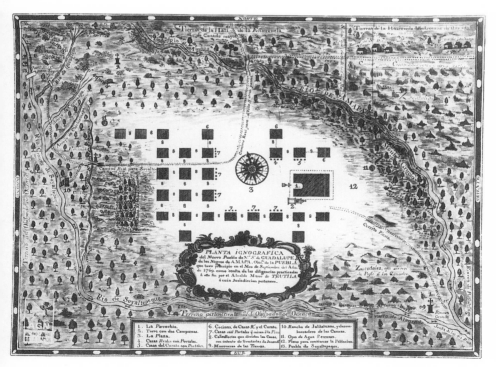

FIGURE 6. Plan of Nuestra Señora de Guadalupe de los Negros de Amapa. Courtesy of the Archivo General de la Nación, Mexico City.

runaways and specifically their stated motivations for their flight in New
Spain through 1769.

Individual Slave Flight

Domingo de la Cruz, a mulatto slave born and raised in Puebla, had been
a house servant in Don Juan Páez's household for nearly three years when
he ran away in 1693. He fled to the port city of Veracruz where, claiming
to be a Spanish soldier named Francisco de la Torre Ponce de León, he
joined a fleet and set sail for Havana, Cuba.[21] He subsequently married
three times: in Havana, in New Spain near Puebla, and in Guatemala.
After his various travels, Domingo attempted to reconcile with his second
wife in Puebla and settle down. He apparently confessed his bigamy to
his confessor, who refused him absolution until he denounced himself
before the Inquisition. That self-denunciation begins Domingo's trial
as a bigamist. His story raises a number of important questions about
the institutional stability of slavery and the mindset of slaves themselves.
How typical was his experience? Was it as easy to successfully escape
slavery and pass as a free person (and a Spaniard to boot) as his story
suggests? Did his flight represent the bold, pubic declaration of a more
generalized slave radicalism that rejected the legitimacy of slavery as a
social institution?

Bigamy trials like that of Domingo's are a rich and yet underutilized
source that begin to answer to such questions. Slaves accused of bigamy in
New Spain were overwhelmingly runaways and were a fairly homogenous
group on the surface. While three slaves, among the twenty-five surviving cases, were forcibly separated from their first spouse by sale, seventeen
had fled their servitude.[22] Excluding the anomalous case of one African
woman, slave bigamists in New Spain after 1640 were all creoles, and they
were all males, and the great majority self-identified as mulatto.[23]

Although it has been argued that their bigamy is evidence of the per-
sistence of African patterns of polygamy, lack of Christianization, or of
social deviancy, in fact it was clearly tied to the fact that they had fled
their servitude.[24] In all but Domingo's case, these runaway bigamists
were married prior to their flight. In many cases, they left not only their
first wives but also children when absconding, highlighting the weight of
the decision to flee.[25] Slave bigamists rarely married in the same village,
town, or city twice. Rather, they tended to flee a significant distance before

integrating themselves into society and marrying a second time. Finally, in a overwhelming number of cases, the men married for a second time at least five years or more after being separated from their first wives. For example, Francisco Balderas married Gertrudis, another slave, in Mexico City in 1705. In 1713, he ran away to Querétaro, where he eventually married a free mulatta named Francisca in 1719.[26]

Assessing rates of long-term slave flight in New Spain is near impossible. Censuses from sugar plantations provide a potential starting point, however. Of ninety-five censuses from colonial ingenios I examined for this study, twenty-two included references to runaway slaves, 3.7 percent of all slaves (totaling 2,186) being listed as absent at the time of the census. In addition, four of these censuses include information about changes in slave population over a specific lease period that allows for an estimation of the rate of slave flight. These four haciendas experienced an average rate of flight of one-half of one percent, or one in two hundred slaves, per year.[27]

We cannot assume that these figures reflect rates of flight across the colony, but they do suggest that long-term flight was much less common than Domingo's example might lead us to believe. Inquisition records are rife with accusations by masters that their slaves were runaways, but in many of those cases flight was a short-term tactic as opposed to a long-term strategy to escape slavery permanently. A number of the bondspeople discussed in the chapter 4 absconded for short periods of time before being recaptured or returning of their own volition. For example, Juan Bautista had fled his master's panadería only to return voluntarily after fifteen days.[28] Slaves often ran away for short periods of time to escape punishment, ill treatment, and even the ramifications of domestic disputes, but long-term flight does not appear to have been in the forefront of slaves' minds as they negotiated their daily lives. In other words, Domingo's successful escape and integration into free society appear to be truly exceptional.

We are still left to decipher what motivated slaves to run away when they did. Slave bigamists often spoke to the particular circumstances that led to their flight, and those testimonies provide windows into the daily operation of slavery. The trial transcripts for slave bigamists indicate those few slaves who ran away did so for reasons rooted in their lived experience, not in response to any institutional weakness in slavery and not in the pursuit of freedom in the abstract sense. Domingo's testimony, for

example, suggests that most bondsmen and bondswomen were not waiting for an opportunity to flee. Rather, flight was usually a response perceived breakdowns in the master-slave relationship or abusive treatment.
Domingo fled after overhearing that because he had pale skin and light
hair, his master planned to brand him on his face to mark him as a slave.
Similarly, Marcos Ramírez testified that although his master frequently
severely punished him for the slightest offense, he only ran away following a brutal thrashing with a stick followed by a vicious beating about
the head with the butt of a knife.[29] Complaints about mistreatment and
ongoing abuse were a common refrain in slave bigamists' explanations of
why they fled. They, like many of slave blasphemers, vehemently rejected
what they perceived to be the arbitrary or sadistic use of physical coercion.

Master-slave relations were a two-way street, however, and the increasing brutality of slave owners was not the only cause of their dete-
rioration. Catalina testified that her husband, Francisco Xavier, ran away
because of his worsening relationship with his master, caused in large part
by his own drunkenness, which resulted in his frequently being punished.
This example suggests that slaves were just as capable of contributing to
the vitiation of a stable, working relationship as were masters.[30]

It might be tempting to treat slaves' testimony that they fled their
servitude as a result of ongoing abuse as a rhetorical ploy to redirect the
attention of the Inquisition from their sin—bigamy—and perhaps place
blame for their situation elsewhere. Herman Bennett makes a compelling
argument that slaves' creolization in New Spain enabled them to better
navigate colonial institutions like the Inquisition and to manipulate their
testimony for their own benefit and to the detriment of others.[31] In that
light, one might argue that in claiming "mistreatment" as the cause of
their flight, these slaves demonstrated a highly sophisticated understanding of the dominant moral discourses in the colony.

There are multiple reasons for believing, however, that these slaves
were not attempting to deflect the attention of inquisitors but were simply
recounting the experiences that led to their flight in the first place. Other
witnesses, some of whom had not seen the runaway bigamist for years,
often corroborated the runaway bigamist's contentions of abuse. In many
cases, when the first wives of slave bigamists were questioned about their
husbands' flight, they echoed charges of maltreatment and deteriorating
master-slave relations. Like Catalina, Gertrudis, the wife of Francisco
Balderas, testified that her husband ran away because he had learned his

master planned to punish him.[32] Equally importantly, such claims rarely deflected the attention of inquisitors from the slave-in-question's transgressions because inquisitors almost never considered abusive master-slave relations as a mitigating factor when prosecuting and punishing slave-bigamists.[33]

While inquisitors largely ignored claims of abuse by slaves, they were much likely to take seriously the possibility that a runaway slave had erroneously contracted a bigamous marriage. Numerous slave bigamists testified that they married a second time *only* after being led to believe that their first wife, whom they had deserted when running away, had died in the interim. For example, Francisco Balderas testified that he married the second time in Querétaro only after hearing that his first wife was deceased. Six months later, he testified, he learned that she was in fact still alive, and so then he confessed his sin.[34] Runaways proved willing to fabricate such stories to try to escape the wrath of the Inquisition. In one example, Marcos Rodríguez admitted to lying to inquisitors to "minimize and excuse his sin" of entering into a bigamous marriage when he testified that he had learned of his first wife's death from her uncle in Chiapas. Silverio Joseph also admitted that he lied when he told inquisitors that his brother-in-law had informed him of his wife's death. He testified that he assumed she had died because he left her afflicted with the pox (*viruelas*).[35] Lorenzo de la Cruz spent over two years in jail waiting for inquisitors to corroborate his testimony that two friends had informed him in Guatemala of his first wife's death in Puebla. Felipe de Santiago initially confessed that he fled after finding, and subsequently attacking, his wife and her lover in bed, leaving them both for dead. When questioned further about this testimony Felipe admitted that he had fabricated the story. The real cause of his flight, he testified, was escalating tensions between him and his overseer.[36] These examples suggest that slaves were generally testifying truthfully when attributing their flight to perceived abusive treatment or a general breakdown of master-slave relations

The testimony and actions of other slave bigamists illustrate the complicated relationship between slavery and freedom in colonial Mexico, suggesting the possibility that freedom did not figure largely in the daily conflicts between masters and slaves and in how the enslaved envisioned their social position. In a tear-filled confession taken on July 9, 1742, Gregorio de la Cruz denounced himself as a bigamist. According to his testimony, nearly eleven years prior, he had run away from his master's livestock ranch near Zacatecas, abandoning his first wife, because of the "inhumane treatment" he suffered at the hands of his owner. Gregorio made his way to Nieves, near Durango, and after establishing himself as a free person there, he married a second time.[37]

What makes Gregorio's story of particular interest, however, is not that he successfully escaped and then integrated into free society but rather that after living in Nieves for nearly eight years as a free man, he returned to slavery of his own free will. Following the death of his second wife, his sense of guilt at abandoning his first became so great, he testified, that he returned to her and his master in Zacatecas and reenslaved himself. Importantly, Gregorio's teary confession came three years after he returned to her and his enslavement, which, I believe, lends credibility to his assertion that he returned because he felt he had greatly wounded his first wife by leaving her.

That a slave who had successfully escaped his servitude would return of his own volition defies expectations. Although this is only one case, Gregorio's actions speak volumes about how slaves potentially viewed their condition in the era prior to the Atlantic revolutions. Gregorio did not describe slavery as unfair or illegitimate, and his actions (particularly returning of his own free will) indicate that he did not conceive of slavery as insufferable, even after having lived as a free person for nearly eight years.[38] At least three other slaves, including Domingo de la Cruz, denounced themselves before the Inquisition as bigamists, and as runaway slaves, thereby guaranteeing their return to slavery. In each case, the guilt of being a bigamist, and perhaps remorse over betraying the trust and love of their first wife, drove the runaways to do something that is unthinkable from the modern perspective: to put themselves in a position where they were sure to be returned to chattel status.[39]

In another case in which a slave appears to eschew freedom for love, Capitán Andrés Dávalos, a peanut vendor and a slave owner, accused Juana, the slave of the Conde de Miravalle, of witchcraft before the Inquisition. Dávalos and Juana had been having an illicit affair and had lived together for nearly ten months. During that time, he had tried time and time again to give Juana money so that she might purchase her freedom. She, however, rejected his offer and demanded that they marry. Although Dávalos repeatedly rejected the possibility of marriage and tried to provide Juana the means to free herself, she refused. According to Dávalos, when it became apparent that he had no intention of marrying

Juana, she bewitched him, causing him to fall ill. Juana's rejection of his offer to buy her freedom and her demand for marriage suggests that personal liberation was not the foremost thing on her mind or at the core of her identity.[40]

The case of Joseph de la Cruz, a runaway tried by the Inquisition for blasphemy, highlights the ideological strength of slavery and underscores the possibility that the pursuit of personal liberty may not have been a central motivation for slave flight. Joseph had grown up in Mexico City in the home of Inquisitor Francisco de Estrada y Escobedo, where he was taught to read and write and where he was apprenticed as a tailor. On the inquisitor's death, however, Joseph was sold to a sugar plantation, where he found life unbearable. He asserted that they worked him too hard, beat him too rigorously, and would drip boiling sugar on his wounds after flogging him. He eventually ran away to escape further maltreatment. It is tempting to think that Joseph simply decided to flee slavery altogether, as did many of the bigamists discussed herein, because conditions were too harsh. However, his testimony points to a more complicated rationale. According to Joseph, he fled the sugar plantation for Mexico City in order to seek out a new owner, and he even went so far as to name three potential buyers he had located. He hoped to find someone in Mexico City who would purchase him from the ingenio and thereby free him from his suffering but not his servitude. Admittedly, this testimony could be justification after the fact. Joseph may have hoped to integrate himself into Mexico City as a free person when he fled but was forced to make up the story about seeking out a new master after being captured to minimize the implications of his flight. Yet other slaves likewise associated their flight with a desire for a new master. For example, Diego Rincón similarly testified that he had approached his "abusive" master to seek permission to find a new master before fleeing. They proved unable to agree on a price. Rincón's master demanded 400 pesos while he could only find potential buyers willing to pay 300. In light of both that and the deteriorating relations with his master, Rincón made the decision to abscond.[41] Joseph's and Diego's desires were framed by the Spanish legal code. They also highlight the fact that there were bounds on what slaves could aspire to. Those limits speak to slave identity. Colonial law did guarantee a slave the right to seek out a new owner in cases of mistreatment. But in invoking that protection, slaves used their agency to improve conditions within slavery rather than to escape or destroy it.

One last bigamy case highlights the limited vocabulary pertaining to liberty available to slaves in New Spain. Antonio de la Cruz's is the only case that specifically mentions the pursuit of liberty as the motivation for a slave's flight. Antonio had originally run away to Mexico City, leaving his wife and children behind, so he could pursue a case against his master, Don Domingo de Rebellar, over an unfulfilled promise of manumission. While his first wife, María, did not mention the suit when explaining why he had fled, other witnesses did corroborate his motive.[42] His case suggests that the pursuit of freedom in an abstract sense was not necessarily fundamental to slave agency and identity.

Ironically, the stories of runaways like Domingo and Gregorio de la Cruz who successfully integrated themselves into free society serve to illuminate the ideological health of slavery in colonial Mexico. They suggest that the end of the slave trade and the growing free majority among people of color did not translate into a sense among the enslaved that slavery was in ideological decline and weakening institutionally. The reality that chattel slavery was not the dominant form of production in the colony does not appear to have been transmuted into a form of slave radicalism that called for escape from slavery or the destruction of it as an institution. Nor did slaves' continued contact with free people, particularly those of African descent, appear to have generated such radicalism in New Spain.

The "Great Escape" from Calderón

On August 9, 1763, nearly fifty slaves armed with indigenous hoes, sickles, and machetes frantically descended the stairs from the main house of the ingenio Santa Barbara de Calderón and fled the hacienda. Founded in the first decade of the sixteenth century, Calderón was one of the oldest and largest sugar plantations in the heart of a key sugar-producing region near Cuautla de las Amilpas in the modern state of Morelos when Don Asencio González purchased it in 1758.[43] More than one hundred slaves lived and labored there across the eighteenth century, making it significantly larger than the average ingenio in central New Spain.[44]

The problems began earlier that fateful day, when the overseer ordered the entire slave population—totaling 104 men, women, and children—to leave the fields where they were working for the main house so they could be appraised as part of the settling of the last will and testament of González, who had recently died. According to the alcalde mayor in charge of the appraisal, the slaves' "insolent" refusal to lay down their tools upon their arrival at the main house was the first sign of trouble.[45] Once the evaluation was completed, the slaves, still armed, were told to return to work. They, however, refused to leave and demanded to know who, exactly, would become their new owner. The alcalde mayor informed them that Don Manuel Ruiz de Castañeda, the husband of Don Asencio's daughter and heir, Doña María Ignacia González, was their new owner. The slaves then cried out "in a single voice" that they did not want Don Manuel as their master. They refused to recognize anyone other than Don Juan Felipe Díaz Cano, Don Asencio's friend and executor, as their rightful owner. Then, powerless to stop them, Don Manuel, the alcalde, and the other assessors watched the slaves leave the house, flee the hacienda, and take off down the road in the direction of Mexico City.

The conflicts generated by this moment of collective action that are described in the records provide further insight into the realities of slavery, and particularly into the negotiation of both mastery and slavery, in New Spain. The documents include a written account of events leading up to the mass flight by Don Manuel Ruiz de Castañeda as well the testimonies of six slaves taken during their criminal trial, and the comparison of these contradictory versions of events brings to light bondsmen's and slaveholders' competing visions of mastery and slavery.

In the testimonies taken as part of the criminal investigation of the Calderón incident, the six slaves identified as the leaders of the mass flight admitted that they came to the appraisal with their tools. They argued afterward that they had not been allowed to return their tools to their homes prior to being evaluated as part of the probate. They added that they refused to lay them down because they feared they might be lost or stolen. Such probate evaluations were a fairly common occurrence in the lives of ingenio slaves. It seems likely, therefore, that they knew what was about to transpire when the mayordomo ordered them to the main house, which could indicate that their refusal to give up their tools was aimed at intimidating the appraisers.

The slaves also admitted that they, as a group, demanded to know who their new owner was and that on learning it was to be Don Manuel they "respectfully and peacefully" left the house en masse and took to the road for Mexico City. Two slaves who initially fled the hacienda with the group had a change of heart and quickly returned. These two slaves, Domingo and Eusebio, informed Don Manuel that the group was going to Mexico City. They planned to present a petition before the viceroy or the royal audiencia—the highest-ranking political official and highest court in the colony, respectively. In it they planned to request that living and labor conditions on the hacienda be returned to what they had been prior to Don Asencio González's death. Don Manuel and the other appraisers all intimated, however, that the slaves went to Mexico City to find Don Juan Felipe Díaz Cano.

The group who fled the plantation—including at least forty-six slaves (twenty-four males over sixteen years of age, including the two who returned to the hacienda, nineteen women, and six boys between eight and twelve years of age) and seven free laborers (five men and two women, both of whom were married to slaves)—arrived in Mexico City two days later. They set up camp in the plaza directly in front of the viceregal palace in hopes of receiving an audience before the viceroy or the audiencia. This was perhaps an odd choice, given that this was the same plaza where thirty-five slaves had been executed following an aborted slave rebellion in 1612.[46] The slaves testified that in the course of their journey, they had sold their tools in order to buy food. It is reasonable to assume, however, that the slaves recognized that carrying their tools would be perceived as a hostile gesture, as they likely intended when they arrived with them for the appraisal, and thus abandoned them so as to appear nonthreatening to colonial officials. On August 12, 1763, they were taken into custody and put in the royal jail. Six slaves, five men and one woman, were identified as the leaders of the rebellion and separated from their compatriots. They were interrogated that same day.

Although the Calderón slaves' actions were out of the ordinary, the issues that drove them to act, and their subsequent demands, were not. Their concerns were common points of contention between slaves and masters throughout New Spain. Their decision to flee en masse but not to try to escape into the countryside and establish a runaway community, their belief that they could successfully present their case before viceregal authorities, and their later willingness to return to slavery on the ingenio reinforce the account of the nature of master-slave relations in New Spain I have been developing.

The principal complaint of this group of slaves was that life had become insufferable since Don Asencio González's death and that the current owners, Don Manuel and Doña Ignacia, were complicit in, or at least indifferent to, the abuses they suffered. Joseph Roberto, the first of the slave leaders to be interrogated, testified that they made the decision to flee for Mexico City despite a real fear that they might be killed for leaving the hacienda. They were moved to such action, he asserted, because conditions on the ingenio had simply become unbearable.[47] The slaves indicated that what they regarded as acceptable master-slave relations was rooted in their prior lived experience and also made it clear that they viewed Don Asencio as kind and fair. They argued that the slaves of Santa Barbara de Calderón were the envy of the other ingenios of the region because, owing to Don Ascencio's benign mastership, they had a reputation as good and faithful workers. Moreover, the slaves' testimony suggests that they were perfectly willing to peacefully go back to the hacienda, and thereby to their status as slaves, if conditions were returned to those that obtained prior to Don Asencio's death.

The slaves testified that they had been given every indication by Don Asencio that Juan Felipe Díaz Cano would take over the ingenio on his death. According to five of the slave leaders, Don Asencio never told them that Doña Ignacia and Don Manuel would inherit them. Their preference for Don Juan apparently stemmed from their belief that he would be a more benevolent owner, a belief that was encouraged by his having given each slave a gift of 1 or 2 reales (a real was one-eighth of a peso) during a Christmas-season visit to the hacienda. Based in part on that visit, the slaves thought Don Juan would be a much more acceptable and caring master than Don Manuel had proven himself to be. The slaves' ultimate hope could have been that Don Manuel might be replaced with a more acceptable owner, perhaps even Don Juan, but their complaints focused on improving conditions on the hacienda.[48]

All six leaders testified that following Don Asencio's death, the average daily labor requirement for field workers had been increased significantly. Under the new regime the workload for slaves was in effect double what it had been. The overseer demanded that enslaved workers complete in one day what a free wage laborer was given two days to finish. These new allotments were, they suggested, significantly higher than those imposed on any other slave population in the region. Joseph Hilario, one of the slave leaders, testified that slaves would have to rise before daybreak and work until after nightfall without taking a break, even for food or water, in order to finish their quotas.[49]

The slaves also complained that they were being forced to work on Sundays and festival days. According to church law, those days were normally set aside for rest and prayer, and that had indeed been their experience under Don Ascencio's mastership.[50] As noted in chapter 1, slave owners who violated the prohibition of working their slaves on official days of rest could and did find themselves before the ecclesiastical courts or the Inquisition on charges of abuse. Slaves clearly understood that Sundays and festival days were not workdays, and they consistently opposed any attempt to infringe on their limited free time.

Not only were slaves expected to work on Sundays, the leaders testified, but the workload for Sunday was the same as for the other days of the week. Manuel Antonio Roque stated that on Sundays, the slaves would begin working at the same hour as other days. At eleven in the morning they would return from the fields to hear mass, the only concession to the religious requirement on Sundays. Around two in the afternoon, after a lunch break, they would return to the fields. At around eight in the evening, the slaves left the fields, prayed on the rosary, and then went to their homes for the night.[51] Working seven days a week from dawn until dusk was in their minds insufferable.

Beyond oppressive labor demands, the Calderón slaves also balked at the new demand that skilled slaves, who normally worked in the crushing mill and *casa de purgar* (boiling house) only, labor in the fields.[52] Customarily, skilled slaves, overwhelmingly men, did not do fieldwork. That task generally fell to women, children, and young men. Forcing skilled slaves to work in the fields might have threatened the internal hierarchies of the Calderón slave community. More concretely, however, compelling skilled workers to labor in the fields violated expectations based both on their past experience and the normal operation of sugar plantations throughout the region.

Most importantly, in the eyes of the slaves, they had been happy and obedient workers under the benevolent hand of Don Asencio. The differences in their experiences under the two regimes are evident in their references to their increased workload and to their being forced to work on Sundays and holidays. In order to drive this point home, Ana María testified that when it rained Don Asencio would send blankets to the fieldworkers to protect them from the downpour. In the case of torrential rain and fierce storms, Don Asencio would bring all the workers in from the fields. The new owners, however, required the slaves to work in the fields even in the most violent of rainstorms and would not even offer them blankets. Despite these circumstances the slaves were still expected to complete the increased daily workload.[53]

These deteriorating labor conditions represented the principal complaint of the slaves and one of their primary reasons for fleeing the hacienda. Equally important, in their eyes, was the abusive physical coercion of the overseer, Pedro de Luna. All six slaves swore that following the death of Don Asencio, Pedro de Luna had become sadistic. First, he increasingly resorted to violence to compel the completion of the augmented daily workload. Joseph Roberto testified that the slaves would be punished for the slightest mistake or if they stopped for rest. Tomás Aquino added that the slaves were often unable to eat the tortillas that they brought with them to the fields for fear that they would be severely beaten because they dared to stop working long enough to eat. Reflecting the close-knit nature of the slave community, the witnesses testified that those slaves who completed their labors early would assist their compatriots in completing their quotas rather than rest so that no slave would have to face Luna's lash.[54]

The slaves also accused Luna of beating them with whips and sticks dipped in burning embers and/or lye. His express intent, they contended, was to significantly increase the amount of pain he inflicted. In fact, "in his cruelty" Luna had recently beaten three slaves so severely that two had subsequently died of their wounds. Uncle Joseph died with "pus coming from his nose and ears," presumably owing to a beating about the head and shoulders. In similar fashion, Luna smashed Uncle Pedro Ramón over the head and about the body with large stick. Pedro subsequently died from his infected wounds. Moreover, all the slaves indicated that at the time they had left the hacienda another slave, Uncle Esteban, was very ill on account of a thrashing he had taken from Luna. So ill, in fact, that Joseph Roberto, among others, testified that he would not be surprised if Esteban had died from his wounds in the time since they had fled the plantation. That all three abused slaves were called "uncle" (*tío*) might suggest that they were community leaders.[55]

Slaves understood that whippings were to be expected when they were insolent, if they ran away, or if they failed to complete their assigned labors. Yet they also knew what was legitimate and what was inhumane. Beatings, if not excessive and not too frequent, were simply a part of the life of a slave.[56] Yet Pedro de Luna's desire to inflict additional pain by beating them with a stick or whip dipped in embers or lye went beyond the pale of acceptability from the slaves' perspective. The differences between acceptable and unacceptable violence were not determined by law or the master's will but rather in the ongoing test of wills between masters and slaves. In the Calderón case, the overseer was abusive because his use of physical violence far exceeded the limits of legitimate and moderate punishment established in the slaves' lived experiences under Don Asencio and the by the way slaves on neighboring ingenious were treated.

Making matters worse, and undergirding their petition for a new master, Don Manuel and Doña Ignacia refused, according to the slaves, to intervene on their behalf. Ana María spoke to her hope that Doña Ignacia would treat the slaves as her *criados*. The term translates as "servants" but implies a level of protection and care provided by the master not generally associated with slavery. However, when they complained to Doña Ignacia, she "put her hands in her belt" and did nothing to protect her slaves from the abuses of the mayordomo. Joseph Roberto, identified as a *maestro de azúcar* in the census of 1763, similarly asserted that their complaints to Don Manuel had fallen on deaf ears.[57] The lack of action on the part of their new owners may have led the slaves to believe, perhaps rightly, that Don Manuel and Doña Ignacia were complicit in the cruelties that they suffered.[58]

Don Manuel himself predictably painted a completely different picture in describing the breakdown of order and authority at Calderón. Immediately following the departure of the slaves, he wrote a letter recounting his version of events leading up to the mass flight. In it, he claimed the slaves were insolent and disobedient workers, charging that they worked only at their own whim and with little or no respect for those who ran the hacienda. He asserted that his slaves preferred dancing and getting drunk to working, even though the hacienda prohibited slaves from engaging in these activities. Their insolence had grown so great, he suggested, that they had openly discussed how they would refuse to recognize anybody other than Don Juan Felipe Díaz Cano as their owner. And he reported rumors to the effect that if Cano were not placed in charge of the hacienda the slaves would kill all those currently in charge. Don Manuel also insinuated that Don Juan may have pressed the slaves to make noise about how they would recognize no master other than him in order to further his quest to gain control of the hacienda. Moreover, he complained that recent interventions into hacienda discipline by colonial authorities, who had twice sent dispatches reprimanding Don Manuel to treat the slaves better (the Calderón slaves had successfully petitioned the audiencia to admonish their owner and his staff), had emboldened them in their recalcitrance and unwillingness to submit to his dominion.[59]

Echoing common slaveholder remarks in testimony describing contests with their slaves, Don Manuel defended his administration of the hacienda by arguing that he was dealing with chattel, a rude and simple people who were predisposed to being troublesome and who violently resisted their subjugation to a new owner. To excuse them from their servitude would result in serious damage to the interests of the hacienda. Moreover, their very nature made it necessary, he wrote, to commit "grave excesses" to compel them to carry out their normal and customary labors. To subdue his slaves, who, he believed, were united against him, and to put them in their proper place, it was necessary to intimidate and dominate three or four them. His letter reads both as a justification of how he managed the hacienda (including the way he dealt with "uncles" Joseph, Pedro Ramón, and Esteban) and as a plea for colonial officials to show no leniency in dealing with the runaways and thereby reinforce his own authority. To that end, he requested that the audiencia separate the leaders out from the rest and punish them. This, he asserted, would serve as an example to the rest of his bondspeople and assist him in securing the good, tranquil, and functional administration of the hacienda.[60] Don Manuel tacitly admitted that he had ratcheted up the workload and the levels of physical coercion on the hacienda in order to, in his own words, resubjugate the slaves to their servitude.

Comparing the statements of the six slaves identified as the leaders of the rebellion with that of their new master provides insight into the hidden transcripts of both masters and slaves and reveals the interaction of the competing visions of mastery and slavery that underwrote the negotiated character of power in master-slave relations. Don Manuel viewed the slaves as simple and obstinate and felt that coercion and violence were the best means to secure their obedience. His apparent failure to understand the intricacies of master-slave relations may have owed to his relative inexperience as a slaveholder. He clearly felt that the violence he employed was required to secure the level of control over his chattel needed to operate a productive ingenio. The slaves, in turn, recognized that their social position obligated them to labor, made physical violence part and parcel of daily life, and placed them under the authority of their master and overseers. They did not, however, believe that the power of masters was unlimited. Their understanding of slavery was not grounded in abstract notions of fair play but rather in slave materialism, the interaction of the imposition of mastery from above and their lived experience(s). Their recollections of conditions under Asencio González and their knowledge of conditions on neighboring plantations clearly shaped their expectations. Even in the face of what they considered to be a brutal regime, these slaves appear to have been very comfortable in expressing their concerns to their owners and overseers. When those complaints fell on deaf ears they felt vindicated in trying to bring them before the colonial authorities. They neither viewed master authority as absolute and unchallengeable nor were they so cowed that they would not voice their complaints in public.

The Calderón slaves' belief that the viceroy or the audiencia would intervene on their behalf was based in experiences in their recent and collective memory. For example, between the death of Don Asencio González in April and the mass flight in August as many as six slaves had already absconded from the hacienda. This group included Joseph Romero, who was also interrogated as a leader of the mass exodus. The earlier runaways had apparently fled in order to complain to colonial authorities regarding their treatment. Some, like Joseph Romero, then seem to have returned to the hacienda. The documents do not clearly indicate if those runaways were punished for running away. The audiencia responded by sending at least two dispatches back to the hacienda warning its managers to treat the slaves better. Nearly all of the slaves claimed that although they were still forced to work Sundays and festivals days, the severity of mistreatment and overwork subsided after the dispatches had been received. Yet, based on their testimony and the decision to flee, despite their fear that they could be executed for doing so, it seems that conditions had not returned to normal or acceptable levels in their eyes. The fact the slaves could recall instances where the viceroy and/or audiencia interceded on their behalf in their past no doubt figured in their decision to flee en masse.

From Don Manuel's perspective, however, this intrusion by colonial authorities into hacienda discipline made the slaves recalcitrant and unwilling to submit to his or the mayordomo's authority. According to Don Manuel, the slaves could not be forced to complete any more work than what they believed to be acceptable. Any attempt on his part or that of his mayordomo to extract additional labor was met with threats from the slaves that they would once again take their complaints to colonial authorities in Mexico City. Despite Don Manuel's sense that such insolence was out of bounds, neither openly defying a master's authority nor complaining about workloads was an exceptional occurrence in New Spain. Nor were they predicated solely on the state's previous interventions into hacienda discipline.

Don Manuel and his representative in Mexico City, Don Joseph Antonio de Santander, asserted the slaves, as an armed mass, had threatened their owners and overseers on other occasions in the recent past. Following the receipt of one of the dispatches from the audiencia admonishing the overseers to treat them better, the slaves entered the main house en masse and, brandishing their weapons and tools, daringly cried out that someone would pay for the death of two or three of their compatriots (presumably "uncles" Joseph and Pedro Ramón). This testimony suggests that the slaves' refusal to lay down their arms on August 9 was probably an effort to intimidate their appraisers, as in this earlier confrontation.[61]

Another incident in the collective past of the Calderón slaves may have led them to believe that outside assistance was available and that they could get away with trying to bully their owners with the threat of violence. In this case, the Calderón slaves availed themselves of the authorities to prevent what they feared would result in the disruption of their community. On May 26th, 1728, following another appraisal related to the apparent bankruptcy of the ingenio, the Calderón slaves, armed with their tools including knives and machetes, surrounded one of the evaluators, Don Martín de Cabrera, as he left the plantation. They begged Cabrera to intervene on their behalf regarding their "great grief" and fear that their community was about to be broken apart. Don Martín, the administrator of the nearby ingenio San Joseph de Cocoyoc, testified that the slaves were very concerned that control of the hacienda was going to pass to the owners of the neighboring Casasano and Hospital ingenios. The slaves feared that the owners of these neighboring ingenios would break up their slave community and disperse them throughout the other haciendas in retaliation for the alleged theft of some cattle by the Calderón slaves.[62]

The following day the slaves presented their grievances before Bachiller Don Miguel de Nava, the judge and inspector of the testaments, chaplaincies, and pious works of the archbishopric of Mexico.

"In distressed and distraught voices, with the women screaming and crying," the slaves begged that the hacienda be reentrusted to Don Diego Barrientos, who currently leased it, or that a member of the chaplaincy be placed in charge rather than being leased to the owners of Casasano or Hospital. If the hacienda fell under the control of the owners of Hospital and Casasano, they said they would to burn the ingenio to the ground and "send it all to the Devil."[63] They vowed that they would never accept official transfer of the hacienda, and therefore their community, to anyone they did not deem an acceptable owner. In addition, they asked that four of their compatriots, apparently the leaders of this mutiny, be freed.

Nava successfully pacified the slaves by assuring them that they would not be placed under the control of either Hospital or Casasano. Whether or not the actions and threats by the slaves in fact affected who subsequently took charge of the hacienda is not important, because since the hacienda did not get leased to Hospital or Casasano, the slaves could certainly have arrived at the conclusion that their actions had preserved their community and families. It is also possible that some of the slaves living on Calderón in 1763 had lived through the tumult in 1728. But even if not, it is more than likely that stories of that incident were passed from generation to generation of slaves and served as a blueprint for collective action in 1763.

The course of events in both 1728 and 1763 clearly indicate that one of the more potentially distressing aspects of slavery was the effect that major changes in a slave owner's life could have on the psyche of the enslaved. Bankruptcy, financial difficulty, and even death left slaves, as individuals and communities, open to a myriad of negative and unwelcome repercussions. Communities and families could be ripped apart with the sale of children, spouses or lovers, and extended kin. This may have been most frightening for the slaves because unlike in the case of workloads and levels of physical punishment, the normal operation of master-slave relations did not provide slaves an opportunity to negotiate in these instances. Slaves were at their most powerless when it came to changes in the circumstances of their owners.

On August 12, 1763, Don Manuel's lawyer requested that the leaders of the rebellion—whom he identified as Joseph Hilario, Joseph Roberto, Ana María, Francisco Ramón, Vicente Ferrer, Tomas de Aquino, and Antonio Manuel (aka el Cojo)—be separated from the rest of the slaves in order to prevent them from further influencing their fellow runaways.[64] In another petition dated August 19, he requested that the slaves be escorted back to the hacienda as quickly as possible. According to that application it was the height of the harvest (which was unlikely, as it was the rainy season), and without the slaves to cut and process the sugarcane, the hacienda faced financial ruin. The petition cautioned that slaves could not be expected to return of their own volition; if they were freed with instructions to return they would surely take flight instead for places where they could never be recovered. To insure that the slaves would be obedient and well behaved in the future Don Manuel requested that the six leaders be punished in front of their fellow runaways. That, he thought, would impress on them what they would face if their insubordination continued. Furthermore, the ringleaders were not to be returned to the hacienda but, in accordance with Don Manuel's request, were to be placed in an obraje in Mexico City until a suitable buyer could be found for them. Almost sarcastically, the petition noted that the slaves had requested permission to seek out a new master.

Measuring the success or failure of the mass flight from the perspective of the Calderón slaves is difficult. On August 19, the five male leaders of the mutiny were brought before the rest of the slaves who had fled to Mexico City, tied to a post, and given no more than six lashes apiece. Ana María was spared this punishment, apparently owing to her sex. This beating prompted the remaining slaves to ask to be returned to the hacienda where they promised to live obediently. The leaders were then sent to an obraje to await sale. As fathers, mothers, husbands, wives, and friends of those who remained on the hacienda, their loss meant the disruption of family and community. Many of the complaints brought forth by the Calderón slaves in 1728 and 1763 arose squarely in their desire to protect and maintain the slave community on the plantation. The loss of these six slaves likely represented a severe blow.

Yet the same court order that prescribed this punishment also upbraided the owners and mayordomos of Calderón again, admonishing them to treat their slaves better, beginning immediately. In fact, the audiencia demanded that the slaves not be punished in any excessive manner and that they not be forced to complete any more work than what was customarily expected on all the haciendas throughout the region. Finally, the judges recommended that the mayordomo, Pedro de Luna, be replaced with someone who would treat the slaves better, which would help secure the smooth operation of the hacienda.[65]

This might appear to be a victory of sorts for the slaves, but it was not uncommon for the audiencia or other civil, ecclesiastical, and inquisitorial courts to caution slave owners to treat their chattel better in instances of apparent abuse. Colonial officials had issued similar warnings to Don Manuel and his mayordomo in the recent past. But did colonial authorities actually enforce their rulings? The slaves' decision to run away and seek redress in Mexico City suggests they were not convinced that the reprimand by the audiencia would restore the living conditions they were used to under Don Asencio's mastership. They testified that conditions had improved since their initial complaint but that they were not what they had been during Don Asencio's lifetime. On the other hand, perhaps they simply saw a hearing with officials in Mexico City as an opportunity to make their wish that they wanted Don Juan, whom they believed would be a benevolent master, to take control of the hacienda known.

This case provides an extraordinary example of the ordinary negotiation of mastery and slavery in New Spain. Owners and their chattel contested with each other over what amounted to acceptable behavior for both; this give-and-take can be understood as the unequal interaction of the private transcripts of slaves and masters in public, resulting in the hegemonic processes of rule. The intervention of the state into those relations potentially exacerbated the problem by checking the theoretically absolute authority of masters (guaranteed, and yet circumscribed, by the *Siete Partidas*), thereby giving the slaves a false sense of agency. That was certainly the argument of Don Manuel Ruiz de Castañeda. But the hubris created by the theoretically complete authority that Don Manuel believed he possessed as a slaveholder caused him to misread social reality and to rely too heavily on coercion. By ignoring the initial complaints from his bondsmen regarding acceptable levels of treatment and work, he allowed master-slave relations to spiral out of control.

Interestingly, and perhaps perplexingly from the modern perspective, the Calderón slaves did not pursue their collective liberation by running away, forming a palenque, and entering into negotiations with the state for their freedom as did the runaways from Córdoba. Nor did they demand to be treated as free wage laborers. Rather, they limited their demands to being permitted to state the conditions under which they would return to slavery, which speaks to the extent of the ideological domination they faced. and helps explain why their radicalism did not take the form that we might have anticipated. Conversely, their ability to reject parts of that subordination underscores the limits of that domination. And the fact that they could and did effect change by giving public expression to those aspects of their enslavement that they rejected speaks to their limited agency to affect the nature of rule.

Conclusion

The resolution of the Calderón and Amapa slave rebellions clearly demonstrates the willingness of the Spanish colonial state to interject itself into certain types of disputes, to serve as a mediator between masters and slaves, planters and runaway slaves. Historians have long treated Latin American slavery as distinctive because of the limited legal protections extended to the enslaved and the fact that slaves could appear in legal proceedings as plaintiffs and witnesses (even against their masters), neither being a privilege that was generally afforded to slaves in British North America.[66] A key component of the Spanish colonial order was the deployment of civil, ecclesiastical, and even inquisitorial courts, which literally and figuratively represented the state's authority to mediate disputes, resolve conflicts, make decisions, and impose punishments in the name of colonial stability. By allowing all colonials—regardless of their race, class, gender, or status (free vs. enslaved)—access to these colonial institutions the Spanish defused dissent and thereby weakened the ability of colonial subjects to mount a radical challenge to colonial structures.[67]

The ability of the Calderón slaves to engage the state, to make their demands and declare their expectations of how slavery should operate in colonial courts, and the fact that the Mandinga runaway slaves could successfully petition the colonial state for their freedom and citizenship provide clear evidence of the negotiated nature of power relations in the colony. Each of these cases is extraordinary, but the negotiations themselves were not. Negotiation between masters and slaves did not only occur in those instances in which the state intervened. Rather such interventions, although exceptional, produced historical documents that bring into view the ongoing contestations, the normal social dynamics, of master-slave relations. In other words, master-slave relations cannot be characterized simply by compliance or rebellion, total power or powerlessness. but rather as a process of continual negotiation that had the potential to lead to rebellious or violent action.

A number of important conclusions can be drawn from the comparison of the Calderón mass flight with moments of individual slave flight, the string of rebellions in Córdoba, and the subsequent creation of Amapa. The destruction wrought by the slave rebellion of 1735 illuminates the danger that the flight of the Calderón slaves represented had they taken up arms or had slaves from neighboring plantations been inspired to follow suit. It serves as a stark reminder that slaves, like masters, also had recourse to violence. That threat of rebellion served to check the unabated repression of the enslaved in most cases. In addition, the creation of Amapa highlights another road that the Calderón slaves could have but did not take.

Comparing these moments of collective slave action also brings to light the danger in conflating the motivations and desires of palenque residents, who in this case were seeking to formalize their freedom, and those of slaves like those found at Calderón, who were struggling to improve the conditions under which they lived and labored. Put plainly, slaves who had successfully escaped bondage and become cimarrones—either fighting or negotiating for their continued freedom—had undergone a change in subject position. Their actions were no longer representative of slaves but of runaway slaves. The lack of testimony from the slaves involved in the Córdoba rebellions underscores the uniqueness of the sources on the conflicts at Calderón. Individual runaways and even the collective runaways from Calderón repeatedly articulated that they were running from something, from unbearable treatment and deteriorating master-slave relations, rather than running to something, freedom. It should not be surprising, then, that the slaves in the Calderón mass flight did not undergo a change in subject position similar to that of those runaways who negotiated with the state for their freedom. That group never appears to have considered themselves anything other than slaves and sought only to improve their living conditions under slavery rather than to escape it.

The Calderón slaves did, like individual runaways, however, exhibit slave radicalism. It just was not aimed at the escape from or the destruction of slavery. Rather than a war against slavery it seems more appropriate, in the novohispano case, to speak of a war within slavery. We might assume that the Amapa runaways provide evidence that the Calderón slaves had the potential to strike against their own enslavement. The slaves' apparent response to the emancipation rumor in 1735, which was likely the news that negotiations between the cimarrones and the state had failed, to transform it into a rumor that local planters were blocking the liberation of all the enslaved in Córdoba, proves that slaves could be ready recipients to such discourses. It may also provide evidence that an antislavery position could emerge from within slavery itself. But without testimonies as to why the Amapa cimarrones fled in the first place (which might be different from the justifications for flight given by other runaways) it would be mere conjecture to categorize it as such. The goal is not to diminish the agency of slaves by labeling it prepolitical but rather to suggest the limited ways that their agency impacted the structures of power that they lived within. My position does not preclude the possibility of radicalism among slaves that sought the destruction of slavery or that such an agenda could have emanated out of slavery itself.

Treating the imposition of rule as the result of unequal interaction between the private transcripts of the elite and those they dominate allows for an account of planter power that shows that it was not unlimited. Potential slave actions were determined by a larger structure of power relations, structures that slaves helped maintain and yet also altered through their daily contestations with their masters. Slaves, basing their critiques of the application of power in their own lived experiences, worked through both confrontation and accommodation to manipulate the system to their "least disadvantage."[68] Still, the Calderón slaves, who escaped their enslavement, did not demand liberty like the runaway slaves from Mandinga, who successfully negotiated their personal emancipation. Despite slaves' clear connections with the free population of African descent as well as the possibilities of manumission, the majority of slaves focused their attention and energies on making slavery as livable as possible, not on escaping it. Therefore the quest for personal liberation does not appear to have been fundamental to their identities as slaves. Why? The complicated answer, which is that freedom did not play as an important role in the ways that slaves conceptualized their social position as did other issues and that discourses of personal liberty were less significant within the sociocultural language of colonial New Spain than we might expect, is explored in depth in the following chapter.

CHAPTER 6

"The Liberty He Promised Me"

The Complicated Relationship Between
Slavery and Freedom

✤ ON MARCH 16, 1658, CATALINA DE LA CRUZ, A BLACK SLAVE (perhaps of Congolese descent) presented an incredible petition before the Inquisition regarding her freedom and that of her two sons Felipe and Miguel. In it she demanded that she and Felipe be recognized as freed and demanded the restitution of monies that she assumed that she had paid for Miguel's liberation.[1] At the heart of her suit lay the fact that her previous owner, Doña Isabel Tristán, had been tried, convicted, and relaxed (turned over to secular authorities for execution) in the great Mexico City auto-de-fé of 1649 as a crypto-Jew. Catalina's petition asserted that when Tristán committed heresy by practicing Judaism she immediately vacated her *dominio* (dominion) over her slaves. At that very moment, Catalina argued, she and Felipe (Miguel had not yet been born) became free.

The claim itself is remarkable, but the intervening years between the time that Catalina and Felipe were removed from Tristán's control in 1642 and the completion of their case in 1659 are equally significant for our understanding of the implications of her story for the lived experience of slavery in colonial Mexico. As was customary, the Real Fisco de la Inquisición (The fiscal branch of the Inquisition) seized the estate of Doña Isabel once she was formally accused of being a crypto-Jew. Catalina and Felipe were subsequently sold in 1645 to Eugenio de Saravia, a secretary for the Inquisition, and soon thereafter Catalina gave birth to her second son, Miguel.

According to Catalina, at a certain point she began saving money that she hoped to use to free herself and her sons, entrusting some 200 pesos to the care of Don Martín de Aeta, an accountant for the Inquisition. Catalina made clear in her petition that she initially hoped to use the courts to force Saravia to liberate herself and her sons in return for the 200 pesos but to date only Miguel had been liberated. In seeking out advice on how best to proceed, however, "multiple people" suggested that she pursue her case on the grounds of Tristán's heresy. Her appeal to inquisitors, therefore, also included her demand for the restitution of the 200 pesos she had deposited with Aeta. Here she was likely assuming that if she had been freed before Miguel's birth, he would have been born free and it would have been unnecessary for her to purchase his freedom. She demanded an additional 40 pesos in recompense for her service to Saravia over the previous fifteen years.

Savaria countered that when he purchased Catalina and Felipe, dominion passed to him and therefore he should not be held responsible for Doña Isabel's infraction. Secondly, he argued that he knew nothing of the 200 pesos entrusted to Aeta and thus that he had no agreement with Catalina granting her the privilege of purchasing her freedom. The lack of such an agreement would have severely limited her access to the courts to press for her liberty and may explain the advice she received to pursue her case based on Tristán's heresy. Saravia also claimed to have already manumitted Miguel gratis in 1647 and provided the court a copy of a carta de libertad for him. He likely presented Miguel's carta to underscore that he had not offered Catalina the possibility of purchasing her liberty or that of other son and thus had no knowledge of the 200 pesos. Unfortunately for the historian, Catalina did not state exactly when she began saving money or if her plan to purchase her freedom and that of Felipe actually predated Miguel's manumission in 1647.[2]

After reviewing the testimony and various petitions, Inquisitor Pedro de Medina Rico found her case meritorious and ordered Catalina and Felipe freed on July 10, 1659.[3] The legal rationale behind his accepting Catalina's argument is not clear in the case file largely because colonial

magistrates were forbidden to issue written explanations of their decisions.[4] The *Siete Partidas* did, however, prohibit Jews from owning
Christian slaves and stipulated that any slaves owned by non-Christians
would be liberated upon the slave's baptism.[5] However, the decision
was more likely connected to the fact that Medina Rico was a *visitador*
(inspector) sent from Spain to determine if officers of the Holy Office
in New Spain were misrepresenting acquisitions from property seizures
to the Supreme Holy Office of the Inquisition in Madrid. Eugenio de
Saravia, Catalina's owner, and Martín de Aeta, the person she entrusted
her money to, became the primary focuses of that inquiry and were eventually punished for corruption.[6] Saravia apparently died in the middle
of Catalina's case, on December 8, 1658, which may have also impacted
Medina Rico's decision to grant her petition in July of the following year.[7]

Catalina's pursuit of liberty certainly resonates with a modern audience. That she was saving money to purchase her freedom, that she sought
out the advice of powerful members of society about how best to secure
her and her child's liberation, and that she presented such an innovative
argument before the courts all suggest that the quest for freedom might
have been central to her identity and agency. Cases like Catalina's, in
which the enslaved sued their masters over liberty, provide an excellent
means by which to explore the contours and implications of slave conceptions of freedom. These suits represent one of the few instances where
master-slave conflicts were explicitly about access to liberty and where
slaves evoked the word *libertad* (liberty or freedom) in colonial Mexican
documentation. In such cases, slaves or their representatives used
ecclesiastical, civil, or inquisitorial courts to press their masters for their
personal liberation.[8] How slaves like Catalina conceived of libertad and
how such conceptions impacted slave identity and agency remain open
questions.[9] Their suits allow for further consideration of issues surrounding the nature of slave radicalism and the question of how slaves might
have understood their own agency introduced in the preceding chapters.

Historians have taken up the task of exploring the complicated
relationship between freedom and slavery in Latin America, particularly
during the time leading up to, and including, the independence era (1810–
20s). They have found that the rhetoric of freedom for slaves assumed
particular importance in the context of the Bourbon reforms (1750–1810)
and the independence movements. These changes were due in large part
to the introduction of Enlightenment discourses relating to slavery and

freedom throughout the Atlantic world.[10] Slavery, defined as the most extreme example of an individual denied natural rights and serving as a metaphor for tyranny, was a key rhetorical weapon in the rejections of European colonialism articulated by independence fighters throughout the Atlantic world. As such, Peter Blanchard argues that "the liberators' call for freedom with its associated slavery metaphor found favor at all levels of society, but it struck an especially resonant chord within that sector of the Spanish American population who in fact and by law were enslaved."[11]

What of the period prior to the Atlantic revolutions? What of a context like New Spain, where slavery was already in decline by the onset of the major Bourbon reforms (the onset of which coincided with the reign of Charles III [1759–88]) and the Atlantic revolutions? Most scholars are comfortable stipulating that slaves in the Atlantic world conceived of freedom *and* that they *yearned* for their own personal liberation even before the revolutionary period.[12] Their accounts of the impact of that desire on slave agency are much more complicated. For many, the majority writing in the 1970s and 1980s, that desire provided the wellspring of slave resistance and a superstructural explanation for slave agency.[13] More recently, however, some scholars have been willing to disaggregate the two, arguing that while slaves longed for liberty, their agency had "little to do with abstract freedom."[14]

Even so, we continue to associate slave agency with freedom. Christine Hünefeldt argues that slaves were able to win "fractions of freedom" through their contests with masters over day-to-day issues. Those fractions "spurred the dissolution of the slave system (i.e. emancipation)" in nineteenth-century Peru.[15] María Elena Díaz sees that process at work even the seventeenth and eighteenth centuries. Díaz hypothesizes that read against Orlando Patterson's notions of "social death," any "enactment of a social or even territorial tie outside the master-slave bond may be read as a de facto recovered fragment of 'human rights' and a piecemeal achievement of *freedom* in a person's life, even if it coexisted with major aspects of enslavement."[16] The desire to read slave agency as aimed at securing fractions of freedom is likely shaped by two important historical and historiographical impulses, the recognition of the righteousness of the end of slavery (which is undeniable) and the laudable desire to make slaves key actors in the destruction of slavery. But, for the sake of argument, let us imagine that history stopped in 1770. If emancipation did

not then loom on the horizon, how would slaves have understood their
own agency prior to that date? What discursive tools, and social spaces,
were available to slaves to express that sense of agency? Would they have
articulated their small victories in master-slave conflicts in terms of piecemeal freedoms?

A more sophisticated definition of freedom may be needed to frame
our discussion of the relationship between liberty and slavery in the minds
of the enslaved themselves in New Spain. Patterson presents what he calls
a chordal triad of notes, or core meanings, of freedom in Western thought.
The first note is personal freedom, understood as the antithesis of slavery,
defined as the absence of coercion or restraint. If one has personal freedom, one feels able to do as one pleases and is restricted only by the desire
of others to do as they please.[17] The second note, civic freedom, speaks
to the ability of adult members of a community to participate in its life
and governance. It can take on political (voting) and economic (property
ownership) connotations, among others. Last, Patterson introduces the
notion of sovereignal freedom, the power to act as one pleases, regardless
of the wishes of others. He is very clear that this note includes the domination and exploitation of others.[18] In this note, the individual who has
the most power is the most free, and the exercise of sovereignal freedom
always entails the disadvantaging of someone else. This third variant is
potentially problematic, from the modern perspective, because it appears
to be a threat to personal freedom.[19] But sovereignal freedom could be
understood as the definition of mastery itself. Patterson, employing his
musical metaphor, suggests that each of these notes of freedom have coexisted in Western sociopolitical thought since they were first articulated
as a triad in ancient Greece but that in a given historical context one note
dominates the others.[20]

Even before the Atlantic revolutions, each of these three types of
freedom existed in New Spain, but their salience depended on rank and
social position. Manumission deeds clearly articulate that the slave being
freed received both the personal and civic liberties legally denied to them
as chattel. Such records often include the phrasing that the slave in question was freed from "all captivity and servitude" or "the dominion of
others," language that corresponds to notions of personal liberty.[21] The
same cartas often included language that the ex-slaves received the right
to buy and sell property, make out a will, enter into contracts, and so
forth, which is civic liberty or the ability to participate in civil society. Yet

the third type, sovereignal freedom, was what slave owners were actually relinquishing when they liberated a slave. As chapters 4 and 5 suggest, it was sovereignal freedom, perhaps better understood as power, with which slaves had daily contact.

There is little evidence that Patterson's notion of personal freedom as it existed in Spanish juridical thought was understood as an inalienable right or was even highly esteemed by individual colonial subjects, including slaves in New Spain prior to the 1770s.[22] In his study of litigation initiated by Indians in seventeenth-century New Spain, Brian Owensby suggests that the claims he encountered were aimed at mitigating the "intrusive" or what Patterson would define as the sovereignal freedom of others and were clearly "bounded by the law." Litigants were not invoking *personal freedom* in these cases, and they understood libertad as a conditional, not an absolute, privilege that arose out of one's fulfilling the obligations commensurate with one's position in the social hierarchy.[23] This restricted notion of libertad was the one that prevailed in New Spain, he contends, and petitions filed by castas and slaves differed very little from those of Indians.[24]

To assess whether or not slaves seized on existing discourses surrounding libertad and radicalized them requires the following: 1) a thorough accounting of how Spanish law articulated access to freedom for slaves; 2) a careful examination of patterns found within manumissions to uncover how and why particular slaves received personal emancipation; and 3) a close reading of actual "liberty suits" like the one brought by Catalina de la Cruz to understand the specific nature of the claims a slave could make on the state regarding liberty. Those comparisons suggest that for the overwhelming majority of slaves, the institutional and ideological constraints on libertad severely restricted how slaves may have perceived it. That conception was so circumscribed that that it played little if any role in how slaves negotiated their daily lives. Slaves were nearly incapable of forcing their masters to free them.[25] The overwhelming majority of "liberty suits" are best understood as cases brought by people who presumed themselves or their loved ones to be, categorically, *freed*, and who demanded recognition of that status, insisting that it was correct, according to the law and shared concepts of justice.[26] Similar to the Mandinga runaways, these potential ex-slaves had undergone a change in subject position and legal standing that allowed them to demand recognition of their status as freed persons. There is little in the record to

indicate that slaves were mobilizing notions of freedom in their contests
with their masters outside the specific arenas covered in Spanish law.

Law and Freedom in Spanish America

The work of Frank Tannenbaum and subsequent scholars has led many
to the conclusion that Spanish American slaves were entitled by law or
custom to manumission. The process of *coartación*, defined as "the right
of the [slave] to demand that his price be publicly set by a court of law
and . . . to pay off his price in several installments," plays a central role in
these conceptions.[27] Alejandro de la Fuente, for example, argues that such
protections had been "firmly established and protected in Spanish legislation and claimed by slaves" in Cuba and perhaps in other Spanish colonies
since the sixteenth century.[28]

Yet Spanish imperial law and customary legal practice in the colonies
did not guarantee slaves the right to manumission. Although the *Siete
Partidas* stipulated "that all laws of the world should lead towards freedom"
they stopped short of guaranteeing slaves the right to emancipation.[29] The
section entitled "Concerning Liberty" does not include any language that
might allow slaves to press for their own liberation.[30] Nor did subsequent
Spanish American slave legislation—including that in the *Recopilación
de leyes de los reynos de las Indias* (1681) and Charles IV's Instruction on
Slavery (1789)—codify a slave's right to manumission.[31] Rather, it would
be a better to say that these laws outlined the processes by which masters,
or the state, could free slaves.

Furthermore, coartación, which appears to have been a uniquely
Cuban institution for much of the colonial period, must be distinguished
from self-purchase. The term underwent a process of definition throughout the colonial period until it became codified in 1842 in Cuba as the
legal right of slaves to *force* masters to accept their self-purchase and to
make partial payments toward that manumission and apparently the right
of *coartados* (those in the process of purchasing their freedom) to demand
to be sold to a new master if they so wished. The codification of this
process in the 1840s appears to have emerged out of a customary right
regularly protected by courts in the late colonial period.[32]

Spanish legal tradition clearly defined the circumstances under which
a slave might turn to civil, ecclesiastical, or inquisitorial courts to press
for his or her own liberation prior to the nineteenth century. Echoing

the *Siete Partidas*, Emperor Carlos I issued a *cédula real* (royal order) in 1540 that stated, "We order our Royal Audiencias that if any black man or woman or anyone else, held as a slave, proclaims liberty, that they be heard, given justice, and be protected from mistreatment by their masters for doing so."[33] The wording of that royal order is critical because it limited slaves' access to the courts to instances when they claimed to be wrongfully enslaved and were therefore theoretically already free(d). The meaning of that decree becomes clearer when compared to how the *Siete Partidas* articulated the circumstances under which a slave could bring suit against his or her master over liberty:

> There are, however, certain special cases in which [a slave can bring suit against his master]; as, for instance, when someone makes a will in which he orders that a certain slave of his be emancipated, and he who is directed to do this fraudulently conceals the will, in which the grant of emancipation was made.[34]

In other words, if a promise of freedom in a testament went unfulfilled, the slave had recourse to colonial courts to see it enforced. Even this protection was conditional, however. Another section of the *Siete Partidas* clearly prohibited masters from freeing slaves if it meant defrauding creditors. Colonial courts, as we will see, clearly valued the rights of creditors over access to freedom for slaves.[35] Thus, even promised manumissions could be overturned if they infringed on the civic freedom of others. The *Partidas* further specify the conditions under which a slave might bring suit over *libertad*:

> We, moreover, decree that, where any slave has money which does not belong to his master but which he has received from some other party, and gives it to someone to be kept for him, trusting in him, with the understanding that he will purchase him of his master, and afterwards set him at liberty; and bought him, is unwilling to set him free; we declare that, under circumstances of this kind, the said slave has a right to appear in court . . . and force [the other party] to keep the contract entered into with him. The same rule applies where a slave makes a contract with anyone to purchase him of his master, and set him free after he has repaid the money which he gave for him, and after this

contract was entered into, he, having purchased the said slave, refuses to receive the money for his emancipation, or, having received it, refuses to set him free, as he had agreed to do.[36]

Here again, the law is quite specific that a slave had recourse to colonial courts only if promises of assistance in achieving personal manumission were unfulfilled. Catalina de la Cruz may have initially sought to bring her suit under this protection.

The implications of relationship between the conditions under which a slave might bring suit as defined in the royal order of 1540 and those set out in the *Siete Partidas* are more clearly identifiable in the section in the *Siete Partidas* that prescribes when a slave might name an attorney to represent himself:

> Where anyone *appears to be a slave* and is in the power of another, even though he may wish to institute legal proceedings against the party having control of him in order to be liberated from slavery *by stating that he is free*, under these circumstances, we decree that though he can appear in court in his own behalf, he cannot appoint an attorney. . . .

> We also decree that, where any relative of the *alleged slave* desires to conduct his case, he can do so. . . Wise men attached so much importance to freedom, that they . . . deemed it proper that relatives should have the authority to conduct suits for persons *wrongfully held as slaves.*[37]

Spanish legal tradition, therefore, articulated liberation as a possibility and only sought to guarantee slaves' access to the courts *to prove* that a promise of freedom remained unfulfilled or that a person was being wrongfully kept as a slave. Manumission was, therefore, a possibility totally under the purview of mastery. For slaves, however, once manumission was offered, it was transmuted into something more closely associated with the modern conception of a privilege, something that could be defended in colonial courts. But were slaves able to use courts to litigate for personal freedom without cause? Did the possibility of slaves employing the state to force their masters to accept their personal liberation emerge as a customary right in New Spain? Or did practice closely follow the letter of the law?

Before we can answer those questions, however, we must explore how manumission operated in New Spain.

Manumission in Practice

Manumission, the legal mechanism by which a master transferred owner-ship of a slave to the slave himself or herself, has long been held up as a defining characteristic of slavery in Latin America. Manumission has been understood as representative of the more humane nature of slavery in Catholic colonies (among specialists, however, the notion has largely been dispelled), as a powerful form of social control employed by masters over their chattel (the promise of manumission, or even hope of manumission, resulting in better behaved slaves), or, as means to measure the capacity of slaves to confront their own domination. In all three cases, however, manumission is understood as central to the operation of slavery as an institution in Latin America.

Manumissions generally took one of four forms: purchased (immediate for payment); gratis (immediate without compensation); "upon death" of the owner; or conditional (with the imposition of extra service often beyond the lifetime of the manumitting master). The upon death and conditional forms were often granted in last will and testaments, while the purchased and gratis forms were often conveyed via formulaic cartas de libertad sworn out before a notary public. For a breakdown of manumissions in New Spain by sex, age, and form see table 6.1.[38]

There was a noticeable rise in the importance of purchased manumissions over time in New Spain.[39] That pattern is significant because the prevalence of purchased manumissions might appear to be a measure of slave agency in achieving their dream of personal liberation (table 6.1).[40] Some cartas indicate that slaves had requested (*ha pedido*) their freedom, offering a particular self-purchase price, rather than waiting for masters to offer manumission of their own accord. For example, Juan de Guzmán and Luisa de Guevara allowed their thirty-year-old mulatta slave María de la Candelaria to purchase her freedom for 300 pesos in 1676 after she "begged" them to do so.[41] Such notations were rare but the rate of incidence of slaves petitioning to buy their freedom does appear to have increased in Mexico City from the 1670s to the 1720s. Yet, even with the rise in purchased manumission, the majority of manumissions were not purchased and coartación rarely if ever occurred in colonial Mexico. Only

TABLE 6.1. Sex, Age, and Form of Manumitted Slaves in New Spain

	Mexico City 1580–1650	Mexico City 1673–76	Mexico City 1723–26	Guanajuato 1699–1750
Sex				
Male	38.5%	34.9%	38.3%	44.7%
Female	61.5%	65.1%	61.7%	55.3%
TOTAL	(104)	(238)	(204)	(226)
Age				
>0–5	41.5%	17.7%	15.8%	19.1%
6–14	12.3%	14.0%	12.2%	18.5%
15–45	33.9%	53.0%	54.7%	54.3%
46+	12.3%	15.2%	17.3%	8.1%
TOTAL	(65)	(165)	(139)	(173)
Manumission Type				
Unconditional	--	21.6%	25.5%	26.5%
Upon Death	--	39.0%	23.5%	24.3%
Conditional	--	10.6%	8.8%	8.4%
Purchased	--	28.8%	42.2%	40.7%
TOTAL		(236)	(204)	(226)

Sources: AN, 1673–76 and 1723–26; AHG, PC, 1699–1750; Mexico City, 1580–1650: Bowser, "The Free Person of Color in Mexico City and Lima," 350.

1 of the 675 manumissions from Mexico City and Guanajuato I analyzed was the result of a process that resembled coartación.[42] And truth be told, it is near impossible to determine if many purchased manumissions were initiated by masters or slaves.

The growing importance of purchased manumissions may be more than a simple reflection of an increase in the number of slaves pursuing their own liberation, however. In a context like New Spain marked by a decreasing number of slaves, it might also be a sign of the increasing reluctance of slaveholders to free their chattel without payment. The number of wills that did not free slaves but instead provided specific instructions about who was to inherit them rose significantly from the 1670s to the 1720s.[43] The declining incidence of manumissions granted via wills could be an indication that slave owners were now less willing to deprive their heirs of slaves without compensation. Still, self-purchase was not the dominant form of manumission in New Spain whatever owners' motivations were.

Slave women and children accounted for between two-thirds and three-quarters of all freed slaves with known ages. Female slaves dominated, receiving between 55 and 65 percent of all manumissions. Children under the age of fifteen also represented a substantial portion of liberated slaves in colonial Mexico (table 6.1). A focus on who was being freed by whom and what motivated masters to free the particular slaves they did sheds light on the relevance of liberty in the everyday lives of slaves in New Spain, revealing that a great majority of manumissions resulted from long-term relationships between masters and their slaves and not the active pursuit of personal liberation by slaves.

A common argument has been that slave women exploited their sexuality and pursued relationships with free men, even their masters, in order to gain access to freedom for themselves and their children.[44] That conception is grounded in the belief that a desire for liberty played a key role in slave agency. It also has explanatory value in accounting for the predominance of women and children among the liberated. Slave-owning women, however, freed a significant portion of slaves in New Spain, undermining the significance of the paternity/lover thesis. The quantity of bondspeople freed by women seems to have been much greater than the proportion of slaves they owned. Men largely dominated economic life in colonial Spanish America, and thus we might expect that there would be more male than female slave owners and that men would own more slaves, on average, than would women. The lack of census materials frustrates any attempt to measure the extent of female ownership of slaves in New Spain, but it is clear that women freed slaves at much higher rates than they bought or sold them. Female slaveholders manumitted 48–53 percent of bondsmen and bondswomen in Mexico City in the 1670s and 1720s. Yet they only purchased approximately 19 percent and sold about 29 percent of slaves in that city in both 1675 and 1725.[45] If these patterns of buying and selling provide a rough indicator of slave ownership by sex, then it appears that slaves owned by women had a much better chance of achieving freedom than did those with male masters.[46]

An exploration of who mistresses liberated suggests that women and children were proportionally more important among slaves freed by women than by men. In Mexico City mistresses freed an outright majority of women and children—nearly six in ten—in the 1670s and the 1720s. In Guanajuato things were a little more complicated. Unlike in Mexico City, men freed a clear majority of slaves (56 percent) and as a result they also freed more women and children than did mistresses. However, slave women and children represented a larger proportion among those freed by mistresses than among those liberated by men. For example, 61 percent of slaves freed by women were female compared to just over half of those liberated by men.[47] Similarly, men freed 58 percent of children in Guanajuato. But children still were proportionally more significant among slaves freed by women (43 percent) than those by men (36 percent). The strongest associations were between female slave owners and their slave women and children, on one hand, and between male slave owners and adult male slaves, on the other. The fact that slave women and children were more likely to be freed by women than by men indicates that even if sexual relations between masters and slaves influenced manumission patterns by male masters, it accounts for only a small proportion of slaves freed overall.[48] Therefore, we must put to rest the presumed causal connection between manumission and male master–female slave sexual relations, which in turn undermines the implicit associations of the pursuit of liberty with manumission, in New Spain at least.[49]

Explanations by mistresses as to why they freed particular slaves highlight the impact of the shared social universe of mistresses, their female slaves, and the children of both on manumission. One important pattern that emerges from these explanations is that the motivations behind particular manumissions were clearly related to the caregiving roles, particularly the child-rearing functions, of women, both slave and free. This suggests that access to liberation was normally the result of a lifetime of faithful service rather than the culmination of a lifelong, active pursuit of manumission by slaves.

Numerous mistresses freed bondswomen in remuneration for wet-nursing and/or raising their children. Bernarda Fernández de Guevara freed Rosa, her thirty-seven-year-old mulatta slave, for her assistance in raising her daughters. Magdalena de Soria manumitted Agustín, her one-year-old slave, in compensation for the good service of his mother Juana de San Antonio.[50] Serving as wet nurses and nannies to masters' children increased the likelihood of liberation for slave women and their children.

An exploration of child rearing from another perspective further underscores the importance of the shared social universe of mistresses and their slaves within the domestic sphere. Mistresses often made reference to surrogate maternity when manumitting slaves, particularly children, and did so much more often than men. For example, Nicolasa de Guevara y Orellano, a widow from Mexico City, freed her eleven-year-old slave María de Cristo, because "she was born into my hands and grew up in my home."[51] Explanations such as this should be interpreted metaphorically; they speak to the privileged position of slaves who operated within the same social space as their female owners.

Men could and did reward slave women for fulfilling maternal roles within their households, but they did not do so as often as women. Juan López de Rivera freed a two-year-old slave named Francisco as compensation for the care and love with which Francisco's mother had raised his daughters.[52] Examples like this should not, however, obfuscate the fact it was women—mistresses and slaves alike—who shared the experiences of bearing and raising children and providing care for other members of the slaveholding family, especially during illnesses, within the domestic sphere. Those shared experiences in social reproduction created bonds not possible between slave women and male masters in most cases and resulted in a sense of social intimacy. That familiarity, in turn, increased the likelihood that slave owners, particularly women, would liberate their slave women and their children. Therefore, it appears likely that intimate daily interactions between female slave owners and their slaves represented the single most significant determinant as to which slaves were freed and why.

Similarly, the means of manumission could be multiple; the relationship between masters and their slaves that grew out of their shared domestic universe could compel masters to grant their slaves the power to purchase their manumission. Alonzo Roma y Sotomayor freed his thirty-one-old-year old slave, Francisca de la Concepción, on January 8, 1723, in return for 300 pesos paid to him by Lorenzo Fabián de Puga. Don Alonzo explained that Francisca had "served him with much love and goodwill, raising his daughter." In another complicated example from 1673, Doña María Benítez Tamayo promised to liberate six-year-old María de la Trinidad and two-year-old Catarina de San Ildefonso, because they "had grown up in her arms, and she loved them like her own daughters." And yet she also required payment, in the form of 50 pesos for each girl, from their aunt, a free woman named Dominga Rodríguez. She also required that both girls continue to serve her and her daughter, María Guerrero, until both were deceased. Doña María clearly expected that to occur in the distant future, as she added the caveat that any children born to young slave girls were to be considered freeborn. In these cases, relationships created within the domestic sphere, payment, and future service all figured into the manumission equation.[53]

These examples underscore the potential danger in treating purchased manumissions as evidence of slave agency aimed at obtaining personal liberty. The act of manumission might be best understood not simply as the seizure of freedom by slaves but also as the renunciation of dominion, or mastery, by slaveholders. This way of conceptualizing manumission is lent support by the *Siete Partidas*, which lay out the means by which a person could divest themselves of dominion over a slave but does not spell out how a slave might actively pursue liberation. By thinking of manumission in this light, we avoid the tendency to situate the history of the enslaved within larger metanarratives that tell the story of how Atlantic slavery was superseded by freedom and that subsequently treat slave agency as part of a broad history of the attempts of the enslaved to gain their freedom. Such metanarratives valorize modern sensibilities about "freedom" and overlook the ways that slaves imagined the history they were making.[54]

"Liberty Suits"

A consideration of the liberty suits brought by slaves further deepens our inquiry into slave conceptions of freedom in colonial Mexico and helps divorce them from teleological metanarratives of emancipation. Slaves brought "liberty suits" on four distinct but potentially overlapping grounds. Most common were "breach of promise" suits over unfulfilled offers of manumission. Adhering to the strictures of the *Siete Partidas*, these cases centered on either promises of manumission in testaments or on contracts between slaves and free people who had offered to purchase the slave with the stated goal of liberating them. A second type consisted of "free birth" claims, wherein the mother of a presumed slave claimed that she was free, or had been freed, before her child was born. Thus, the child in question was freeborn because status followed the womb. Third were accusations of abdication or violation of "dominion" that charged a master with violating his or her rights of ownership. Last were requests to establish the "just price" of a slave so that someone might purchase his or her freedom.[55] The overwhelming majority of cases surrounding libertad for slaves in New Spain were clearly grounded in the specific protections the *Siete Partidas* afforded slaves.

In a prototypical "breach of promise" suit, a free mulatto named Francisco Camargo appeared before the Inquisition on July 31, 1661, to present a petition on behalf of Juan and Ursula Clemente and their daughters Lucía and María regarding their freedom. That petition began a joint suit brought by nine slaves against the estate of Pedro de Soto López, an accountant for the Inquisition. Two additional petitions were filed on behalf of Carmargo's wife and their three sons as well as another unrelated slave child named Sebastian de Soto. The substance of all three petitions was very similar. De Soto, they claimed, had freed all nine slaves on his deathbed and that he had been unable to draft a properly notarized will or carta de libertad due to his poor health. The slaves' petitions, however, suggested that numerous witnesses would provide testimony supporting their claims.

Pedro de Castro, the attorney for Pedro de Soto's estate, countered that the slaves in question were part of de Soto's estate and that freeing them would prejudice his creditors by diminishing the assets available to satisfy his debts, thereby implicitly invoking the *Siete Partidas*. According to Brian Owensby, Juan Félix de Galbes, the *procurador* (advocate) for the slaves, countered that "liberty is so 'favored' a principle in law that it might not be dispensed with to satisfy debts."[56] Galbes's claim represents one of the few rhetorical flourishes regarding the value of liberty in an abstract sense found in any of the case files consulted for this study. In March 1663, the tribunal of the Inquisition rendered its verdict, ruling that Galbes had successfully proven de Soto's intent to free the slaves. The ruling added that freeing them in no way prejudiced the estate because it was large enough to settle all debts against it without the plaintiffs. These nine slaves' freedom and their ability to engage colonial institutions to protect it was fundamentally grounded in Pedro de Soto López's decision to manumit them. There is nothing in the documentation to suggest that the slaves were actively pursuing freedom or that access to liberty framed their relations with their owner.[57]

Manuel Muñoz, another slave owned by de Soto, had also brought a successful liberty suit in 1649, suggesting perhaps that the nine slaves who brought suit in 1661 had reason to believe that the court would protect offers of liberation. Muñoz claimed that de Soto had promised him his freedom on numerous occasions in return for his good service before selling him, in a fit of anger, to Tomás de Contreras, the obrajero from Coyoacan. Manuel petitioned that the sale be voided and that he be declared freed. Interestingly, de Soto supported Manuel's claim, writing that "it is true that in return for his continual good service I [promised] him his freedom on multiple occasions, and although I sold him out of anger it has always been my desire to give him his freedom." After some wrangling over price, Contreras agreed to sell Manuel back to de Soto, and on August 29, 1650, Manuel received his carta de libertad.[58] This case represents one of the rare instances in which a slave brought suit against a living owner as opposed to challenging the estate of a deceased owner, as did the nine other slaves freed by Pedro de Soto López.

The two cases initiated by slaves of Pedro de Soto López expose a number of issues that underscore the contingent and precarious nature of slaves' access to freedom in New Spain before the 1770s. First, the core element of these cases was an offer of liberty by de Soto. In them, the slaves were not simply attempting to use the courts to free themselves. This was true of the great majority of freedom suits. Second and equally importantly, these ten slaves owned Pedro de Soto López represented nearly one-sixth of the number of slaves who brought suit against their masters and more than one-third of all slaves who successfully won their freedom in available documentation for New Spain from 1604 to 1769.[59] This could suggest that slaves' access to the courts was significantly more limited than the number of cases might indicate.

De Soto's slaves must have known about the successes of Manuel Muñoz in 1649 when they brought suit against his estate in 1661. That possibility indicates, perhaps, that knowledge concerning the courts and how to access them was spread from individual slave to individual slave and may not have been something that all slaves were necessarily aware of. The fact that the case of Catalina de la Cruz did not set a precedent that other slaves followed lends further support to the idea that this level of legal savvy was not widespread. In the context of a significant crackdown against accused crypto-Jews in the early 1640s, the Inquisition had confiscated some fifty-three slaves, including Catalina and her son. There is no evidence that any of these other slaves won their freedom based on their masters' heresy as did Catalina and Felipe.[60] These cases in combination illustrate the possibility that slaves, even those who had been promised liberation, were not by and large fully aware of the legal options available to them.

The number of cases that do not center on offers of manumission that had been made by masters are quite limited in number, representing, at most, five of twenty-nine found suits. In two such examples, free people sought to use the courts to free enslaved loved ones even though they had not been offered manumission. In August 1757, Juan José de la Higuera, a free pardo, requested that a "just price" be established for Lorenza de Iriate, the slave of Don Pedro de Iriate and Doña Juana María Dávalos, so that he might purchase her freedom in order to marry her.[61] The court complied, and two assessors appraised Lorenza's value at 125 pesos. The case ends without any indication that the established purchase price was ever met, but it seems safe to assume it was. It is important to note, however, that although Juan José petitioned the court to establish her just price, there is no evidence that her owners contested his petition. If, however, they had decided to do so, they could have fought him, arguing that there was no compelling reason for them to be forced to free or sell Lorenza. Oddly, Lorenza never testified in the course of the judicial proceeding that was brought in her name. This request also dates to quite late in the colonial period, underscoring how rare such requests to establish "just price" for manumission (which could be read a precursor to coartación) were in New Spain.

A much more complicated example of a free person trying to win the liberation of an enslaved family member absent an offer of manumission comes from Querétaro in 1717. Miguel Altamirano, a free mulatto, brought an ultimately unsuccessful suit based on charges of "violation of dominion" on behalf of his daughter María de los Dolores against the convent of Santa Clara de Jesús. Madre Gertrudis de San Buenaventura had tried, against her father's expressed wishes in his testament, to sell María. Don Alonzo de Estrada Altamirano had stipulated in his will that upon his death María should serve his daughter in the cloisters until the slave's death, specifically prohibiting María from being sold. Miguel first petitioned to prevent the sale. On June 2, Don Joseph de Torres de Vergara, a lawyer for the audiencia, found that Madre Gertrudis had not received "absolute dominion" over María and thus ordered that she was not to be sold.[62] Miguel then initiated a second case, arguing that Madre Gertrudis and her abbess had violated the limited dominion they enjoyed over María when they attempted to sell her. As a result of that violation, he petitioned that María should be freed. Torres de Vergara, the same judge who decided in María's favor in the first suit, concluded that Miguel's new petition was without merit, and declared that María would not be freed.[63] There is nothing in the file to suggest that María was a driving force behind the attempt to win her liberation, and she did not appear on her own behalf.

There are only three cases in which slaves were clearly actively pursuing their own liberation *prior* to receiving an offer of manumission from their masters. In 1686, Teresa Rodríguez, a mulatta slave, appealed to ecclesiastical authorities in Mexico City to establish her "just price" and to allow her to purchase her freedom. She testified that a recent appraisal of the sugar hacienda where she labored assessed her value at 50 pesos. Yet she asked the court to order the executors of her master's estate to accept 150 pesos for her freedom. She likely offered triple what she was worth because she believed that amount of money would have seemed more valuable to her master's estate than an old slave woman. Teresa argued that she was unable to work owing to her advanced age and many illnesses. She also added that she had given birth to twelve children during her life on the hacienda. The judge ordered that the executors of the estate accept the 150 pesos and free her.[64] Teresa's case represents the single example wherein a slave won his or her freedom in this manner, namely, by forcing a living master or executor to liberate him or her. That reality certainly undercuts the notion that coartación was a customary right in New Spain prior to 1770.

In only two other cases, is it obvious that slaves initiated their pursuit of freedom on their own, without a offer from their master. Each legal proceeding, however, revolved around offers of assistance in achieving liberty from a third party, something that was clearly covered by the *Siete Partidas*. One of these suits was Catalina de la Cruz's. The other was one brought by Juan Esteban against Andrea de la Riva, a free parda, who claimed to be his owner.[65] While laboring on a *rancho* owned by his previous master, Don Antonio de Prados, Juan Esteban was able to grow some 469 pesos worth of corn and beans in 1734. He entrusted that produce to Dr. Antonio de Sosa Betancourt to sell on his behalf. The proceeds of that sale were to be used to purchase Juan, after which Betancourt promised to free him. Betancourt used those monies to purchase Juan for 250 pesos, but he failed in the intervening four years before his death to provide Juan his carta de libertad or the remaining 219 pesos. After Betancourt's death de la Riva, his heir, refused to recognize Juan as a free person, claiming that she inherited the slave as part of the Betancourt's estate. Juan successfully petitioned that Andrea provide him his carta and the outstanding 219 pesos. On September 9, 1738, Juan was declared free.[66] Juan's case raises a number of important questions, many of which cannot be answered. First, how did he first come to the decision to pursue his own liberation? Second and even more perplexingly, why did he continue to live, for all intents and purposes, as Betancourt's slave for nearly four years? Why did he not demand his carta and the remaining funds the moment that Betancourt purchased him using the monies from selling the produce?

Juan Esteban and Catalina de la Cruz were clearly pursuing their liberation prior to an offer from their masters, although their ability to bring suit to secure that freedom was predicated on the offer of assistance from a third party. As was the case with Pedro de Soto López's liberated slaves, however, in the overwhelming majority of cases liberty suits were predicated on a promise of manumission by a slave owner. Once slaves learned that they had been offered freedom they could become fanatical in its pursuit. Following the death of Licenciado Félix Pérez, Mateo Camacho ran away from a sugar plantation where he labored in Izúcar, Puebla. He made his way to Mexico City apparently to seek the assistance of Don Diego Joseph de Bustos, an accountant for the Inquisition, in securing the manumission that Pérez had promised him, along with six other slaves, in his will. Pérez's estate was likely in probate, and his heir, Capitán Martín Calvo, could not execute those manumissions until the inventory had been completed. Mateo interpreted Calvo's failure to follow through on the promise of manumission as an attempt to deny him his freedom, prompting him to abscond.

Mateo's story took a sensational twist on August 9, 1695, when, after learning that Calvo had arrived in Mexico City, Mateo stabbed himself in the neck and stomach five times with a knife. Mateo later testified that he acted out of desperation because he was afraid that Calvo had come to recapture him, return him to the sugar plantation, punish him for his flight, and deny him his liberty. Mateo found himself jailed in an obraje for nearly two years waiting for his case to be adjudicated. He ultimately attacked numerous coworkers, threatening to kill them, as the stress of waiting having driven him into a near homicidal rage. He was ordered released from the obraje and freed from his bondage on September 25, 1697.[67] No matter how dramatic the story, however, Mateo's actions emanated out of an unfulfilled promise of manumission. Although he ran away from his new master and nearly committed suicide rather than be returned to his enslavement, nothing from his case file suggests that liberty was a key component of his daily struggles before he learned of the offer from Pérez.

Freed slaves could invoke such promises to petition for the freedom of their children. In September 1660, Leonor, a freed Angola who had been owned by Pedro de Soto, requested that her son Juan de la Cruz be declared free. According to her petition, Pedro de Soto granted Leonor her freedom in his testament written in 1639. That testament ordered that Leonor would enter into the service of his daughter Madre Inés de San Pedro, confessed in the convent of Our Lady of Balbanera in Mexico City, upon his death and that she was to be freed from her servitude upon the nun's death. The will also stipulated that Leonor provide Madre Inés a daily wage and that the nun could not, under any circumstances, sell her. Madre Inés had recently passed away, and Leonor subsequently received her carta de libertad as promised in de Soto's will. Her petition concerned her son Juan, who had been born in 1648, after Don Pedro's death. She argued that Juan should be considered freeborn. The convent countered that Pedro de Soto's will did not specifically speak to the status of any children that Leonor might give birth to between his and his daughter's deaths. As such, they argued, Juan de la Cruz should be considered a slave because his mother was still enslaved when he was born. The alcalde found merit in this argument and dismissed Leonor's case in 1660.[68]

But Leonor would not be deterred. Showing the typical tenacity of a slave who believed that she, or a member of her family, was wrongfully enslaved Leonor continued to press her case. Four years later, in February 1664, she appealed the first ruling to the episcopal court. In the appeal, she changed her tactics slightly. She now argued that while de Soto's testament specified that she would be freed upon Madre Inés' death, it did not in fact grant the nun ownership over her. Instead, the language of the will stipulated that Leonor was required to provide Madre Inés with one real per day until her death. If Leonor was unable to meet that condition, the nun could not sell her but could only rent out her services/labor to pay for her own upkeep in the convent. Thus, Leonor argued, she wasn't technically a slave when her son was born. Don Pedro had granted his daughter income from Leonor but not dominion over her. The convent attempted to counter these arguments, but the episcopal court found Leonor's case meritorious and ordered Juan freed. He was released from the convent into the custody of his mother in 1667.[69] Her successful claim can perhaps be traced to a provision in the *Siete Partidas* that stipulated that when testators bequeathed the service of a slave to another person, they were not actually granting them dominion or ownership of said slave.[70]

In similar case, this one from July 1736, Clara Rosa, a recently freed mother, sought to win the manumission of her child. Clara explained that she and her daughter belonged to the recently deceased Doña Gertrudis Bravo de Agüero, who had stipulated in her will that Clara would be freed upon her death. Her daughter María Micaela, on the other hand, was to be inherited by Agüero's daughter Juana Lorenza and would be freed, like her mother before her, only when Juana Lorenza died. Clara Rosa, however, hoped to speed her daughter's release and thus she petitioned that she be allowed to purchase the girl's freedom early. In carefully crafted language Clara argued that Doña Juana and her guardian, Doña Petra Bravo de Agüero, abused young María. She pleaded with the court to act as "a father of the miserable and destitute, and those who have been tyrannized" and force Doña Juana Lorenza and Doña Petra to set a just price that she might pay to secure her daughter's liberation.[71] She was clearly trying to combine the legal protection that abusive masters could be forced to sell maltreated slaves with the offer of freedom in Agüero's will. Doña Petra countered Clara's charge of abuse, suggesting that they treated young María more like their child than a slave. She added, however, that they would gladly accept 200 pesos in return for María's liberation. Clara countered that 100 pesos seemed a more reasonable price to her. The court eventually ordered that two assessors evaluate María's value. One set her value at 175 pesos while the other at 150 pesos.[72] The case file ends with the assessments, and therefore we don't know if a manumission price was set by the court and if Clara Rosa was able to meet it. This case, like Leonor's, illuminates the ingenuity that some recently freed people exhibited in their attempts to win the freedom of their enslaved children. And yet, at the same time, it also underscores the near limitless nature of master power regarding manumission and the severely restricted access slaves had to liberation and to the courts to press for personal emancipation, short of an offer by their masters.

Another interesting trend that points to the circumscribed nature of access to freedom in New Spain is that an overwhelming majority of cases (twenty-five of twenty-nine cases involving fifty-two of fifty-seven slaves) were brought against the estates of deceased owners.[73] More often than not, cases against estates arose out of unfulfilled promises of manumission in testaments or from deathbed declarations of slaveholders. But even Teresa Rodríguez, who convinced the court to allow her to purchase her own freedom for 150 pesos, waited until after her owner's death to bring her petition. Slaves appear to have been nearly powerless to employ the courts to press their living masters for their own liberation. Those who did appeal to the courts for their freedom did not typically do so while the master-slave relationship was ongoing but only once the person who had direct dominion over them had died. This may indicate that they recognized the limited access they had to freedom.

Only one case appears, on the surface, to have been a potentially fraudulent claim of unfulfilled manumission, and that is in large part because the slave's claim was unsubstantiated by any documentary evidence or witness testimony. Juan de la Cruz appeared before an alcalde to initiate a case against his current owner, Licenciado Francisco Sánchez Pichardo, on May 7, 1664, while being held in jail as a runaway.[74] Luis de Sezeña, appointed as Juan's legal advocate, argued that his client had fled from his master in order to press his claim in court. He charged that Sánchez had violated the restricted dominion imposed by his previous owner, Juana Pérez, in her will. Sezeña suggested that her testament included a provision that if Juan could provide 200 pesos to her estate, he was to be freed. In the event that Juan was unable to do so he was to be sold to Sánchez, with stipulation that if he could provide the 200 pesos in the future, then he was to be freed. Such a clause would not have been uncommon in New Spain. Sezeña went on to argue that owing to this stipulation, Sánchez never received *directo dominio* (absolute dominion) over Juan. Thus, when Sánchez branded Juan on the face, the petition continued, he violated the limited dominion he had acquired over the slave. Therefore Juan should be freed. Sánchez's agent submitted a copy of the bill of sale dated January 30, 1642, which included none of the restrictions suggested in Sezeña's petition.[75] The court found against Juan, and his case was dismissed. Without a copy of Perez's will, which it is surprising the court did not locate, it is impossible to know if this claim had merit. It is difficult to know, therefore, if in this case there was a genuine offer of manumission or whether it was an instance of a slave lying to officials in the hopes of being freed or perhaps the innovative (but ultimately ineffective) arguments of a Spanish procurador (the legal argument that Sánchez had only "limited" dominion was most likely devised by Sezeña and not Juan).

Colonial courts proved quite thorough in trying to substantiate claims brought by slaves against their deceased owners, or their estate, that an offer had been made, the experiences of Juan de la Cruz notwithstanding. The burden of proof, however, fell squarely on the slaves. As a result, slaves were not able to simply falsely insinuate they had been freed as a means to win access to the courts and, more importantly, to manumission.

An even more salacious example highlights the significant burden of proof on slaves to substantiate an unfulfilled offer of manumission. Leonora Sarándola, a recently freed mulatta, presented a petition to secular authorities in Querétaro on August 21, 1761, demanding that Bachiller Joseph de Asas free her son Joseph Martín. In addition, she requested the return of some 120 pesos that she had paid for the freedom of her daughter María Lucía. According to Leonora's petition, Don Manuel de Asas, the priest's father and her previous owner, had promised to free her if she would agree to have a sexual relationship with him while she was his slave. She argued that she had refused Don Manuel's advances countless times in the past and only acquiesced after he promised to liberate her.[76] They then began a long-term sexual relationship that resulted in the births of María Lucía and Joseph Martín.

Numerous witnesses testified on behalf of Leonora and her children. Juan Antonio Hinojosa and Joseph Manuel de Córdoba both testified that they believed Don Manuel had fathered the children. Perhaps most powerfully, Fray Joseph de Santa María, from the convent of San Agustín, testified that Don Manuel had told him of his plans to free his children. Fray Joseph added, however, that Don Manuel had also lamented that he could not fulfill his promise to liberate his slave lover because of the public scandal it would create, particularly for his wife.[77]

In order to avoid such public embarrassment Don Manuel sold Leonora to Don Joseph Flores in 1747, apparently without her children. She was eventually sold again to Don Bernardo Curballo, who

subsequently freed her upon his death for good service. She testified that
when she approached Joseph de Asas to make good on his father's promise
he flatly refused. Therefore, she requested that the court declare Joseph
Martín free and order that Asas repay her the 120 pesos that she had paid
for María Lucía's freedom.

Asas responded that Leonora's claim about the offer of liberation
was groundless and that her subsequent demand that he return María
Lucía's manumission price was outlandish. His father, he argued, had not
forced Leonora into a sexual relationship, he was not the father of her
children, and he had never offered Leonora and her children their freedom. Asas insisted that rather than having an affair with his slave, his
father frequently beat Leonora "to punish her for her prostitutions" and
for sneaking out of his house at night to spend time with the children's
real father, whom he did not name. Further, he countered testimony that
his father had commissioned a wet nurse for both María Lucía and Joseph
Martín out of paternal feelings. He conceded that his father had hired
the wet nurse but only because Leonora was unable to breastfeed her own
children. He concluded by noting that María Lucía had not been freed by
her mother, but by Don Rafael de Zarate, who had initially received her
as collateral for a 120-peso loan to his father.[78]

Despite the corroboration of Leonora's claims by Fray Joseph, the
case remained unresolved. The final document in the file is a petition
from Leonora dated July 20, 1765, nearly four years after her initial petition, pleading that someone review and decide her case. The salacious
affair aside, this suit turned on one simple issue: Leonora's claim that her
children had been promised freedom by her master (and their father). The
basis of her argument was, therefore, that her children were wrongfully
enslaved. As was the case in many other liberty suits, Leonora's appearance in court was not the culmination of a lifelong pursuit of freedom
but rather the result of an offer of manumission by her master. There
is nothing from the case file to suggest that manumission and freedom
were central to Leonora's understanding of her daily life and struggles,
that she would have pursued liberation without having been offered it.
Leonora also seems to have been unable to approach the courts to enforce
the manumission of her children until she herself had achieved freed
status and perhaps until after Manuel de Asas' death, which illustrates the
circumscribed access that slaves had to the courts.

In many cases, heirs challenged claims of manumission by bonds-people, highlighting that decisions to free particular slaves often were the result of bonds that had been formed in long-term personal relationships between the master and the enslaved, bonds that were not shared by heirs and the slave in question. The trend of heirs contesting the freedom of recently inherited slaves reveals a series of other important patterns in such cases. The burden of proof for substantiating offers of manumission was quite high. Slaves had to supply evidence to prove the claim that they had been offered manumission, and although they received assistance from officers of the colonial courts, who could be quite meticulous in seeking out proof of such an offer, word of mouth and even unnotarized offers of manumission were challenged, often successfully, by slave owners or their representatives.[79]

Another unsuccessful breach of promise suit that demonstrates the burden on slaves to verify offers of manumission comes from Antonio de Guzmán and Agustín de Benito in 1749. Don José de Bustamante had purchased the two slaves from an obraje in Querétaro and sent them to work in his silver mine in Pachuca. At that time, they insisted, Bustamante had offered to manumit them when they had paid him their original purchase price. He also promised that they could earn money toward self-purchase over time by delivering their *partido*—the share of ore miners were entitled to as part of their wages—to him. The audiencia conducted a very thorough investigation to determine if it was common for slaves to work in the Pachuca mines, if they performed the same duties as free workers, if they were entitled to a partido if they did, and, if so, what the value of that partido was. In the end, however, the audiencia was unable to substantiate Antonio and Agustín's claim that Bustamante had promised them their freedom. The final decision was, therefore, that Bustamante was not obligated to free them. The verdict also stated that owing to substantiated accusations of abuse by the slaves Bustamante was required to sell them to a master who might treat them better.[80] Like Leonora's case, this one turned on a single issue, whether or not Bustamante had promised the two slaves their freedom. Their lack of success resulted, in large part, from their inability to prove such an offer had ever been made. Equally importantly, the court was not moved by the confirmed abuse that Antonio and Agustín had suffered to force Bustamante to free his slaves. This suggests that the property rights of masters, even abusive ones, were considered more sacrosanct than slaves' opportunities to achieve personal liberation.

In a similar petition, on December 2, 1728, Gertrudis de Bocanegra requested that she, her two daughters María Josefa and Micaela Marina, and another woman named Gertrudis de la Encarnación be declared free based on an agreement they had with their recently deceased mistress, Doña Juana de Güemez. When Güemez entered the convent of Santa Catarina de Saena in Mexico City following the death of her husband in 1721, she had promised to free her slaves upon her death if they would faithfully remit her a *jornal*, or a daily wage. Nicolas Palacios and Ramón de la Rosa both made similar petitions in October 1729. Now that Señora Güemez had died, the slaves requested that their freedom be realized.[81] Alférez Fernando Güemez, Doña Juana's sole heir, responded that the slaves' claims were false and that his sister intended that he should inherit all her bondspeople upon her death.[82] Numerous witnesses testified they had overheard Doña Juana proclaim her intention to free her slaves. However, the case ends without resolution for all the slaves except Nicolas. Juan de Bengoa, an attorney for the audiencia, concluded that Nicolas should be freed because he was actually able to provide a carta de libertad from Señora Güemez. In the face of multiple, seemingly credible, witness testimonies that supported the other slaves' claims and the fact that the slaves in questions had lived ostensibly as freed people outside the bonds of a formal master-slave relationship for nearly six years, the audiencia still had not decided their case by 1734 when the case file ends, some five years after they demanded their freedom.[83]

Even slaves who could produce written offers of manumission from their masters found their claims contested if the offers were not notarized. Leonor Reyes, who had been a slave on the Amanalco ingenio near Cuernavaca, received a written but unnotarized offer of manumission from her owner, Melchor Arias Tenorio. That document, dated April 17, 1650, granted her "liberty so that she may enjoy it so long as she shall live, which I give her with all my will so that at no time will anyone be able to interfere with said liberty but rather she will be able to enjoy it."[84] Francisco Arias Tenorio, Melchor's brother and the executor of his will, eventually ratified the carta on May 15, 1658. Despite this, Leonor found herself working at Amanalco as a slave, unable to leave. On May 21, 1658, she approached an alcalde mayor in Cuernavaca in the hope of gaining official recognition of her liberty.[85]

The Inquisition denied her initial petition in 1662. Andrés Gamero León, the administrator of Amanalco, had successfully argued that the written offer of manumission was part of Melchor Arias Tenorio's attempts to defraud his creditors.[86] In one fell swoop, Gamero cast doubt on the veracity of the offer and pitted Leonor's access to personal freedom against the civic freedom of Arias's heirs and debtors, making an argument that was valid under the *Siete Partidas*. Leonor filed an appeal in 1670. In 1673, the Supreme Council of the Inquisition in Madrid overturned the 1662 decision. Leonor was declared free some fifteen years after her manumission first came into question. That unnotarized written offers of manumission could be challenged by slave owners or their heirs accentuates the reality that slaves' access to personal freedom was severely limited by the civic and sovereignal freedom of others (and not just their immediate owners).

That freeing a slave would prejudice the creditors or heirs of an estate was a common refrain in liberty suits. Gertrudis, a mulatta slave, and her son Salvador claimed to have been offered freedom by their owner, Don Juan Enríquez Magariño, on his deathbed. However, in the process of settling his will, the two slaves were first pawned and then ordered sold to Joseph Gómez de Valdez to cover some 1,250 pesos of estate debt. Gertrudis, however, petitioned the audiencia that she and Salvador be freed, as stipulated in Don Joseph's unnotarized will. Making matters even more interesting, Don Juan's testament read that he wanted to free Gertrudis and Salvador "because [Gertrudis] was the natural daughter of [his] father, Don Gaspar Ruiz de Cáceres . . . and as his natural sister she had been assisting, serving, and nourishing him for over twenty-seven years."[87] Doña Elena Carrillo Barrientos, Don Juan's widow, challenged the will, however, claiming that it was void because her husband had been unable to sign it before he died. She added that freeing the slaves would make it more difficult to settle his significant debts. Neither Don Juan's promises of manumission nor his admission that Gertrudis was his sister deterred Doña Elena from defending her estate and inheritance. After the parties exchanged a series of petitions, the audiencia issued a interesting ruling on December 11, 1711, some seventeen months after Gertrudis and Salvador initiated their complaint. In an attempt to protect Doña Elena's property rights and to provide the slaves a path to liberty, Gertrudis and Salvador would be granted their freedom once they paid 100 pesos and 200 pesos, respectively, to Juan's heirs.

In other examples the courts struck down well-documented promises of manumission on account of questions about the estate of a deceased slave owner without providing the slaves in question an alternative path to liberation. In July 1708, Marcos de Pantoja filed a petition that he be allowed to purchase his freedom for 100 pesos as offered in the will of his deceased owner, Doña Juana de Santander. The court rejected Marcos's application, however, because Don Pedro de Valdez y Portugal, Juana's son and heir, had had her will declared null and void in order to cover a substantial debt she owed before Marcos made his application.[88]

The courts commonly placed a higher value on the obligation to settle a slaveholder's debts or on the rights of an heir to inherit his/her full legal share than on the liberty of a slave. Fernando de Olivares y Carmona, procurador for the Real Fisco de la Inquisición, argued this point when he wrote in the initial decision against Leonor Reyes that a creditor's "right is so privileged that it forbids debtors from granting liberty to their slaves except upon receipt of an amount equal to their value and price."[89] The discourse of "personal freedom" clearly did not dominate judicial proceedings in New Spain, even if the idea did find expression in sociojudicial language. The *Siete Partidas* clearly articulated the relationship between civic and personal freedom by prioritizing the rights of creditors relative to promises of manumission made to slaves. It appears then that access to personal freedom for slaves was contingent. We might then ask what the implications of that contingency were for the identity and agency of slaves.

One last case, heart-wrenching as it is, reinforces the conclusion that discourses surrounding personal freedom for slaves were not paramount within the judicial system and may not have resonated with slaves in novohispano society in ways that we might have expected. Justa Rita de Villaseñor, a mulatta, accused her master Francisco Hernández of repeatedly raping her for years, beginning when she was thirteen, and claimed that she became pregnant as a result of his attacks. Justa Rita's complaints to Francisco's wife about the rapes resulted in more violence. At some point during her ordeal Rita's mother apparently approached Francisco to beg him to liberate her. Francisco rejected that request but intimated that Rita would be freed after he and his wife died. Rita closed her petition with a demand for justice and requested that she be granted the manumission Francisco had promised her upon his death.[90]

When interrogated, Francisco denied raping Rita (he claimed the sex was consensual) and rejected the assertion that he had promised her freedom. When Rita's mother appealed to him, he explained, he had told her not to worry because Rita would not likely be a slave for long. He told her that as he was old, he would die soon and that because he and his wife were childless, it was likely that Rita would only be a slave until his wife's death, when she would likely be freed.

The judge believed Francisco culpable for the rape and referred the case to the Inquisition in Mexico City. He ordered an *embargo de bienes* (lien) against Francisco's estate. He also ordered that Rita be removed from Francisco's custody. The case then descended into a legal debate as to whether Francisco could be punished for raping Rita because he was not her legal owner. A bill of sale, dated January 26, 1750, clearly stated that Francisco's wife, Juana de Aguirre, had purchased Rita. Because she, and not her husband, was Justa Rita's rightful owner she requested that the slave be returned to her custody. Despite the accusation of rape the case ends without resolution. Justa Rita's access to freedom was circumscribed by Juana's rights of ownership, by questions about whether or not she could be held accountable for her husband's transgressions, and most fundamentally by uncertainty over whether or not Justa Rita had actually been promised her freedom. Again, as was the case with Antonio de Guzmán and Agustín de Benito, even abuse was not enough to move courts in New Spain to free slaves, even those that claimed to have been offered access to manumission by their abusive masters.

Numerous historians have argued that manumission afforded masters power over their slaves. Because a promise of freedom potentially provided masters a means of controlling or manipulating their servants, it may be tempting to conclude that such offers were common.[91] Because these offers were quite rare, however, one can only conclude that masters did not in fact need to rely on promises of manumission to control their slaves. The significant number of deathbed manumissions would further seem to undermine the idea that masters used manumission as leverage against their slaves. That reality reduces the likelihood that offers of manumission, or even the possibility of offers of manumission, were central to the discourses that framed master-slave relations.

There are also a few examples of slaves who did not learn for many years that they had been offered freedom or even had been liberated.

On November 11, 1740, Eugenia Jerónima petitioned that her daughter Felipa be named freeborn and thus not the slave of Doña Juana de la Vera. Eugenia had recently been freed following her mistress's death. Eugenia claimed that her daughter should be considered freeborn despite the fact that Doña Juana de Escamilla's will, written in September 1740, claimed Felipa as a slave and stipulated that Doña Juana de la Vera would inherit her. But it turned out that Doña Escamilla had freed Eugenia on September 25, 1734, although she had not informed her slave of that fact. Eugenia would not learn she was in fact a freed woman until after her mistress's death, meaning that she continued to live as a slave, believing herself as such, for over five years, during which time, in February 1735, she gave birth to Felipa.[92] Once she learned that she had been freed prior to Felipa's birth, meaning that her daughter was born free, she approached Señora de la Vera to secure the girl's status as a freeborn child. She did not make direct reference to the *Siete Partidas*, but her request was clearly associated with the law that stated that a child's status followed that of the womb of its mother. In her petition, she claimed that Doña Juana then demanded payment of 70 pesos for Felipa's liberty. In a second petition, Eugenia summarized the origins of her case by noting that "of the forms of servitude, nothing is worse than slavery" and argued that "because status follows the womb, and because [my daughter] was born to a freed slave . . . she is the same as I am." On reading Escamilla's will, which stated that she had freed Eugenia in 1734 *and* stipulated that any children that Eugenia might bear subsequent to her own death would remain her slaves (a contradiction), the audiencia found for the ex-slaves and ordered Felipa freed immediately. Similarly, Marcos de Pantoja did not learn of this mistress's offer of manumission (which had been subsequently declared null and void) until nearly nineteen years after her death in 1689. When he brought his case in 1708 that he be allowed to purchase his liberty for 100 pesos, as stipulated in Doña Juana de Santander's will, he argued that he had not been informed about the clause in her will until recently.[93] These two cases, in which masters never informed their slaves of their intention to free them, reduce the likelihood that manumission was central to the discourses that framed and mediated master-slave relations.

In summary, in twenty-six of twenty-nine cases an unfulfilled offer of manumission was central to the slave plaintiff's suit and his or her ability to appear before colonial authorities. Twenty-one cases (involving forty-nine slaves) unambiguously center on such unfulfilled promises of manumission. Two other suits involving three slaves were predicated on offers of third-party assistance, if we include that of Catalina de la Cruz. Another single case involved a freed mother trying to expedite the freedom of a daughter who had been promised future manumission. To these we can add the two suits that revolved around freed women seeking to prove that they had given birth to their "enslaved" children after they themselves had been liberated and thus their children should have been considered freeborn and not enslaved at all. The importance of master prerogative in these cases reflects trends within manumissions as well, the great majority of which appear to have been initiated by slave owners wishing to free their slaves rather than by slaves seeking liberty.

If the majority, or even a significant minority, of these cases had been found to have been initiated by slaves demanding their freedom in the face of the legal, social, and procedural restrictions on their access to manumission, then we might have been able to conclude that the idea of personal freedom was more powerful than the restrictions placed on it. But in only one case, that of Teresa Rodríguez, do we find a slave in New Spain using the courts to request freedom absent a prior offer from his or her master or an offer of assistance from a third party, and even Teresa did not bring her suit against a living slaveholder.[94] In two other cases, those of Catalina de la Cruz and Juan Esteban, it is clear that slaves were pursuing their own liberation prior to receiving an offer from their masters, and yet their ability to appear in court was predicated on their contracting the assistance of a third party. None of the other twenty-six found cases meet the criteria of a slave requesting freedom outright; they all insinuate that there was a standing offer of manumission. Therefore, the most reasonable conclusion seems to be that the legal restrictions on slaves' access to freedom helped frame their conceptions of liberty.

The close reading of colonial law, manumission records, and liberty suits casts strong doubt on the possibility that personal freedom was central to slave identity and agency in New Spain. First, manumission was not a right or privilege guaranteed by customary or codified law. Slaves were unable to employ the courts to force masters to grant them manumission against their will. Second, slaves overwhelmingly brought their cases against dead, rather than living, owners. This indicates, perhaps, that liberty did not factor into the daily contests between masters and slaves in any meaningful way. Third, the burden of proof fell squarely on the shoulders of slaves, and the courts often ignored or rejected credible and notarized written offers of manumission. This emphasizes how precarious even real promises of freedom were in practice. These suits thus highlight how divorced the potential for liberation was from slaves' daily realities in colonial Mexico. They symbolize the primacy of a master's sovereignal and civic freedoms over a slave's access to personal freedom, a primacy that stemmed precisely from the nature of the legal restrictions, which made slaves' access to freedom a function of the owner's, and not the slave's, prerogative.

Unlike the natives studied by Owensby, slaves proved unable to employ libertad to escape or mitigate the arbitrary and capricious power of others; their status as slaves made that a near impossibility. These cases proceeded on terms clearly articulated in the Spanish legal tradition, which severely limited the conditions under which slaves could press for liberty. If we accept that slaves' skills at navigating colonial institutions came from their immersion in structures of society and the discourses that animated them, then their restricted access to personal freedom must have affected how they perceived liberty, and how they perceived liberty must in turn have informed their agency.[95] In other words, institutions, religion, law, and so forth (i.e., the state) provided "the common material and meaningful frameworks" within which domination and resistance take place.[96] The hidden transcripts of slaves were intimately connected to, and influenced by, those official spaces. Therefore libertad did not play as significant a role in how slaves negotiated their social status as we might have assumed.[97]

Despite the novel circumstances of Catalina's case, hers and others like it highlight the circumscribed nature of slaves' conceptions of freedom in seventeenth- and eighteenth-century New Spain. Her long-term pursuit of freedom was truly exceptional. Perhaps then, from the slave's perspective, liberty was a nearly impossible dream. However, when a master offered a slave his or her freedom, that nearly impossible dream was all of a sudden real, and so many became relentless in its pursuit. It follows then that whatever conceptions of liberty slaves had played little part in how they understood the history they were making and the battles they fought with their masters and how they sought to improve their lives on a daily basis. These suits brought by slaves to secure their freedom should not be seen as evidence of their absolute desire for liberty. Rather, they should be understood as exemplifying the extent to which slavery was a conflict-ridden relationship in which slaves sought to expand their control over myriad matters at the expense of their masters. In other words, these contests were to win degrees of personal autonomy and to reduce by degrees the sovereignal freedom their masters enjoyed over them. The temptation to label those contests as being over "fractions" of freedom or "piecemeal" freedoms is a strong one, but it should be resisted because it makes things murkier by equating agency within slavery with liberty (which we have defined as the absence of slavery). In the rare case, that pursuit could be transformed into the unmitigated quest for personal liberation. Underneath all the incredible stories recounted in this book is the essential tension that slaves had to prove that they were wrongfully enslaved—either by showing that they were born to a free mother or that a promise of freedom remained unfulfilled—in order to press for their own liberation within the legal system in New Spain prior to the 1770s.

Conclusion

✦ IF WE RETURN TO THE TWO STORIES FROM THE CALDERÓN INGENIO that opened this study we see how well those slaves' actions to defend their families and communities and their ability to contest the application of master authority serve as powerful indicators of the nature and forms of slavery in colonial Mexico. The metanarrative that emerges from those historical moments and thus from this study is a story about the ability of slaves to contest, negotiate, and accommodate themselves to particular elements of their oppression, generally within the structures of that domination. Thus, I have tried to locate slave agency within the particular social, cultural, political, and ideological contexts in which novohispano slaves operated. The tendency to equate agency with demonstrations of slaves' humanity proves too facile. The debates as to whether or not slave actions devoid of "revolutionary goals" represented slaves' capitulation to their domination are also less than helpful. Neither approach captures how slaves envisioned and articulated their own agency. The actions of slaves recounted herein highlight the need to redefine what we mean by slave radicalism in order to divorce it from the pervasive and powerful discourses of emancipation and the assumption that freedom naturally followed slavery.

The temptation to read the actions of seventeenth- and eighteenth-century slaves as part of the metanarrative of the destruction of slavery is powerful and understandable. In truth, I wish that I had encountered a nascent or, even better, a fully fluorescent sense of "personal freedom" among slaves in seventeenth- and eighteenth-century New Spain. I had hoped to find that such conceptions provided a superstructure on which we could understand slaves' contests with their masters. Not having found them, however, moved me to try to understand how slaves saw their own social power, how they approached their contests with their masters, and what the limitations were on how they conceptualized and exercised that agency. I have argued that slaves in New Spain prior to 1770 envisioned their position in society and their access to the courts very differently from slaves in republican Peru, in Brazil after the official abolition of the slave trade in 1850, or even in late colonial Guayaquil and Cuba. Appreciating that reality helps us avoid being teleological and ahistorical, forces us to focus on change over time, and urges us to redouble our search for the exact moment when slaves began to employ a lexicon of liberation to challenge their personal enslavement and the legitimacy of slavery as an institution.

On some level, we may be asking too much of our historical subjects in our search for revolutionaries. A brief comparison between how we approach the histories of women and those of slaves in the colonial period illustrates this possibility. Steve Stern writes that gender relations in late colonial New Spain "were a bitterly contested world of gender right and obligation. In this world women . . . did not challenge the principles of patriarchal dominance as such but reinterpreted their operational meanings so markedly that conflict ensued on the practical issues that defined the meanings and limits of patriarchal authority in everyday life."[1] Why doesn't the argument that women did not challenge the principles of patriarchy elicit the same negative internal responses as would a similar assertion that slaves did not challenge the principles of slavery? To argue that slaves reenvisioned the "operational meanings" of mastery and slavery so markedly that conflict ensued would encapsulate the nature of master-slave relations as discussed herein. But to make that argument potentially opens one up to denying slave agency, the very thing that I have been trying to uncover and understand from the perspective of slaves.

The nature of Spanish colonialism provides the framework within which we must approach slavery in New Spain. The ability of slaves to avail themselves of colonial institutions to make claims contrary to the wishes and advantage of their owners is often held up as the defining characteristic of Spanish American slavery. It is worth noting, however, that slaves appear in colonial documents as defendants much more often than as plaintiffs. For example, we find over one hundred slaves accused of blasphemy before the Inquisition. Compare that to the twenty-nine examples of liberty suits or the eight found maltratamiento cases in various civil, criminal, ecclesiastical, and inquisitorial courts. This may indicate that access to colonial courts was more circumscribed that we thought. Courts operated to maintain the colonial order, and slaves fell under their jurisdiction just like other colonial subjects.

Yet all of those cases provide windows into the day-to-day realities of slavery and mastery in the colony. Let us move backward. The relevant bits of imperial law indicate that access to manumission in New Spain was in theory severely circumscribed, and liberty suits and the manumissions that were in fact granted provide evidence that up to 1770 this indeed was the case. Slaves were able to bring suit against their masters but only in situations clearly prescribed and circumscribed by Spanish legal codes. Only in extremely rare situations were slaves able to act independently of the will of the masters and seek personal liberation. An important function of Spanish jurisprudence was to define what was realistic and what was unrealistic and to "drive certain aspirations into the realm of the impossible."[2]

From that perspective, manumission was defined as a near impossibility. That reality helps us understand the lack of discourses relating to liberation among runaway slaves like those from Calderón and the individual runaways who appear in the historical record because they committed bigamy. Their testimonies suggest that rather than running to something, freedom, they were generally fleeing from what they perceived to be abuse and/or the breakdown of master-slave relations. So slaves did seize on opportunities to run away, but they did not necessarily conceptualize flight as a means to achieving personal liberation. The great majority of slaves stayed and suffered in slavery, and in part my goal has been to understand why.

The nature of slave flight helps us in turn understand the commonplace conflicts, negotiations, and accommodations between owners and their bondspeople through which mastery and slavery in the colony were redefined over time. Slaves clearly participated in those articulations; they had power to influence their masters. Slaveholder fear of slave witchcraft provides clear evidence of that agency. The radicalism of slaves' actions lies in their willingness to employ that agency in public, to interject their private understandings of the proper operation of mastery and slavery into the open and force their owners to engage those visions. These daily conflicts come to the fore in the blasphemy cases considered herein.

Even within the rigid structures of their enslavement, novohispano bondspeople still had considerable autonomy, which allowed them to construct lives and cultures not entirely controlled by those who dominated them. Through marriage and spiritual kinship Africans and their descendents constructed social networks grounded in shared ethnic and racial identities and developed common cultural visions. Even though demographically overwhelmed by free people, and particularly Indians, Afro-Mexican slaves constructed a distinctive cultural identity in New Spain. Their ability to build families and communities within the confines of colonial society bespeaks the same types of agency that allowed slaves to contest acceptable workloads and reasonable levels of physical violence. They adopted the ethnic monikers imposed by their enslavers like "Angola" and colonial institutions like marriage and adapted them to fit their needs. Novohispano slaves, therefore, exhibited significant radicalism as they accommodated and contested the institutional and individualized elements of their oppression, seeking, for the most part, to make their enslavement as livable as possible.

Appendix

TABLE 1.1A. Slave Populations from Sugar Plantations in Central New Spain, 1648–86

Hacienda	Year	Pop	Men	Women	Ratio (M/W)	Children <15	Children as % of Total Pop	Women 15–44	Ratio	Reference
Amanalco, Santa Ana	1658	86	53	33	1.61	15	17.4%	16	0.94	AGN, Civil, vol. 2124, exp. 1, fs. 35–40
	1666	104	66	38	1.74	17	16.3%	18	0.94	AGN, Civil, vol. 1711, exp. 6, fs. 559–72
Nuestra Señora de los Ángeles	1648	36	26	10	2.60	5	13.9%	1	5.00	AGN, Tierras, vol. 3285, vol. 1, exp. 38–39
Atlihuayan, San Diego	1672	87	44	43	1.02	29	33.3%	12	2.42	AGN, Tierras, vol. 114, fs. 204–6
	1684	122	67	55	1.22	34	27.9%	17	2.00	AGN, Tierras, vol. 2051, exp. 1
Barreto, San Diego Ticumán	1676	46	28	18	1.56	10	21.7%	9	1.11	AGN, Tierras, vol. 1742, f. 153
Chiconaguapa, Santa Inés	1676	91	60	31	1.94	12	13.2%	17	0.71	AN, #6, vol. 20, fs. 460–83
Nuestra Señora de la Concepción	1679	82	48	34	1.41	10	12.2%	20	0.50	AGN, Tierras, vol. 131, exp. 1, fs. 18–21
Guajoyuca	1680	65	34	31	1.10	22	33.8%	14	1.57	AGN, Tierras, vol. 239, fs. 84v–86
Pantitlan, San Nicolás	1658	112	60	52	1.15	31	27.7%	20	1.55	AGN, Civil, vol. 2124, exp. 1, fs. 5–12
San Joseph (Amilpas)	1676	45	24	21	1.14	17	37.8%	8	2.13	AN, #379, vol. 2507, fs. 166–94
Santa Anna	1667	23	16	7	2.29	4	17.4%	5	0.80	AGN, Tierras, vol. 3460, exp. 52, fs. 222–24
Suchiquesalco	1669	36	19	17	1.12	14	38.9%	8	1.75	AGN, Tierras, vol. 1735, exp. 1, f. 64
Temisco, Nuestra Señora de la Concepción	1682	113	57	56	1.02	35	31.0%	22	1.59	AGN, Tierras, vol. 3445, caud. 7, fs. 19–25

	Year									Source
Tenango, Santa Ana	1672	100	60	40	1.50	22	22.0%	17	1.29	AGN, Tierras, vol. 1732, exp. 1, fs. 81–88
Tilapa, San Joseph	1656	65	34	31	1.10	12	18.5%	15	0.80	AGN, Tierras, vol. 3482, exp. 1, fs. 16–17
	1663	101	54	47	1.15	31	30.7%	21	1.48	AGN, Tierras, vol. 3190, exp. 2, fs. 77
	1670	99	65	34	1.91	32	32.3%	16	2.00	AGN, Tierras, vol. 3483, exp. 1, fs. 787–89
	1677	98	65	33	1.97	26	26.5%	9	2.89	AGN, Tierras, vol. 3483, exp. 1, fs. 787–89
	1679	88	58	30	1.93	27	30.7%	11	2.45	AGN, Tierras, vol. 3190, exp. 2, fs. 42–44
Tlacomulco, San Antonio	1661	34	18	16	1.13	6	17.6%	5	1.20	AGN, AHHJ, vol. 93, exp. 1, fs. 14–17
	1670	55	34	21	1.62	12	21.8%	10	1.20	AGN, AHHJ, vol. 93, exp. 1, fs. 14–17
	1679	57	38	19	2.00	14	24.6%	12	1.17	AGN, AHHJ, vol. 93, exp. 2, fs. 29–33
Tolentino, San Nicolás	1648	126	88	38	2.32	19	15.1%	14	1.36	AGN, Tierras, vol. 3285, exp. 1, fs. 24–29
	1663	123	82	41	2.00	12	9.8%	23	0.52	AGN, Tierras, vol. 3285, exp. 1, fs. 236–38
	1677	121	90	31	2.90	9	7.4%	18	0.50	AGN, Tierras, vol. 3170, fs. 8–11
Zacatepec	1676	68	38	30	1.27	9	13.2%	14	0.64	AN, #336, vol. 2200, fs. 9–42
Running Total		2183	1326	857	1.55	486	22.26%	372	1.31	
			60.7%	39.3%						
Mean		81								
Median		63								
Xochimancas	1653	240				73	30.4%	58	1.26	Berthe, "Xochimancas," 88–117
TOTAL w/Xochimancas		2423				559	23.07%	430	1.30	

TABLE I.2A. Slave Populations from Sugar Plantations in Central New Spain, 1687–1724

Hacienda	Year	Pop	Men	Women	Ratio (M/W)	Children <15	Children as % of Total Pop	Women 15–44	Ratio	Reference
Amanalco, Santa Ana	1700	52	30	22	1.36	19	36.5%	15	1.27	AGN, Tierras, vol. 3106, fs. 122–23
	1701	50	27	23	1.17	18	36.0%	16	1.13	AGN, RFI, vol. 33, exp. 11, fs. 279–83
Nuestra Señora de los Angeles	1702	46	22	24	0.92	15	32.6%	8	1.88	AGN, Tierras, vol. 235, exp. 1, fs. 14–16
	1704	49	24	25	0.96	18	36.7%	8	2.25	AGN, Tierras, vol. 235, exp. 1, fs. 193–95
Apanquisalco, Nuestra Señora de la Concepción	1703	53	36	17	2.12	10	18.9%	5	2.00	AGN, Tierras, vol. 3095, exp. 11, fs. 269–70
Atlihuayan, San Diego	1689	115	66	49	1.35	40	34.8%	17	2.35	AGN, Civil, vol. 251, exp. 5
	1701	91	51	40	1.28	24	26.4%	25	0.96	AGN, Civil, vol. 251, exp. 5
Atotonilco, San Nicolás	1690	24	19	5	3.80	0	0.0%	3	0.00	AGN, Tierras, vol. 3040, f. 326
	1699	28	23	5	4.60	1	3.6%	4	0.25	AGN, Tierras, vol. 3040, fs. 430–32
	1711	32	21	11	1.91	7	21.9%	1	7.00	AGN, Tierras, vol. 3042, exp. 3, fs. 162–63
Barreto, San Diego Ficuman	1702	21	13	8	1.63	3	14.3%	2	1.50	AGN, Tierras, vol. 1742, f. 175v
Capila, San Nicolás Xavier	1703	18	8	10	0.80	9	50.0%	6	1.50	AGN, Tierras, vol. 211, exp. 1, f. 9
Cocoyoc, San Joseph	1702	75	47	28	1.68	12	16.0%	17	0.71	AGN, Tierras, vol. 201, exp. 1, f. 148–51
	1714	56	36	20	1.80	8	14.3%	6	1.33	AGN, Tierras, vol. 1564, no exp.
Mártir, San Pedro	1710	55	30	25	1.20	22	40.0%	10	2.20	AGN, Tierras, vol. 3340, exp. 2
	1717	171	79	92	0.86	56	32.7%	38	1.47	AGN, Tierras, vol. 2880, exp. 2, fs. 66–76
Pantitlan, San Nicolás	1700	71	41	30	1.37	13	18.3%	19	0.68	AGN, Tierras, vol. 3106, fs. 125–26
	1701	44	24	20	1.20	12	27.3%	8	1.50	AGN, RFI, vol. 33, exp. 11, fs. 169–302

San Joseph (Izúcar)	1689	134	85	49	1.73	26	19.4%	17	1.53	AGN, Tierras, vol. 151, exp. 1, fs. 115–18
Santa Bárbara de Calderón, fs. 70–82	1708	130	69	61	1.13	36	27.7%	30	1.20	AGN, Bienes Nacionales leg. 908, exp. 11,
Santa Inés, fs. 64–70	1702	64	45	19	2.37	11	17.2%	6	1.83	AGN, Bienes Nacionales leg 700, exp. 15,
Temilpa, San Francisco	1710	106	63	43	1.47	32	30.2%	15	2.13	AGN, Tierras, vol. 1812, exp. 1, fs. 60–69
	1712	76	49	27	1.81	20	26.3%	11	1.82	AGN, Tierras, vol. 1813, caud 2, fs. 177–80
Temisco, Nuestra Señora de la Concepción	1711	97	44	53	0.83	37	38.1%	25	1.48	AGN, Tierras, vol. 3275, exp. 1, fs. 16–18
Tenango, Santa Ana	1714	94	43	51	0.84	41	43.6%	20	2.05	AGN, Tierras 3265, exp. 1, fs. 275–78
	1689	56	35	21	1.67	10	17.9%	10	1.00	AGN, Tierras, vol. 1732, exp. 1, fs. 201–2
	1693	50	30	20	1.50	12	24.0%	9	1.33	AGN, Tierras, vol. 1980, exp. 2, fs. 134–36
	1699	55	28	27	1.04	16	29.1%	14	1.14	AGN, Tierras, vol. 1980, exp. 2, fs. 273–75
	1709	106	69	37	1.86	26	24.5%	23	1.13	AGN, Civil, vol. 23, exp. 1, fs. 30–46
Teripitio	1707	155	76	79	0.96	52	33.5%	40	1.30	AGN, Civil, vol. 1681, fs. 172–73
Tilapa, San Joseph de	1709	55	36	19	1.89	10	18.2%	6	1.67	AGN, Tierras, vol. 3190, exp. 2, fs. 42–44
	1722	42	27	15	1.80	10	23.8%	2	5.00	AGN, Tierras, vol. 207, exp. 1, fs. 17–20
Tlacomulco, San Antonio	1693	53	34	19	1.79	17	32.1%	8	2.13	AGN, AHHJ, vol. 93, exp. 1, fs. 79–82
	1721	79	52	27	1.93	25	31.6%	12	2.08	AGN, Tierras, vol. 1965, exp. 1, fs. 70–6
	1722	79	52	27	1.93	26	32.9%	13	2.00	AGN, Tierras, vol. 1981, exp. 5, fs. 74–86
Tolentino, San Nicolás	1693	155	116	39	2.97	19	12.3%	25	0.76	AGN, Tierras, vol. 3170, fs. 55–59
	1698	150	110	40	2.75	23	15.3%	18	1.28	AGN, Tierras, vol. 3206, caud. 2, fs. 155–67
RUNNING TOTAL	2787	1660	1127		1.47	736	26.4%	512	1.44	
Mean		75								
Median		56								

TABLE 1.3A. Slave Populations from Sugar Plantations in Central New Spain, 1725-63

Hacienda	Year	Pop	Men	Women	Ratio (M/W)	Children <15	Children as % of Total Pop	Women 15-44	Ratio	Reference
Atlihuayan, San Diego	1732	86	48	38	1.26	29	33.7%	15	1.93	AGN, Tierras, vol. 522, exp. 5
Cocoyoc, San Joseph	1730	104	60	44	1.36	18	17.3%	18	1.00	AGN, Tierras, vol. 1566, exp. 3, fs. 19–24
	1738	89	55	34	1.62	18	20.2%	13	1.38	AGN, Tierras, vol. 1938, exp. 5, fs. 35–43
	1743	54	32	22	1.45	19	35.2%	11	1.73	AGN, Tierras, vol. 1566, exp. 12
	1746	63	37	26	1.42	28	44.4%	14	2.00	AGN, Tierras, vol. 1566, exp. 11
	1749	73	40	33	1.21	36	49.3%	15	2.40	AGN, Tierras, vol. 1972, exp. 2, fs. 27–35
	1752	66	36	30	1.20	27	40.9%	11	2.45	AGN, Tierras, vol. 1974, exp. 2, fs. 88–90
Nuestra Señora de Guadalupe	1739	49	20	29	0.69	26	53.1%	9	2.89	AGN, Tierras, vol. 1941, caud. 2, fs. 7–10
	1741	45	18	27	0.67	24	53.3%	9	2.67	AGN, Tierras, vol. 1941, caud. 6, fs. 33–36
Mártir, San Pedro	1731	55	26	29	0.90	23	41.8%	12	1.92	AGN, Tierras, vol. 1972, exp. 2, fs. 20–23
Miacatlán	1737	72	44	28	1.57	23	31.9%	8	2.88	AGN, Tierras, vol. 1972, exp. 2, fs. 20–23
Palapa	1750	256	127	129	0.98	95	37.1%	69	1.38	AGN, HH, vol. 307, exp. 9
Santa Bárbara de Calderón	1735	101	53	48	1.10	29	28.7%	17	1.71	AGN, Bienes Nacionales leg 98, exp. 2
	1763	104	64	40	1.60	35	33.7%	17	2.06	AGN, Tierras, vol. 1935, fs. 48–50
San Gaspar	1738	75	40	35	1.14	38	50.7%	16	2.38	AGN, Tierras, vol. 2420, exp. 1
San Nicolás	1751	92	50	42	1.19	37	40.2%	17	2.18	AGN, HH, vol. 329, exp. 8

San Vicente-Matlapán	1756	50	23	27	0.85	21	42.0%	11	1.91	AGN, Tierras, vol. 1951, caud, 3 f. 25
Temilpa, San Francisco	1735	56	36	20	1.80	11	19.6%	6	1.83	AGN, Tierras, vol. 1813, caud 2, fs. 177–80
	1758	31	17	14	1.21	8	25.8%	6	1.33	AGN, Tierras, vol. 1962, exp. 1, fs. 49–50
Temisco, Nuestra Señora de la Concepción	1728	89	43	46	0.93	40	44.9%	21	1.90	AGN, Tierras, vol. 3428, exp. 1, fs. 20–25
	1738	82	36	46	0.78	41	50.0%	22	1.86	AGN, Tierras, vol. 3432, caud. 8, fs. 47–50
Tilapa, San Joseph de	1730	28	20	8	2.50	3	10.7%	4	0.75	AGN, Tierras, vol. 206, caud 3, fs. 73–74
	1736	24	15	9	1.67	5	20.8%	1	5.00	AGN, Tierras, vol. 564, exp. 1, fs. 38–39
Tlacomulco, San Antonio	1731	62	41	21	1.95	18	29.0%	10	1.80	AGN, Tierras, vol. 1981, exp. 5, fs. 74–86
	1741	59	40	19	2.11	20	33.9%	8	2.50	AGN, Tierras, vol. 1981, exp. 5, fs. 74–86
	1753	51	28	23	1.22	15	29.4%	11	1.36	AGN, Tierras, vol. 1965, exp. 1, fs. 179–86
Tlilapan, San Juan Bautista	1727	57	33	24	1.38	17	29.8%	9	1.89	AGN, Tierras, vol. 458, exp. 3, fs. 1–41
Tolentino, San Nicolás	1730	133	90	43	2.09	29	21.8%	22	1.32	AGN, Tierras, vol. 1935, fs. 34–85
RUNNING TOTAL		2106	1172	934	1.255	733	34.8%	402	1.82	
Mean[a]		68								
Median[a]		63								

*Excludes Palapa.

TABLE 1.4A. Hacienda Censuses from Central New Spain That Include Slave Prices, 1670–1759

Hacienda	Year	Source
1670–99		
Atotonilco, San Nicolás	1690	AGN, Tierras, vol. 3040, f. 326
San Joseph (Amilpas)	1676	AN, #379, vol. 2507, fs. 166–94
Tolentino, San Nicolás	1698	AGN, Tierras, vol. 3206, caud. 2, fs. 155–67
Zacatepec	1676	AN, #336, vol. 2200, fs. 9–42
1700–29		
Pantitlan, San Nicolás	1701	AGN, Tierras, vol. 3106, fs. 125–6
Barreto, San Diego Ficuman	1702	AGN, Tierras, vol. 1742, fs. 175v
Apanquisalco, Nuestra Señora de la Concepción	1703	AGN, Tierras, vol. 3095, exp. 11, fs. 269–70
Nuestra Señora de los Ángeles	1704	AGN, Tierras, vol. 235, exp. 1, fs. 14–16
Amanalco, Santa Ana	1701	AGN, Tierras, vol. 3106, fs. 122–23
Atotonilco, San Nicolás	1711	AGN, Tierras, vol. 3042, exp. 3, fs. 162–63
Temilpa, San Francisco	1704	AGN, Tierras, vol. 1761, exp. 1, fs. 228–30
	1710	AGN, Tierras, vol. 1812, exp. 1, fs. 60–69
Temisco, Nuestra Señora de la Concepción	1714	AGN, Tierras, vol. 3265, exp. 1, fs. 275–28
	1728	AGN, Tierras, vol. 3428, exp. 1, fs. 20–25
Tilapa, San Joseph de	1722	AGN, Tierras, vol. 207, exp. 1, fs. 17–20
Cocoyoc, San Joseph	1714	AGN, Tierras, vol. 1564, no exp.
1730–59		
Atlihuayan, San Diego	1732	AGN, Tierras, vol. 522, exp. 5
San Gaspar	1738	AGN, Tierras, vol. 2420, exp. 1, fs. 35–59
San Vicente-Matlapán	1756	AGN, Tierras, vol. 1951, caud. 3, f. 25
Temilpa, San Francisco	1758	AGN, Tierras, vol. 1962, exp. 1, fs. 49–50
Temisco, Nuestra Señora de la Concepción	1738	AGN, Tierras, vol. 3432, caud. 8, fs. 47–50
Cocoyoc, San Joseph	1749	AGN, Tierras, vol. 1972, exp. 2, fs. 27–35
	1752	AGN, Tierras, vol. 1974, exp. 2, fs. 88–90
Chiconcuac, Santa Catarina	1745	AGN, Tierras, vol. 1969, exp. 1, fs. 102v–10

TABLE I.5A. Hacienda Censuses from Central New Spain That List Skilled Slaves, 1727–58

Hacienda	Adult Men	Skilled Men	Prices Listed	Source
Atlihuayan, 1732	31	6	X	AGN, Tierras, vol. 522, exp. 5
Cocoyoc, 1738	44	6		AGN, Tierras, vol. 1938, exp. 5, fs. 35–43
San Gaspar, 1738	16	7	X	AGN, Tierras, vol. 2420, exp. 1, fs. 35–59
San Vicente-Matlapán, 1756	13	8	X	AGN, Tierras, vol. 1951, caud 3, f. 25
Temilpa, 1758	14	5	X	AGN, Tierras, vol. 1962, exp. 1, fs. 49–50
Temisco, 1728	20	7	X	AGN, Tierras, vol. 3428, exp. 1, fs. 20–25
Tilapa, 1730	17	4		AGN, Tierras, vol. 206, caud 3, fs. 73–74
Tlacomulco, 1741	27	13	X	AGN, Tierras, vol. 1965, exp. 1, fs. 179–86
Tlilapan, 1727	23	19		AGN, Tierras, vol. 458, exp. 3, fs. 1–41
TOTAL	205	75		

TABLE 2.1A. Marriage Patterns of Male Slaves, Mexico City, 1640–1749

Afro-Mexican Slave Grooms

Brides	1640–49				1666–89				1690–1719				1720–49			
	Bozal	Black	Mulatto	Total	*Bozal*	Black	Mulatto	Total	*Bozal*	Black	Mulatto	Total	*Bozal*	Black	Mulatto	Total
Slave																
Bozal	58	6	—	64	15	—	—	15	2	1	—	3	1	—	—	1
Black	2	2	2	6	2	7	5	14	3	2	3	8	1	3	—	4
Mulatta	4	3	3	10	1	4	8	13	2	1	9	12	1	2	5	8
Chinese	—	—	—	—	—	—	1	1	—	—	—	—	—	—	—	—
Free																
Bozal	1	—	—	1	—	—	—	—	1	—	—	1	—	—	—	—
Black	—	1	—	1	1	1	—	2	—	1	—	1	—	—	—	—
Mulatta	2	4	2	8	2	14	26	42	2	4	21	27	2	4	13	19
Chinese	1	—	—	1	—	2	—	2	—	—	—	—	—	—	—	—
Mestiza	—	2	7	9	—	7	11	18	—	1	11	12	—	2	8	10
Indian	1	—	—	1	—	5	4	9	—	1	—	1	—	—	4	4
Spanish	—	—	—	—	—	—	1	1	—	—	—	—	—	—	2	2
TOTAL	69	18	14	101	21	40	56	117	10	11	44	65	5	11	32	48
% of Slave Wives	79.2%				36.8%				35.4%				27.1%			
% of Racial Endogamy	90.1%				76.1%				80.0%				66.7%			

Source: AGN, Matrimonios, vols. 1–229.

TABLE 2.2. A Marriage Patterns of Female Slaves, Mexico City, 1640–1749

Afro–Mexican Slave Brides

Grooms	1640–49				1660–89				1690–1719				1720–49			
	Bozal	Black	Mulatta	Total	*Bozal*	Black	Mulatta	Total	*Bozal*	Black	Mulatta	Total	*Bozal*	Black	Mulatta	Total
Slave																
Bozal	58	4	2	64	15	2	1	18	2	3	2	7	1	1	1	3
Black	6	3	2	11	—	7	4	11	1	2	1	4	—	3	2	5
Mulatto	—	4	2	6	—	5	9	14	—	3	9	12	—	—	5	5
Free																
Black	1	—	1	2	—	1	—	1	—	—	—	—	1	—	—	1
Mulatto	—	2	—	2	—	2	8	10	—	1	4	5	—	—	9	9
Mestizo	—	—	—	—	1	2	1	4	—	—	1	1	—	1	2	3
Indian	—	—	—	—	—	—	—	—	—	—	—	—	—	—	—	—
Spanish	—	—	1	1	—	—	—	—	—	—	—	—	—	—	1	1
TOTAL	65	13	8	86	16	19	23	58	3	9	17	29	2	5	20	27
% of Slave Husbands				94.2%				74.1%				79.3%				48.1%
% of Racial Endogamy				98.8%				93.1%				96.6%				85.2%

Source: AGN, Matrimonios, vols. 1–229.

TABLE 2.3A. Marriage Patterns of Male Slaves, Sagrario Metropolitano, Mexico City, 1647–1737

	Afro-Mexican Slave Grooms								
	1647–48			1691–92			1736–37		
Brides	Black	Mulatto	Total	Black	Mulatto	Total	Black	Mulatto	Total
Slaves									
Black	78	1	79	19	2	21	2		2
Mulatta	2	5	7	6	5	11	1	3	4
Chinese	1	—	1	—	—	—	—	—	—
Free									
Black	1	—	1	2		2			
Mulatta	7	4	11	9	17	26	7	14	21
Mestizo	2	7	9	3	4	7	1	7	8
Indian	2		2	1		1		2	2
Spanish	—	—	—	—	—	—	—	2	2
TOTAL	93	17	110	40	28	68	11	28	39
% of Slave Wives			79.1%			47.1%			15.4%
% of Racial Endogamy			90.0%			88.2%			69.2%

Source: AGN, AGH, Sagrario Metropolitano, Cuidad de México, libros de matrimonios de dastas.

TABLE 2.4A. Marriage Patterns of Female Slaves, Sagrario Metropolitano, Mexico City, 1647–1737

| | Afro-Mexican Slave Brides | | | | | | | | |
| | 1647–48 | | | 1691–92 | | | 1736–37 | | |
Grooms	Black	Mulatta	Total	Black	Mulatta	Total	Black	Mulatta	Total
Slaves									
Black	78	2	80	19	5	24	2	1	3
Mulatto	1	5	6	2	5	7		3	3
Free									
Black	3	4	7	—	—	—	—	—	—
Mulatto	1	—	1	—	3	3	1	5	6
Mestizo	1	—	1	—	1	1	—	1	1
Indian	—	—	—	—	—	—	—	1	1
Spanish	—	1	1	—	—	—	—	—	—
TOTAL	84	12	96	21	14	35	3	11	14
% of Slave Husbands			89.6%			88.6%			42.9%
% of Racial Endogamy			97.9%			97.1%			85.7%

Source: AGN, AGH, Sagrario Metropolitano, Cuidad de México, libros de matrimonios de castas.

TABLE 2.5A. Marriage Choice of Male Slaves by Race and Status of Brides

	Slave Grooms							
	Santa Fe, Guanajuato 1669–1723				Sagrario, San Luis Potosí, 1655–1738			
Brides	Black	Mulatto	Total	%	Black	Mulatto	Total	%
Slaves								
Black	—	1	1	1%	10	2	12	7%
Mulatta	4	6	10	7%	3	16	19	11%
Free								
Black	—	—	—	—	5	3	8	5%
Mulatta	12	60	72	52%	15	53	68	41%
Mestiza	2	25	27	19%	4	11	15	9%
Indian	7	20	27	19%	16	28	44	26%
Spanish	—	2	2	2%	—	2	2	1%>
TOTAL	25	114	139	100%	53	115	168	100%

Sources: AGN, AGH, Sagrario, San Luis Potosí, libros de matrimonios de castas, roll 31731, vol. 1, 1655–98, vol. 3, 1698–1704, vol. 4, 1687–97, vol. 5, 1703–22, and roll 31732, vol. 7, 1722–39; ABCG, libros de matrimonios de todas calidades, vol. 1, 1669–83, vol. 2, 1683–96, vol. 3, 1705–1726, vol. 4, 1716–23.

TABLE 2.6A. Marriage Choice of Female Slaves by Race and Status of Groom

	Slave Brides							
	Santa Fe, Guanajuato 1669–1723				Sagrario, San Luis Potosí, 1655–1738			
Grooms	Black	Mulatto	Total	%	Black	Mulatto	Total	%
Slaves								
Black	—	4	4	13%	10	3	13	17%
Mulatto	1	6	7	23%	2	16	18	23%
Free								
Black	—	—	—	—	—	—	—	—
Mulatto	3	8	11	35%	4	24	28	36%
Mestizo	—	5	5	16%	1	9	10	13%
Indian	—	—	—	—	2	2	4	5%
Spanish	—	3	3	10%	—	5	5	6%
Unknown	—	1	1	3%	—	—	—	—
TOTAL	4	27	31	100%	19	59	78	100%

Sources: see table 2.5A.

TABLE 3.1A. Racial Composition of Witchcraft Accusations in the Mexican Inquisition, 1700–99

	Spaniards	Blacks	Mulattoes	Afro-Indians	Mestizos	Indians	Unknown (U)	Total (T)
Adivinación	2	2	7	0	6	2	18	37
Curanderismo	5	9	16	5	14	2	36	87
Hechicería	8	5	24	1	17	8	46	109
Brujería[a]	13[b]	0	10	3	3	1	16	46
RACIAL TOTAL (Rt)	28	16	57	9	40	13	116	
% of Sample (Rt/t)	10%	6%	20%	3%	14%	5%	42%	100%
% of Known Sample (Rt/T-U)	17%	10%	35%	6%	25%	8%	—	100%

[a] Includes accusations of hechicería that involved secondary accusations of making pacts with the devil or engaging in brujería or maleficio.
[b] This number includes three brothers accused a total of seven times over a period of twenty-five years. Each accusation was counted separately because other defendants accused of different crimes at different times and were included in the sample each time.

Source: Universidad de Colima, ARGENA: Base de dato documentos coloniales (México, D.F.: Archivo General de la Nación, Secretaría de Gobernación, 1993).

TABLE 6.1A. Manumissions by Sex of Slave and Master, New Spain

Masters	Slaves		
	Women	Men	Women Manumitted
Mexico City, 1673–76			
Women	86	42	67%
Men	65	39	63%
Mexico City, 1723–26			
Women	66	29	69%
Men	54	49	52%
Guanajuato, 1699–1750			
Women	55	34	62%
Men	70	67	51%

Sources: AN, 1673–76 and 1723–26; AHG, Protocolos de Cabildo, 1699–1750.

TABLE 6.2A. Child Manumissions by Sex of Master, New Spain

Masters	Child Manumission		
	Freed slaves of known age	N	%
Mexico City, 1673–76			
Women	93	31	33.3%
Men	66	20	30.3%
Mexico City, 1723–26			
Women	67	24	35.8%
Men	65	12	18.5%
Guanajuato, 1699–1750			
Women	65	28	43.1%
Men	108	39	36.1%

Source: see table 6.1A.

Notes

Introduction

1. AGN, Bienes Nacionales, vol. 131, exp. 56, f. 2. The plantation, Santa Barbara de Calderón, was located in the jurisdiction of Cuautla, a major sugar-producing and slave-holding region in the modern state of Morelos.
2. AGN, Criminal, vol. 135, exp. 56, fs. 183–214.
3. Ginzburg, *The Cheese and the Worms*, xiv.
4. I understand race and racial identities as historical and social constructs, and I do not employ them herein to refer to biological or fixed social groups. Racial identity, in particular, I understand as referring to a nascent sense of commonality grounded in contemporary understandings of race (as marking divisions within societies based on phenotype) and ethnicity (as marking divisions within societies based on cultural differences that tend to use a language of place of origin). See Wade, *Race and Ethnicity in Latin America*, 13–14, 17–18.
5. AGN, Tierras, vol. 3543, exp. 1, fs. 67, 78.
6. Following the lead of Eric Foner and others, I use "liberty" and "freedom" interchangeably in this study. See Foner, "The Meaning of Freedom in the Age of Emancipation," 437n5; Pitkin, "Are Freedom and Liberty Twins?" It is worth noting that in the Spanish language, there are not two separate words for liberty and freedom. Rather, *libertad* can be translated as both.
7. Bennett, *Africans in Colonial Mexico*, 1.
8. For a discussion of slavery during the height of the slave trade between 1580 and 1640, see Palmer, *Slaves of the White God*.
9. This estimate is based on a beginning population of 17,500 slaves in 1580, the importation of 110,000 slaves over the following sixty years, and an average annual population loss of 2.3 to 3.5 percent, based on Stuart Schwartz's estimates for colonial Brazil (*Sugar Plantations in the Formation of Brazilian*

Society, 368). Palmer and Ngou-Mve agree that 110,000 slaves entered New Spain legally during those years while Palmer estimates that another 40,000 slaves might have been entered illegally (Palmer, *Slaves of the White God*, 28; Ngou-Mve *El África Bantú en la colonización de México*, 97–147). At the low rate of population loss, the slave population would have been approximately 59,700, and at the high rate it would have been 46,700.

I employ the phrase "slaveholding society" to avoid the debate surrounding the differences between "slave societies" and "societies with slaves." For a discussion of those distinctions, see Berlin, *Many Thousands Gone*, 8.

10. Palmer, *Slaves of the White God*, 1–4; Valdés, "The Decline of Slavery in Mexico."

11. For studies that focus on slavery prior to the nineteenth century, see Bowser, *The African Slave in Colonial Peru*; Palmer, *Slaves of the White God*; Schwartz, *Sugar Plantations in the Formation of Brazilian Society*.

12. Blanchard, "The Language of Liberation."

13. Clearly, mine is not the first attempt to employ hegemony as a means to explain master-slave relations. Eugene Genovese, in his masterful *Roll, Jordan, Roll*, asserted that the law served as the primary vehicle by which the ruling class imposed its hegemony, which he argued, "implied the ability of a particular class to contain [class] antagonisms on a terrain in which its legitimacy is not dangerously questioned" (26). Yet, paternalism—defined as a system of reciprocal obligations—and not hegemony served as his model for master-slave relations. Paternalism, as he defined it, was a historical construct specific to the nineteenth-century southern United States and is not applicable to the context of seventeenth- and eighteenth-century New Spain. Instead of treating hegemony as an imposition, I employ it as a model to explore the unequal and ongoing negotiations over the meanings of mastery and slavery by slaves and their owners.

14. Lears, "The Concept of Cultural Hegemony," 570–73. Also see Glassman, "The Bondsman's New Clothes," 282; Scott, foreword, xi.

15. Scott, *Domination and the Arts of Resistance*, 5.

16. Scott, *Domination and the Arts of Resistance*, 111.

17. Ginzburg, *The Cheese and the Worms*, xiv, xix, 60–61.

18. Roseberry, "Hegemony and the Language of Contention," 361.

19. Scott, *Domination and the Arts of Resistance*, 138. He does suggest that the subordinate classes can subtlety "insinuate" their discontent through elementary techniques of disguise—anonymity, euphemisms, and grumbling—or complex forms of disguise—folktales, symbolic inversion, and rituals of reversal such as carnival—but does not expand on how and if those insinuations actually affect relations of power.

20. Foucault, *Discipline and Punish*, 27.

21. Rousse, "Power/Knowledge," 112.
22. Roseberry, "Hegemony and the Language of Contention," 361.
23. Scott, *Domination and the Arts of Resistance*, 21.
24. Since the publication of Frank Tannenbaum's *Slave and Citizen* in 1946 the supposed and real protections offered slaves in Spanish imperial law have fundamentally shaped historians' understanding of the operation of slavery in Spanish and Portuguese America. While Spanish law did fundamentally affect master-slave relations, it did not necessarily result in a more benign form of slavery as Tannenbaum argued.
25. Patterson, *Slavery and Social Death*, 1, 11. According to at least one critic, Patterson presents an "elegant reconstruction of the ideologies of the dominators" rather than a useful model of slavery. See Glassman, "The Bondsman's New Clothes," 280.
26. At least one scholar argues that the private transcripts of slaves in nineteenth-century Demerara (now Guyana) included "the right to freedom, which included the right to the fruit of their labor, the right to constitute and maintain a family according to their own criteria of propriety, the right to never to be separated from family and kin against their wish, the right to move about without constraints, to celebrate their rituals, play their drums—in short, the right to live according to their own rules of decency and respect" (da Costa, *Crowns of Glory, Crowns of Blood*, 73).
27. Hobsbawm, "Peasants and Politics," 13.
28. My thanks to Dr. D. Michael Bottoms for helping me clarify this point.
29. Some sugar was exported from New Spain. See Carroll, *Blacks in Colonial Veracruz*, 165.
30. Jaén, introduction, x.
31. Demographic data from Aguirre Beltrán, *La población negra de México*, 234.
32. Vasconcelos, while paying homage to the "superior . . . spiritual capacities" of "even the blacks," argues that a great benefit of *mestizaje* would be that "the Black could be redeemed . . . by voluntary extinction" (*The Cosmic Race*, 32).
33. For example, see the various essays in *La presencia africana en México*. Also see Aguirre Beltrán, *Medicina y magia*, 109; Alberro, *Inquisición y sociedad en México*, 456; Behar, "Sex and Sin, Witchcraft and the Devil in Late-Colonial Mexico," 48; Cortés Jácome, "La memoria familiar de los negros y mulatos," 128; MacLachlan and Rodríguez O., *The Forging of the Cosmic Race*, 222; Martínez Montiel, "Integration Patterns and the Assimilation Process of Negro Slaves in Mexico," 446; Martínez Montiel, *Negros en América*, 167. Some scholars have placed Afro-Mexicans at the heart of the construction of colonial culture. Arguing that blacks and mulattoes served as cultural intermediaries between the largely distinct Spanish and indigenous cultural worlds, they innovatingly place Afro-Mexicans at the center of mestizaje. See

Carroll, "Los mexicanos negros, el mestizaje y los fundamentos olvidados de la 'raza cósmica' "; Lewis, *Hall of Mirrors*.

34. Recent scholarship emphasizes the cultural interaction, interchange, and exchange among the Spanish and Native American cultural worlds, finding a surprising level of continuity in both. For example, see Clendinnen, *Ambivalent Conquests*; Farriss, *Maya Society under Colonial Rule*; Kellogg, *Law and the Transformation of Aztec Culture*; Lockhart, *The Nahuas After the Conquest*; Stern, *Peru's Indian Peoples and the Challenge of Spanish Conquest*.

35. Bennett, *Africans in Mexico*; Bristol, *Christians, Blasphemers, and Witches*; Germeten, *Black Blood Brothers*; Vinson, *Bearing Arms for His Majesty*.

36. Schwartz, "Sugar Plantation Labor and Slave Life," 39.

37. Blanchard, "Language of Liberation," 500.

38. For examples of studies that contend otherwise, see Owensby, "How Juan and Leonor Won Their Freedom"; Patterson, *Freedom in the Making of Western Culture*.

39. Johnson, "Time and Revolution in African America," 155.

CHAPTER 1

1. For this reason, the state often tried to place convicts in obrajes.

2. AGN, Inquisición, vol. 504, exp. 2, fs. 210–16.

3. Berlin and Morgan, "Labor and the Shaping of Slave Life in the Americas," 1.

4. Cook and Borah, *The Indian Population of Central Mexico*, 48. The Spanish largely stand apart from other early modern European colonial powers for their long concern over the "justice" of their imperial enterprise and the "rights" of the conquered indigenous peoples within it. Many Spanish imperial policies reflected an inherent tension between an indifference to the exploitation of native peoples and a desire to protect them as Christians and vassal of the crown. See Hanke, *The Spanish Struggle for Justice*, and for a more revisionist position, see Seed, "Are These Not Also Men?"

5. Carroll, *Blacks in Colonial Veracruz*, 16.

6. Martin, *Rural Society in Colonial Morelos*, 24.

7. Many scholars argue that these *cédulas reales* (royal orders or decrees) had little impact on obraje operation. See Greenleaf, "The Obraje in the Late Mexican Colony," 233–35.

8. Florescano, "La formación de los trabajadores en la época colonial."

9. Menard and Schwartz, "Why African Slavery?" 99; Palmer, *Slaves of the White God*, 28–30.

10. The consensus regarding the decline of slavery is generally associated with the demographic growth of the indigenous and casta (racially mixed) populations

after 1640. See Carroll, *Blacks in Colonial Veracruz*, 30–34; Florescano, "La formación de los trabajadores en la época colonial," 65; Menard and Schwartz, "Why African Slavery?" 96–101; Palmer, *Slaves of the White God*, 1–4; Valdés, "The Decline of Slavery in Mexico," 167–94.

11. For two studies that highlight the gradual decline of slavery across the eighteenth century in the sugar industry in central New Spain, see Martin, *Rural Society in Colonial Morelos*, 139; Morin, *Michoacán en la Nueva España del siglo XVIII*, 257.

12. Whereas a portion of sugar production was exported from the colony, woolen textiles were consumed domestically. Similarly, in Minas Gerais, Brazil, a burgeoning cottage textile industry, based largely on slave labor, developed after the collapse of mining in the eighteenth century (Libby, "Proto-Industrialization in a Slave Society").

13. Mine owners did initially try slave labor in the late sixteenth century but quickly transitioned to free wage labor. Over 60 percent of workers in the northern mines of Guanajuato, Zacatecas, and San Luis Potosí were African slaves in 1570. By the seventeenth century, however, wages became the primary means of labor recruitment (Palmer, *Slaves of the White God*, 76). Peter Bakewell estimates that in the 1640s approximately one-fifth of the mining labor force in Zacatecas were slaves (*Silver Mining and Society in Colonial Mexico*, 124).

14. Gibson, *The Aztecs under Spanish Rule*, 246.

15. Van Young, *Hacienda and Market in Eighteenth-Century Mexico*, 248; Van Young, "Mexican Rural History since Chevalier," 22–24.

16. Contrary to perceived wisdom perhaps, debt is understood in this context as reflective of the strong bargaining position of labor in the context of a weak labor market (Bauer, "Rural Workers in Spanish America," 36; Gibson, *The Aztecs under Spanish Rule*, 249–55; Taylor, *Landlord and Peasant in Colonial Oaxaca*, 147–52).

17. Gibson, *The Aztecs under Spanish Rule*, 243; Salvucci, *Textiles and Capitalism in Mexico*, 97–98.

18. Few of these studies consider slavery alongside changes in indigenous labor. For some that do, see Brockington, *The Leverage of Labor*; Martin, *Rural Society in Colonial Morelos*; Mentz, *Trabajo, sujeción y libertad en el centro de la Nueva España*.

19. Young, *Hacienda and Market in Eighteenth-Century Mexico*, 249. D. A. Brading describes a similar transition in the Bajío, where small-scale rancheros faced encroachment by expanding "great estates" after 1740, but even that did not result in the complete transformation of rancheros into peons (*Haciendas and Ranchos in the Mexican Bajío*, 173).

20. Mentz, *Trabajo, sujeción y libertad en el centro de la Nueva España*, 361.

21. Barrett, *The Sugar Hacienda of the Marqueses del Valle*, 11; Sandoval, *La industria de azúcar en Nueva España*, 23–35.

22. Carroll, *Blacks in Colonial Veracruz*, 30–34.

23. Naveda Chávez-Hita, *Esclavos negros en las haciendas azucareras de Córdoba, Veracruz*, 22, 179; Naveda Chávez-Hita, "Trabajadores esclavos en las haciendas azucareras de Córdoba, Veracruz," 163–64, 179.

24. Barrett and Schwartz, "Comparación entre dos economías azucareras coloniales," 552.

25. See tables 1.1A–1.3A in the appendix to this book, which include data from ninety-four found censuses of thirty-five ingenios from central New Spain taken between 1648 and 1763. While not ideal, the information available in those censuses does allow us to roughly estimate the size and scope of slaveholdings on the region's sugar plantations. In order to gauge change over time, I created three datasets: 1648–86, 1687–1725, and 1726–63, which make use of all censuses (including multiple censuses for a single plantation in different years) within the timeframe of the dataset. For the first dataset, which uses twenty-seven censuses from seventeen different ingenios, the mean slaveholding was 81 slaves, the median was 63 slaves, and the span was 23 to 126 slaves (STDV=25.7). The 1687–1725 dataset includes thirty-seven censuses of twenty ingenios with a mean slaveholding of 75 slaves, a median of 56 slaves, and the span 18 to 171 slaves (STDV=40.1). Finally, the 1726–63 dataset includes twenty-seven censuses from sixteen ingenios. The mean slaveholding was 68 slaves, the median 63 slaves, and the span 24 to 133 slaves (STDV=31.2).

26. Cheryl Martin is quite clear that in-migration to the ingenios of Morelos began in the seventeenth century but that free labor did not supplant slavery until the eighteenth century; see *Rural Society in Colonial Morelos*, 139.

27. The cotton industry developed very differently than did the woolen industry and did not come to rely on slaves; I do not treat it here. For a discussion of the evolution of the cotton industry, see Bazant, "Evolution of the Textile Industry of Puebla," 66–67; Villanueva, "From Calpixqui to Corregidor."

28. Salvucci, *Textiles and Capitalism in Mexico*, 3, 40–41.

29. For studies that suggest that slaves were too expensive for obrajeros, see Gibson, *The Aztecs under Spanish Rule*, 244; Greenleaf, "The Obraje in the Late Mexican Colony," 233; Miño Grijalva, *La protoindustria colonial Hispanoamericana*, 96–98; Palmer, *Slaves of the White God*, 73; Simpson, *Many Mexicos*, 132.

30. For similar findings, see Chávez Carbajal, "La gran negritud en Michoacán," 103; Super, "Querétaro Obrajes," 206–7.

31. AGN, Archivo del Tribunal Superior de Justicia del Distrito Federal, vol. 5, exp. 44, f. 2.

32. AGN, AHHJ, vol. 319, exp. 12, fs. 54–67.

33. Salvucci, *Textiles and Capitalism in Mexico*, 101; Urquiola, "Empresas y empresarios," 239.

34. AGN, Tierras, vol. 1056, exp. 5, fs. 12–13; AGN, Archivo del Tribunal Superior de Justicia del Distrito Federal, vol. 5, exp. 44, f. 2.

35. Horn, *Postconquest Coyoacan*, 1–13, 218.

36. Aguirre Beltrán, "La esclavitud en los obrajes novoespañoles," 255.

37. Salvucci, *Textiles and Capitalism in Mexico*, 111.

38. For a complete transcription of the inspection, see Edmundo O'Gorman, "El trabajo industrial en la Nueva España a mediados del siglo XVII," 77–85.

39. AGN, Civil, vol. 355, exp. 3, fs. 115–58.

40. AGN, General de Parte, vol. 8, exp. 27, f. 14; AGN, Clero Regular y Secular, vol. 103, exp. 4, f. 169.

41. AN, Almogueras, Andrés de, #11, vol. 50, fs. 48–67.

42. AGN, Tierras, vol. 3221, exp. 1, fs. 31–33; AN, Veedor, Fernando, #687, vol. 4618, fs. 922–25; AN, Veedor, Fernando, #687, vol. 4621, fs. 568–70.

43. AN, Francisco de Valdez, #692, vol. 4700, fs. 322–26. Mexía de Vera paid only 170 pesos per adult male slave, well below market value, but the contract stipulated that he would be forced to pay an additional 130 pesos if he ever sold any of the thirty-four male slaves from his obraje.

44. AN, Anaya, José de, #6, vol. 17, fs. 158–63.

45. These slaves represented the overwhelming majority of the obraje labor force despite the fact that wage labor served as the primary form of labor for the hacienda's ranching enterprises (Konrad, *A Jesuit Hacienda in Colonial Mexico*, 208–10).

46. Super, "Querétaro Obrajes," 206–7.

47. Salvucci, *Textiles and Capitalism in Mexico*, 99.

48. For a discussion of the complicated chronology of labor recruitment in the obrajes of New Spain, see Proctor, "Afro-Mexican Slave Labor in the Obrajes de Paños of New Spain"; Salvucci, *Textiles and Capitalism in Mexico*, 109–11.

49. Barrett and Schwartz, "Comparación entre dos economías azucareras coloniales," 553. Barrett and Schwartz do not provide the value of a kilogram of sugar, only that of a slave, an ox, and a mule calculated in kilograms of sugar. For comparative purposes, it is instructive to note that the value of an ox increased from twenty-three kilograms of sugar in 1600 to sixty-two kilograms in 1700 and eighty-six kilograms in 1800.

50. O'Gorman, "El trabajo industrial en la Nueva España a mediados del siglo XVII," 33–116; AGN, Inquisición, vol. 583, exp. 4, f. 491; AGN, Tierras, vol. 1056, exp. 5, fs. 22v–23; AN, Arauz, Nicolás de, #5, vol. 11, fs. 91–92; AGN, RFI, vol. 22, exp. 7, fs. 125–36.

51. Gibson, *The Aztecs under Spanish Rule*, 245–46.

52. Gibson, *The Aztecs under Spanish Rule*; Salvucci, *Textiles and Capitalism in Mexico*; Van Young, *Hacienda and Market in Eighteenth-Century Mexico.*

53. Palmer, *Slaves of the White God*, 47.

54. Every found census that includes information on sex and age of the slave population is included in the datasets described in n. 25. The censuses were taken at the beginning and end of lease periods of the hacienda in question, when it had been seized for appraisal to settle outstanding debts and/or to be sold.

55. Tadman, "The Demographic Cost of Sugar," 1536.

56. Patrick Carroll found that the slave population on the sugar haciendas in Jalapa, Veracruz, experienced an equalization of sex ratios and a growth in the number of children within the population during the eighteenth century as well. See *Blacks in Colonial Veracruz*, 76.

57. Morgan, *Slave Counterpoint*, 81–83.

58. The nature of the sources makes direct comparisons difficult. While the New Spain data represents a comparison of children zero to fourteen to women fifteen to forty-four years of age, the U.S. information presented by Morgan appears to represent children zero to fifteen and women sixteen to fifty years of age.

59. Philip Morgan also treats any intervals longer than sixty months as anomalous in *Slave Counterpoint*, 89n80.

60. In Puerto Rico and the British West Indies slave women experienced intervals of approximately thirty-six months between births, while those in British North America ranged between twenty-five and thirty months (Craton, "Changing Patterns of Slave Families in the British West Indies," 8; Morgan, *Slave Counterpoint*, 87; Stark, "Discovering the Invisible Puerto Rican Slave Family," 408).

61. Aguirre Beltrán, *La población negra de México*, 219–20. The figures for annual growth rates are my calculations using natural logarithms.

62. For a detailed discussion of slave demography in New Spain after 1640, see Proctor, "Slavery, Identity, and Culture," esp. ch. 3.

63. Scharrer Tamm, *Azúcar y trabajo*, 84–86.

64. Berthe, "Xochimancas," 109–17; *Instrucciones a los hermanos jesuitas administradores de haciendas*, 183. Berthe includes a transcription of the instructions dated March 15, 1664.

65. *Instrucciones a los hermanos jesuitas administradores de haciendas*, 183. Sugar was harvested year round in central New Spain, but the number of days spent harvesting fell somewhere between 120 and 180 days per year in the Caribbean and 300 days per year in Bahia, Brazil. Brazilian mills tended to process cane six days per week, shutting down only on Sundays and religious

holidays, and in some cases operated around the clock. See Schwartz, *Sugar Plantations in the Formation of Brazilian Society*, 103.

66. Berthe, "Xochimancas," 110.

67. Berthe, "Xochimancas," 109–17.

68. In much of the British Caribbean, women dominated field cultivation in the nineteenth century, a pattern tied to the creolization of the slave population and associated changes in sex ratios in favor of women (Beckles, *Natural Rebels*, 24; Higman, *Slave Population and Economy in Jamaica*, 208; Higman, *Slave Populations of the British Caribbean*, 190).

69. For example, in censuses from 1700–29, the average assessed value of female slaves, ages fifteen to forty-four years, was 308 pesos, compared to an average of 305 pesos for unskilled men of the same age group; see table 1.4A in the appendix to this book.

70. Moreno Fraginals, Klein, and Engerman, "The Level and Structure of Slave Prices on Cuban Plantations in the Mid-Nineteenth Century," 1210; Valdés, "The Decline of Slavery in Mexico," 173–74.

71. Bergad, *Slavery and the Demographic and Economic History of Minas Gerais*, 177. The United States was truly exceptional in this regard. There the slave population grew at such phenomenal rates that women's reproductive capacities did not have a positive impact on the potential value of slave women, despite the lack of a regular external slave trade after 1808. See Moreno Fraginals, Klein, and Engerman, "Level and Structure of Slave Prices on Cuban Plantations in the Mid-Nineteenth Century," 1212n49.

72. Martin, *Rural Society in Colonial Morelos*, 138, 142. Also see Scharrer Tamm, *Azúcar y trabajo*, 158.

73. See table 1.5A in the appendix to this book. Adriana Naveda Chávez-Hita found a similar pattern for Córdoba; see *Esclavos negros en las haciendas azucareras de Córdoba, Veracruz*, 103.

74. See table 1.4A in the appendix to this book.

75. Berthe, "Xochimancas," 109–17.

76. Martin, *Rural Society in Colonial Morelos*, 138, 142.

77. Berthe, "Xochimancas," 109–17; *Instrucciones a los hermanos jesuitas administradores de haciendas*, 183.

78. AN, Almogueras, Andrés de, #11, vol. 50, fs. 48–67; AGN, Clero Regular y Secular, vol. 103, exp. 4, fs. 102–216; AGN, Tierras, vol. 3221, exp. 1, fs. 31–33. A number of these positions were guild protected in Spain; see Altman, *Transatlantic Ties in the Spanish Empire*, 57.

79. von Humboldt, *Political Essay on the Kingdom of New Spain*, 189.

80. Salvucci, *Textiles and Capitalism in Mexico*, 123.

81. AGN, Inquisición, vol. 454, exp. 21, fs. 445–54.

82. During the inspection of three Coyoacan obrajeros conducted in 1703, workers testified that the daily workload for slave, free, indebted, and convict wool carders was ten tareas per day. AGN, AHHJ, vol. 319, fs. 54–67.

83. AGN, Inquisición, vol. 441, exp. 5, fs. 503–42, vol. 680, exp. 40, fs. 291–95, vol. 454, exp. 21, fs. 445–54.

84. AGN, Inquisición, vol. 435, exp. 4–5, fs. 287–93, vol. 454, exp. 21, fs. 445–54; AGN, Inquisición, caja 208, carpeta 1, fs. 154v–56; AGN, Inquisición, vol. 431, exp. 9 fs. 265–79.

85. Palmer, "From Africa to the Americas," 229.

86. Cope, *The Limits of Racial Domination*, 95–96.

87. For a discussion of urban women's slave labor in New Spain, see Velázquez, *Mujeres de origen africáno en la capital novohispana*, 161–228. For other Latin American contexts, see Karasch, *Slave Life in Rio de Janeiro*, 207; Socolow, *The Women of Colonial Latin America*, 133–34.

88. AGN, Inquisición, vol. 643, exp. 1, fs. 1–22.

89. AN, Rivera, Francisco de, #559, vol. 3860, fs. 3v–5.

90. AN, Morante, Balthazar, #379, vol. 2507, fs. 48–49.

91. AGN, Inquisición, vol. 498, exp. 50, fs. 50–124.

92. "Real cedula que los gobernadores y justicias no consientan que con los esclavos ejecuten sus dueños excesos ni crueldades (1710)," in *Colección de documentos para la historia de la formación social de Hispanoamérica*, 113–14. Velázquez also includes an interesting discussion about prostitution among Afro-Mexican women in *Mujeres de origen africáno en la capital novohispana*, 217–23.

93. AGN, Inquisición, vol. 454, exp. 39, fs. 475–523; AGN, Reales Cédulas Duplicadas, vol. 18, f. 96; AGN, General de Parte, vol. 8, exp. 71, f. 55, vol. 9, exp. 96, f. 61. Also see Aguirre Beltrán, *El negro esclavo en Nueva España*, 61; Carroll, "Black Laborers and Their Experience in Colonial Jalapa," 122.

94. AGN, Inquisición, vol. 459, exp. 6, f. 688.

95. For changes in the alcabala rates, see Hoberman, *Mexico's Merchant Elite*, 191.

96. Gibson, *The Aztecs under Spanish Rule*, 251.

97. AGN, Inquisición, vol. 576, exp. 5, f. 520. Frederick Bowser found that slave labor was essential in all phases of the colonial Peruvian construction industry (*African Slave in Colonial Peru*, 127).

98. AN, Díaz de Rivera, Juan, #199, vol. 1330, fs. 337v–38. For another example of a slave musician see the case of Francisco Xavier whose wife listed his occupation as a harp player, see AGN, Inquisición, vol. 802, exp. 1, fs. 1–35.

99. AGN, Inquisición, vol. 578, exp. 10, fs. 408–32; vol. 504, exp. 2, fs. 210–16; vol. 477, exp. 23, fs. 241–42.

100. AGN, Inquisición, vol. 431, exp. 9, fs. 466–72.

101. AN, Bernal, Nicolás de, #61, vol. 457, f. 117; AN, Bernal, Nicolás de, #61, vol. 457, fs. 129–30; AN, Bernal, Nicolás, #61, vol. 460, fs. 166–67; AN, Díaz de Rivera, Juan, #199, vol. 1308, fs. 77v–78; AN, Marchena, Juan de, #382, vol. 2529, fs. 11–12; AN, Piedra Cortes, José de, #500, vol. 3372, fs. 57–58; AN, Piedra Cortes, José de, #500, vol. 3372, f. 109; AN, Quiñones, Francisco de, #547, vol. 3706, f. 7; AN, Quiñones, Francisco de, #547, vol. 3708, f. 23; AN, Veedor, Fernando, #687, vol. 4617, fs. 731–32; AN, Veedor, Fernando, #687, vol. 4618, fs. 32–33.

102. AHG, Protocolos del Cabildo, 1725, fs. 234–36; AN, Barreda, Diego, #63, vol. 469, no fol.; AN, Díaz de Rivera, Diego, #198, vol. 1292, fs. 184–86. For an example of a slave blacksmith, see the case of Lorenzo de Ojalora Carvajal, who operated a forge owned by his master in Guatemala City in the 1660s. In the course of his bigamy trial in Mexico City three different local blacksmiths petitioned the Inquisition for the right to his labor. In his application Sebastián Hidalgo argued that Hernando Alonzo and Martín Girbaldo, the other two applicants, already had numerous slaves working in their forges (AGN, Inquisición, vol. 690, exp. 11, fs. 233–385).

103. AGN, Inquisición, vol. 498, exp. 5, f. 120.

104. For a graphic description of the lives of slaves, particularly women, in urban Rio de Janeiro, see Karasch, "Anastácia and the Slave Women of Rio de Janeiro," 79–105.

CHAPTER 2

1. McCaa, "*Calidad, Clase*, and Marriage in Colonial Mexico," 477–78.

2. AGN, Matrimonios, vol. 126, exp. 28, fs. 81–88.

3. Specifically, they testified that the bride and/or groom were not already married, had not taken any religious vow that would prevent them from marrying, and were unrelated to the fifth degree of consanguinity.

4. AGN, Matrimonios, vol. 19, exp. 22, fs. 118–19.

5. Whether or not that knowledge of Catholicism began in Africa (some scholars argue that West Central Africans, primarily in and around the Kingdom of Kongo, were incorporating Catholicism into their cosmological visions as early as the beginnings of the fifteenth century) or in the Americas is not readily evident in marriage applications. See Thornton, "Religious and Ceremonial Life in Kongo and Mbundu Areas."

6. Burke, *History and Social Theory*, 54.

7. For example, Ira Berlin argues that in the United States, status (free vs. slave) was as important as race (black vs. white) in antebellum community formation. Thus, he found a "three-caste" system of slaves, free people of color, and whites who did not regularly intermarry (*Slaves without Masters*, 197). For a

discussion of godparent selection at the baptism of slave children, see Proctor, "La familia y comunidad esclava en San Luis Potosí y Guanajuato, México," 240–49.

8. For the statue guaranteeing slaves the right to marry free from interference, see *Las Siete Partidas*, 4.5.1.

9. Alberro, *Inquisición y sociedad en México*, 456–62; Cortés Jácome, "La memoria familiar de los negros y mulatos," 128; Martínez Montiel, *Negros en América*, 167; Montiel, ed., *La presencia africana en México*.

10. Aguirre Beltrán, *La población negra de México*, 255; Carmagnani, "Demografía y sociedad," 133, 155; Cortés Jácome, "Negros amancebados con indias," 285–93.

11. Bennett, *Africans in Colonial Mexico*, 102; Palmer, "From Africa to the Americas," 223–35.

12. For similar work on race and ethnicity using parish registers in colonial Brazil, see Libby and Frank, "Exploring Parish Registers in Colonial Minas Gerais, Brazil."

13. For an excellent discussion of the changing meanings of race over time in Latin America, see Wade, *Race and Ethnicity in Latin America*, 5–22.

14. Cope, *The Limits of Racial Domination*, 3.

15. Jane Landers ("*Cimarrón* and Citizen") introduces an interesting theory that Afro-Mexicans represented themselves as a distinct república in the early decades of the seventeenth century.

16. Carrera, *Imagining Identity in New Spain*, 36; Cope, *The Limits of Racial Domination*, 24. The origin of the sistema de castas has been dated to the mid-seventeenth century with the appearance of a third group of parish registers, the *libro de castas* or *libro de mestizos, mulatos, y negros*, etc., to accompany the *libro de indios* and *libros de españoles* that until then had represented the theoretically distinct república de españoles and república de indios.

17. Carrera, "Locating Race in Late Colonial Mexico"; Deans-Smith, "Creating the Colonial Subject."

18. Some of these categories had concrete legal and administrative meanings—determining access to guilds, the militia, the clergy, and so forth. The Spanish also imposed sumptuary restrictions on Afro-Mexicans, for example.

19. Carroll, "Los mexicanos negros, el mestizaje y los fundamentos olvidados de la 'raza cósmica,'" 409.

20. All parents of the remaining seventy-nine were mulattos (ABCG, libro de bautizos de todas calidades, libro 14, 1705–9).

21. For those that suggest clear correlations among race, occupation, and social status, see McAlister, "Social Structure and Social Change in New Spain," 36; Mörner, *Race Mixture in the History of Latin America*. Others find that class ordered colonial society and that a person's position in the social hierarchy

was unrelated to race. See Anderson, "Race and Social Stratification"; Chance and Taylor, "Estate and Class in a Colonial City," 482–83; Cope, *The Limits of Racial Domination*. Patricia Seed defines race as the intersection of a cognitive system of racial labels and a division of labor based on the fundamentally different economic functions assigned to Indians (agriculture), blacks (domestic service), and peninsular Spaniards (commerce) ("Social Dimensions of Race," 574). McCaa, Schwartz, and Grubessich rework Chance and Taylors's demographic data and argue that race exerted a strong influence on social stratification ("Race and Class in Colonial Latin America," 433).

22. Aguirre Beltrán, *Medicina y magia*, 109; Alberro, *Inquisición y sociedad en Mexico*, 456; Behar, "Sex and Sin, Witchcraft and the Devil in Late-Colonial Mexico" 48; Cortés Jácome, "La memoria familiar de los negros y mulatas," 128; MacLachlan and Rodríguez O., *The Forging of the Cosmic Race*, 222; Martínez Montiel, *Negros en América*, 167.

23. In the 1792 census, nearly one in nine colonial Mexicans (11.5 percent) and one in three non-Indians (30.5 percent) were listed as black or mulatto. See Aguirre Beltrán, *La población negra en Mexico*, 234.

24. Carrera, *Imagining Identity in New Spain*, 1, 10; Lewis, *Hall of Mirrors*, 22–23.

25. Carrera, *Imagining Identity in New Spain*, 6.

26. Martínez, "The Black Blood of New Spain," 483.

27. Carrera, *Imagining Identity in New Spain*, 10.

28. McCaa, "*Calidad, Clase*, and Marriage in Colonial Mexico," 477–78. Laura Lewis proposes the use of the term "casta," which, she argues, referred to "descent and to putative distinctions carried in blood, ancestry, and color," but she isn't clear as to how it might differ from calidad (*Hall of Mirrors*, 22). Similarly, Patricia Seed presents a definition of "social race" as a combination of physical appearance, economic standing, occupation, and family connections ("Social Dimensions of Race," 574).

29. Carrera, *Imagining Identity in New Spain*, 12–13; Lewis, *Hall of Mirrors*, 29–30. Also see Martínez, "The Black Blood of New Spain," 479–521.

30. Bennett, "Lovers, Family and Friends," 114; Lewis, *Hall of Mirrors*, 31–32.

31. Little consensus exists on the relative importance of "passing" or "racial drift" (i.e., changes in calidad) and on the success of Afro-Mexicans looking to improve their social position. One group of scholars argues that passing was not common and that racial drift, when found, tended to be downward (not upward). The majority of changes that did occur were in degree rather than in kind (e.g., black to mulatto or vice versa rather than mulatto to mestizo or Spanish). See Cope, *The Limits of Racial Domination*, 76–77; McCaa, "*Calidad, Clase*, and Marriage in Colonial Mexico," 497. Another group, however, concludes that when racial variability was measurable the trend was

toward "lighter classification." See Castleman, "Social Climbers in a Colonial Mexican City"; Seed, "Social Dimensions of Race," 594–96. For a nuanced study of passing, see Althouse, "Contested Mestizos, Alleged Mulattos."

32. Bennett, *Africans in Colonial Mexico*, 79–125; Germeten, *Black Blood Brothers*, 11–40; Palmer, "From Africa to the Americas," 223–35.

33. Carroll, "Los mexicanos negros, el mestizaje y los fundamentos olvidados de la 'raza cósmica,'" 403–38. Although she does not focus specifically on Afro-Mexicans, Laura Lewis makes a similar argument in *Hall of Mirrors*.

34. Bristol, *Christians, Blasphemers, and Witches*; Germeten, *Black Blood Brothers*. Ben Vinson's work on the free colored militias is an important exception to this trend. Vinson argues that the militias represented a significant corporate entity "through which racial identity was preserved and expressed" in the late eighteenth century (*Bearing Arms*, 4).

35. There has been considerable debate regarding who—the priest or the petitioner—defined the racial classifications found in parish registers. The growing consensus is now that self-definition outweighed priestly opinion and that this advantage grew over time. This contrasts greatly with the oft-cited inability of witnesses to agree on the racial classification of defendants in criminal and Inquisition records. For examples, see Althouse, "Contested Mestizos, Alleged Mulattos," 151–75; Boyer, "Caste and Identity in Colonial Mexico"; Cope, *The Limits of Racial Domination*, 51–55, 69.

36. Rust and Seed, "Equality of Endogamy," 57.

37. Cope, *The Limits of Racial Domination*, 50; Fields, "Slavery, Race and Ideology in the United States of America."

38. Cope, *The Limits of Racial Domination*, 68–85, quotes, 83.

39. See Wade, *Race and Ethnicity in Latin America*, 21.

40. Bennett, *Africans in Colonial Mexico*, 64–95; Bennett, "Lovers, Family and Friends," 91–104; Palmer, "From Africa to the Americas," 223–35.

41. Data from the Ramo de Matrimonios includes every found marriage of a slave bride or groom and is drawn from vols. 1–229. For a breakdown of slave marriages from the Ramo de Matrimonios by race and status (slave vs. free), see tables 2.1A–2.2A in the appendix to this book.

42. For a general idea of the contours of the debate on the nature of racial and ethnic identity formation in the African diaspora, see Morgan, "The Cultural Implications of the Atlantic Slave Trade"; Thornton, *Africa and Africans in the Making of the Atlantic World*, 186–92.

43. Based on official importation records, over 84 percent of the 150,000–175,000 slaves legally imported prior to 1640 into Veracruz, the principal slave port in New Spain, originated from West Central Africa. See Carroll, *Blacks in Colonial Veracruz*, 32–33, 160; Ngou-Mve, *El África Bantú en la colonización de México*, 97–147. Joseph Miller calculated that 91 percent of

slaves exported from Africa prior to 1650, which corresponds with the height of the trade to New Spain, originated from West Central Africa ("Central Africa during the Era of the Slave Trade," 67).

44. For similar findings on other ethnic monikers employed in the diaspora, see Byrd, "The Slave Trade from the Biafran Interior to Jamaica"; Chambers, "My Own Nation"; Hall, "African Ethnicities and the Meanings of 'Mina'"; Law, "Ethnicity and the Slave Trade"; Lohse, "Slave-Trade Nomenclature and African Ethnicities in the Americas"; O'Toole, "Inventing Difference"; Sweet, *Recreating Africa*.

45. In non-Spanish and non-Portuguese colonies, the term "Angola" referred to slaves taken from bays to the north of the Zaire River. See Miller, "Central Africa," 29.

46. Miller, "Central Africa," 40; Thornton, *The Kingdom of Kongo*, xv.

47. Vansina, "Equatorial Africa and Angola"; Vansina, *Paths in the Rainforests*.

48. Miller, "Central Africa," 35–36; Vansina, foreword, xii; Vansina, *Paths in the Rainforests*, 5, 249.

49. Miller, "Central Africa," 23–27.

50. Thornton, *Africa and Africans in the Making of the Atlantic World*, 191; Vansina, "The Kongo Kingdom and its Neighbors"; Vansina, "Western Bantu Expansion."

51. Chambers, "Ethnicity in the Diaspora," 26. Also see Lovejoy, "Ethnic Designations of the Slave Trade and the Reconstruction of the History of Trans-Atlantic Slavery."

52. Lovejoy, "Identifying Enslaved Africans in the African Diaspora," 9.

53. Herman Bennett cautions, however, that the nature of colonialism forced Africans to employ terms stipulated by their Spanish enslavers, which, in turn, served to set "discursive limits" on their ability to fashion cultural communities of their own (*Africans in Colonial Mexico*, 91).

54. Bennett, "Lovers, Family and Friends," 69, 88; Palmer, "From Africa to the Americas," 233–34. This represents a recalculation of Bennett's data because he counted only marriage applications ("Lovers, Family and Friends," 65), not slaves who married. However, every endogamous marriage application included two slaves. Thus, 660 of 788 (83.4 percent) Angola slaves married endogamously.

55. Bennett, "Lovers, Family and Friends," 66. Importantly, these patterns reflect the general size of the Angola and Congo presence in New Spain; according to Bennett's figures ten times as many Angolas as Congos married in Mexico City prior to 1650.

56. According to Bennett's data, 88 percent of Angolas and 85 percent of Congos married endogamously in Mexico City prior to 1650 ("Lovers, Family and Friends," 66, 69). Studies of Brazil have found a similar pattern whereby

slaves married others from the same slaving region in Africa. See Schwartz, *Sugar Plantations in the Formation of Brazilian Society*, 392; Sweet, *Recreating Africa*, 45–48.

57. The West Central African majority interacted with other ethnic groups of West African origin, which were simply too small to remain completely separate. For example, slaves who claimed Terra Nova or Bran ethnicity tended to marry slaves with the same calidad. But in both cases, the second largest number of spouses for these ethnicities hailed from West Central Africa (Bennett, "Lovers, Family and Friends," 66–69).

58. It is possible to tell from the sources if a particular testigo was testifying on behalf of the bride or groom. Therefore, these figures include only those testigos who testified on behalf of a slave. I excluded testigos for the free spouse because they do not necessarily speak to the intimate relations of the slave in question.

59. AGN, Matrimonios, vol. 172, exp. 170.

60. AGN, Matrimonios, vol. 172, exp. 4.

61. For a discussion of Catholicism in the Kingdom of Kongo, see Thornton, "Religious and Ceremonial Life in Kongo and Mbundu Areas."

62. A lack of data makes it impossible to determine if these patterns were related to average slaveholding sizes for Mexico City.

63. AGN, Matrimonios, vol. 126, exps. 96–97.

64. AGN, Matrimonios, vol. 172, exp. 84. For another example from the 1680s, see AGN, Matrimonios, vol. 67, exp. 59, fs. 291–92.

65. Mullin, *Africa in America*, 161; Slenes, *"Malungu, ngoma vem."*

66. Frey and Wood, *Come Shouting to Zion*, 36.

67. Proctor, "Slavery, Identity, and Culture," 148. For similar findings, see Calvo, *Guadalajara y su región en el siglo XVII*, 91. Unfortunately, similar data cannot be compiled for Mexico City. Legally, only children whose parents were married were defined as legitimate. See Borah and Cook, "Marriage and Legitimacy in Mexican Culture," 947.

68. Beckles, *Natural Rebels*, 171; Fox-Genovese, *Within the Plantation Household*, 49–50; Roddock, "Women and Slavery in the Caribbean," 6.

69. For a study that considers the different implications of these issues by race and class in colonial Brazil, see Nazzari, "An Urgent Need to Conceal."

70. Hünefeldt, *Paying the Price of Freedom*, 150.

71. AGN, Matrimonios, vol. 29, exp. 6, fs. 16–17, vol. 12, exp. 21, fs. 84–88. Interestingly, no free person found herein ever decided not to marry a slave following that warning.

72. We must also keep in mind that marriage, while a sacrament, could be expensive for slaves.

73. Higman, "African and Creole Slave Family Patterns in Trinidad," 171; Higman, "Household Structure and Fertility on Jamaican Slave Plantations," 536.

74. The high number of mulatta slave brides in the parish records further supports this claim. For example, in San Luis Potosí 66 percent (fifty-nine of seventy-nine) of slave brides were mulatta. Similarly, in Guanajuato 86 percent (twenty-seven of thirty-one) of slave brides were mulatta.

75. Hünefeldt, *Paying the Price of Freedom*, 138; Mullin, *Africa in America*, 83.

76. AGN, Criminal, vol. 695, exp. 8, f. 270.

77. Cope's data suggests a similar transition. He found that between 1686 and 1690 56 percent of 214 male slaves married free women. Conversely he found that 80 percent of 119 slave women married slave husbands. Slaves of both genders who listed their race as black were much more likely to marry other slaves than were those listed as mulattoes (*The Limits of Racial Domination*, 84).

78. Cope, *The Limits of Racial Domination*, 81; Hünefeldt, *Paying the Price of Freedom*, 147; Lokken, "Marriage as Slave Emancipation in Seventeenth-Century Rural Guatemala," 178–79; Love, "Marriage Patterns of Persons of African Descent in a Colonial Mexico City Parish," 88.

79. Cope's data shows that 333 slaves married compared to 477 free Afro-Mexicans between 1686 and 1690 in Mexico City's Sagrario parish (*The Limits of Racial Domination*, 82, table 4.10).

80. See tables 2.1A–2.2A in the appendix to this book.

81. Cope, *The Limits of Racial Domination*, 83.

82. That the Spanish words "negro" and "mulato" could have had different meanings and still have referred to a larger community is highlighted by the use of the terms by Afro-Mexicans to designate distinctions within their own community. For example, Ben Vinson III argues for an understanding of the "nuances of color" in his study of the colored militia of New Spain during the eighteenth century. Afro-Mexican militiamen often played the "race card" making clear distinctions between black and mulatto members, reflecting the hierarchical structure of the sistema de castas, in internal struggles for access to privileges within the free colored militia. When faced with external threats, however, racial unity prevailed and the differences among Afro-Mexicans, so prevalent in internal struggles, were subsumed to confront the threat from outside (*Bearing Arms*, 205–7).

83. See tables 2.1A–2.4A in the appendix to this book.

84. There is a clear difference in endogamy rates between black and mulatta slave women and black and mulatto slave men. Cope's data for Sagrario parish from 1686 to 1690 reveals that black slave women married endogamously at a rate of 97.1 percent (N=69); black slave men at a rate of 89.9 percent (N=109);

mulatta slave women at a rate of 86.0 percent (N=50); and mulatto slave men at a rate of 62.0 percent (N=105) (*The Limits of Racial Domination*, 82).

85. AGN, Matrimonios, vol. 14, exp. 28, fs. 73–78.

86. AGN, Matrimonios, vol. 1, exp. 22, fs. 93–96.

87. See tables 2.5A–2.6A in the appendix to this book. Although, one in five slave men in Guanajuato and one in four in San Luis Potosí selected Indian brides, the fact still remains that slaves were much more likely to marry other blacks and mulattos than Indians.

88. Castro Rivas et al., *Desarrollo socio demográfico de la cuidad de Guanajuato durante el siglo XVII*, 62–63; Cope, *The Limits of Racial Domination*, 79, calculated from table 4.7.

89. For example, Cecilia Rabell found that Afro-Mexicans married endogamously in only 35 percent of cases in San Luis de la Paz, Guanajuato, between 1760 and 1810. But she concludes that they were twice as endogamous as would have been expected if marriage were random because they represented less than 10 percent of her sample ("Matrimonio y raza en una parroquia rural," 179–80).

90. The strength of the relationships between slaves who wished to marry and their testigos is measurable. For example, for between 1640 and 1719, less than 10 percent of testigos included in marriages in the Ramo had known the bride or groom who they sponsored for less than six years. The duration of those relationships suggest that testigos were close personal relations of the prospective bride and groom.

91. When a couple applied for marriage they were required to present between two and six witnesses to testify that they were unencumbered and therefore able to marry. In addition, two padrinos served as spiritual sponsors at the wedding ceremonies. As padrinos and testigos served slightly different purposes, the people selected to testigos could, theoretically, be different from those selected as padrinos.

92. In San Luis Potosí, couples married endogamously and selected padrinos from within their casta at exactly the same rate. In Mexico City, on the other hand, rates fluctuated over time, but marriage patterns do not hide the importance of the Afro-Mexican community to slaves to same degree as they do in Guanajuato.

93. ABCG, libro de matrimonios de todas calidades, libro 1, 1669–83.

94. A perplexing pattern within testigo choice emerges in Mexico City in the last sample from the Ramo de Matrimonios for the period 1720–49. In that period, the overall importance of Spaniards as testigos for slaves increased significantly. Spaniards represented 36 percent of all testigos for slaves between 1720 and 1749, compared to only 15 percent between 1690 and 1719. From another perspective, while forty-five of sixty-two slave marriages

between 1720 and 1749 included at least one Afro-Mexican testigo, forty included at least one Spaniard. Yet, slave masters almost never served as a testigo for their own slaves. I found only two examples of masters serving as testigos for their own slaves within the total sample, and both took place prior to 1675. See AGN, Matrimonios, vol. 31, exp. 90, fs. 389–90, exp. 34, fs. 162–64. The causes for this trend are not entirely clear, but it does mirror the increasing importance of Spanish godparents to slaves baptized in Guanajuato and San Luis Potosí in the eighteenth century. See Proctor, "La familia y comunidad esclava en San Luis Potosí y Guanajuato, México," 240–41. Perhaps the Afro-Mexican community was well established by that point, and slaves were seeking patrons from within the white population. On the other hand, a shift may have occurred in which the social status of the testigo, inherently higher in Spaniards, became more important for slaves who sought to marry.

95. Cope found that 119 of 359 (33 percent) black and mulatto men who married were slaves while 214 of 451 (48 percent) women were slaves (*The Limits of Racial Domination*, 83).

96. Cope, *The Limits of Racial Domination*, 79; Rust and Seed, "Equality of Endogamy," 63–65.

97. One might suggest that the castizo and mestizo groups could be combined as well. That is a question for another study, but on the face of it, the connections between the two do not appear as pronounced as those between blacks and mulattos.

CHAPTER 3

1. AGN, Inquisición, vol. 899, exp. 1, fs. 1–17.

2. Aguirre Beltrán, *Medicina y magia*, 253, 256; Behar, "Sex and Sin, Witchcraft and the Devil in Late-Colonial Mexico" 48; Quezada, *Enfermedad y maleficio*, 11, 121.

3. For example, practices like ventriloquism and beliefs like that in spirit possession are traced to African roots (Aguirre Beltrán, *Medicina y magia*, 59–74; Alberro, *Inquisición y sociedad en México*, 297–307; Few, *Women Who Live Evil Lives*, 71–74).

4. Bristol, *Christians, Blasphemers, and Witches*, 149–90. However, Bristol is more interested in witchcraft as an alternative form of authority and power for Afro-Mexican practitioners than she is in it as a means of exploring distinctive variations of colonial culture based in racial identities.

5. Lewis, *Hall of Mirrors*, 150, 174.

6. A comparison of indigenous healing practices with those of their Afro-Mexican, European, and racially mixed counterparts is difficult because

Indians were classified as neophytes and therefore were not subject to the Inquisition. A separate institution known as the Provisorato, or Holy Inquisition of the Indians, was established to hear their religious transgressions. For a discussion of the Provisorato, see Moreno de los Arcos, "New Spain's Inquisition for Indians from the Sixteenth to the Nineteenth Century; Greenleaf, "The Inquisition and the Indians of New Spain." Serge Gruzinski has provided some excellent studies that deal with issues surrounding indigenous healing and magical practices during the colonial period. See *The Conquest of Mexico* and *Man-Gods in the Mexican Highlands*.

7. The temporal focus of this chapter deserves mention. My book in general focuses on the experiences of slaves following the close of the slave trade through the 1760s. This chapter, however, looks at curanderismo over the course of the entire eighteenth century in order to explore the cosmological visions of Afro-Mexicans after creoles and free people of color achieved majority status.

8. Few, *Women Who Live Evil Lives*, 17. Also see Palmer, *Slaves of the White God*, 154.

9. Bristol, *Christians, Blasphemers, and Witches*, 150–51.

10. Delgado, *Concepto y práctica medicinal en el México precortesiano*, 4.

11. Andrews and Hassig, introduction, 29–30.

12. Aguirre Beltrán, *Medicina y magia*, 48–50.

13. Laura Lewis argues that brujería in colonial Mexico was an amalgamation of "flying" by witches and *nagualismo*—using an animal double or turning into a cat, dog, or other animal. See *Hall of Mirrors*, 202n152.

14. For definitions of brujería and hechicería, see Alberro, *Inquisición y sociedad en México*, 297; Ceballos Gómez, *Hechicería, brujería e Inquisición en el Nuevo Reino de Granada*, 84–87; Henningsen, *The Witches' Advocate*, 10–11. Maleficio was understood as the wound the bruja/brujo gave to his/her victim as a result of an explicit pact with the devil. For the definition of maleficio, see Aguirre Beltrán, *Medicina y magia*. Many of these works base their definitions on the ethnographic work on the Azande of Africa by E. Evans-Pritchard. According to Evans-Pritchard, witchcraft, or brujería, represents an "impossible" act while sorcery, or hechicería, represents both a symbolic and real act owing to the material objects employed in it. I am uncomfortable with the "impossible"/"real" distinction because it prioritizes modern over contemporary conceptions of witchcraft. See Evans-Pritchard, "Witchcraft." If the practitioner, the client, and the victim of magic believed in its efficacy, be it brujería or hechicería, then it should be treated as real. For similar conclusions, see Knab, *La guerra de los brujos de la sierra de Puebla*, 7.

15. Divination is a ritualistic action in which supernatural forces are consulted to answer questions regarding occurrences in the natural world. In Nahua, West

Central African, and colonial Mexican cultures divination was employed to discover the cause of illness, tell the future, and locate lost or stolen items.

16. During the sixteenth and seventeenth centuries in Spain, theologians began to refute the reality and efficacy of brujería, and by the end of the seventeenth century in Mexico, inquisitors began to pay less and less attention to accusations of demonic pacts. See Ceballos Gómez, *Hechicería, brujería e Inquisición en el Nuevo Reino de Granada*, 89; Cervantes, *The Devil in the New World*, 136–38; Henningsen, *The Witches' Advocate*, 387–93.

17. Andrews and Hassig, introduction, 31; Aguirre Beltrán, *Medicina y magia*, 29–34; Ceballos Gómez, *Hechicería, brujería e Inquisición en el Nuevo Reino de Granada*, 68–78.

18. Hernández Sáenz, *Learning to Heal*, 43. Also see Lanning, *The Royal Protomedicato*, 334.

19. O'Neil, "Magical Healing, Love Magic and the Inquisition in Late Sixteenth-Century Modena," 91. Also see Christian, *Apparitions in Late Medieval and Renaissance Spain*; Christian, *Local Religion in Sixteenth-Century Spain*, 93–105.

20. MacGaffey, *Religion and Society in Central Africa*, 7.

21. Gruzinski, *The Conquest of Mexico*, 173; Gutiérrez, *When Jesus Came the Corn Mothers Went Away*, 32; Janzen, *Lemba*, 13.

22. Risse, "Medicine in New Spain," 13–14.

23. Gruzinski, *The Conquest of Mexico*, 177–78.

24. Joan Bristol makes a similar point; see *Christians, Blasphemers, and Witches*, 156.

25. For a discussion of traditional medicine in Spain, see Perry, *Gender and Disorder in Early Modern Seville*, 21–23.

26. AGN, Inquisición, vol. 826, exp. 43, fs. 432–46, vol. 1028, exp. 7, fs. 243–45.

27. Poole, *Our Lady of Guadalupe*, 26–7; Taylor, "The Virgin of Guadalupe in New Spain." Kevin Gosner traces the origin of a large-scale Maya revolt in the highlands of Chiapas to the repression of a cult based on a Marian apparition (*Soldiers of the Virgin*).

28. AGN, Inquisición, vol. 790, exp. 3, fs. 288–89, vol. 1210, exp. 4, f. 50.

29. O'Neil, "Magical Healing, Love Magic and the Inquisition in Late Sixteenth-Century Modena," 91.

30. AGN, Inquisición, vol. 1302, exp. 7, fs. 14–15. Rather than punish Juan Manuel for the use of herbs, the Inquisition admonished the secular priests of the pueblos where he prescribed them to redouble their efforts to eradicate idolatry and superstition among the Indians.

31. Juan Manuel was also said to have cured Alberto Martín, an Indian, with the following ceremony, which was clearly related to indigenous practices. Manuel ground fifteen ears of corn before mixing it with water in a gourd.

He placed a burning piece of cotton in the mixture and surrounded the gourd with burning candles. Then he made fifteen tortillas, which he claimed would allow Alberto to live for fifteen years. Juan Manuel then "sucked the sickness" through Alberto's navel with his mouth.

32. AGN, Inquisición, vol. 767, exp. 33, fs. 498–534. The inquisitors were unsure if Juana was a Spaniard or a mestizo, and she escaped before they could question her.

33. AGN, Inquisición, vol. 1300, exp. 12, fs. 192–93.

34. AGN, Inquisición, vol. 1210, exp. 4, fs. 49–65, vol. 1235, exp. 1, fs. 1–187.

35. AGN, Inquisición, vol. 1300, exp. 12, fs. 355–58, vol. 767, exp. 33, fs. 498–534.

36. AGN, Inquisición, vol. 1210, exp. 4, f. 50.

37. For more information on Mexico's boticas, see Hernández Sáenz, *Learning to Heal*, 129–78. For testimony regarding the Virgin, see the testimony of Antonio Valdés, AGN, Inquisición, vol. 1210, exp. 4, fs. 49–65. Among the herbs that he prescribed were laurel, rosemary, *yolochiltique* (perhaps *yolloxochitl*), *marrubio* (horehound), *calaneapatle* (ragwort), *chiquihuite* (*chichiquelite*, or sarsaparilla), *sanquinaria*, *saupalte*, *coeniza* (or *yerba del ángel*), and *tabaco cimarrón*. Similarly, María Tiburcia Reinantes used a wide variety of medicines in her cures. However, one of the most common was an enema made of the leaf of holy palm, a little soap, some ground mammal bone, and *yerba blanca*. See AGN, Inquisición, vol. 1300, exp. 12, f. 355.

38. AGN, Inquisición, vol. 1235, exp. 1, f. 28.

39. AGN, Inquisición, vol. 1210, exp. 4, fs. 50–51. For similar claims about crying in the womb, see AGN, Inquisición, vol. 790, exp. 3, fs. 272–345, vol. 333, exp. 50.

40. It is still believed today that crying in the womb is evidence a child will become a curandero; see Perrone, Stockel, and Krueger, *Medicine Women, "Curanderas," and Women Doctors*, 92.

41. AGN, Inquisición, vol. 1300, exp. 12, f. 202.

42. Craemer et al., "Religious Movements in Central Africa," 458–61.

43. MacGaffey, *Religion and Society in Central Africa*, 196–97. For the argument that West Central African beliefs and practices persisted in Brazil, see Karasch, "Central African Religious Tradition"; Karasch, *Slave Life in Rio de Janeiro*, 255–301; Slenes, "*Malungu, ngoma vem*," 48–67; Sweet, *Recreating Africa*.

44. AGN, Inquisición, vol. 1189, exp. 34, fs. 347–52, 362, vol. 1150, exp. 10, fs. 135–310.

45. Hernando Ruiz de Alarcón cited one occasion when an indigenous curandero used "cupping glasses" filled with cotton, which was then lit on fire to suck the illness from a diseased person (*Treatise*, 175–76). Similarly, Mary Karasch found that the use of cupping glasses was common among healers of West

Central African heritage in Rio de Janeiro (*Slave Life in Rio de Janeiro*, 264–65).

46. Tobacco, in the form of smoke or as an ingredient in medicines and ointments, was considered to a very strong detergent and deterrent against witchcraft (Aguirre Beltrán, *Medicina y magia*, 124–26).

47. AGN, Inquisición, vol. 1189, exp. 34, fs. 347–57, 362, vol. 1150, exp. 10, fs. 135–310. For other Afro-Mexicans who lightly beat their patients, see the cases of María de la Concepción (AGN, Inquisición, vol. 844, exp. 6, fs. 481–543) and Nicolás Candelario de Vargas (AGN, Inquisición, vol. 894, fs. 88–263).

48. For similar practices, see the case against Julián, a mulatto curer from Fresnillo. While preparing to sleep in the home of one of his patients, Julián stuck his knife in the floor at the head of his bedroll and then sprinkled the knife with water, placed an extinguished candle next to it, and sprinkled it with water again. Then he sprayed the walls and floor with water from his mouth before lying down to sleep (AGN, Inquisición, vol. 781, exp. 30, fs. 310–12; also see Aguirre Beltrán, *Medicina y magia*, 187–88).

49. María de la Concepción admitted in her initial testimony that she did not actually remove the cactus spine from Francisco's head. Rather, she found the needle in his hair and then stuck it in his head to give the impression that she had removed it. María faked this because, as she testified, she wanted to impress on Francisco the severity of his condition and the strength of the magic that had been used against him. See AGN, Inquisición, vol. 844, exp. 6, fs. 491–94.

50. Aguirre Beltrán reports that ololiuhqui was a powerful medicine in indigenous systems (*Medicina y magia*, 126–33).

51. Smoke was considered a powerful cleansing and prophylactic agent against witchcraft in African and indigenous societies. The specific use of tobacco and copal, ingredients local to New Spain, likely derived from indigenous practices.

52. AGN, Inquisición, vol. 790, exp. 3, fs. 272–345.

53. AGN, Inquisición, vol. 790, exp. 3, f. 285. According to Aguirre Beltrán peyote had both masculine and feminine manifestations in Nahua cosmology and medicine. He speculates that the feminine form of peyote may refer to the flower of the *peyotl* cactus, while the masculine form may refer to the root. At any rate, in the postcolonial period, the masculine form of peyote became associated with Saint Nicolas, Saint Anthony, and Saint Michael. Similarly, the feminine form was associated with the Virgin Mary and was called Rosa Santa María, Rosa María, Santa María, yerba Santa María, Santa María de peyote, and Nuestra Señora. See Aguirre Beltrán, *Medicina y magia*, 142. Numerous Afro-Mexican curers admitted to using Rosa de Santa

María, most often called simply Rosa María, in their cures. See the cases of Sebastián Hernández (AGN, Inquisición, vol. 781, exp. 54, fs. 609–644); María de la Concepción (AGN, Inquisición, vol. 844, exp. 6, fs. 481–543); Nicolás Candelario de Vargas (AGN, Inquisición, vol. 894, fs. 88–263); Diego Barajas and Juan Ramírez (AGN, Inquisición, vol. 826, exp. 8, fs. 198–212). The only non-Afro-Mexicans encountered in this study who employed Rosa María and peyote were two Indians. In one of those cases the Indian, named María Magdalena, was the curing partner of the mulatto Nicolás Candelario de Vargas just mentioned; see AGN, Inquisición, vol. 894, fs. 22–263. The other, Roque de los Santos, was the curing partner of Manuela Riberos, a mestiza; see AGN, Inquisición, vol. 848, exp. 1, fs. 1–61. In many of these cases as well as in others I discuss, the herb was specifically associated with different religious images of the Virgin Mary.

54. AGN, Inquisición, vol. 790, exp. 3, fs. 282–83, 288–89.

55. For other Afro-Mexicans who claimed to suck the illness from their patients, see the cases of Juan Pavón (AGN, Inquisición, vol. 899, fs. 1–17); José Quinerio Cisneros (AGN, Inquisición, vol. 1189, fs. 345–57, 362, vol. 1150, exp. 10, fs. 135–310); Juan Luis (AGN, Inquisición, vol. 1111, exp. 57, fs. 448–58); María de la Concepción (AGN, Inquisición, vol. 844, exp. 6, fs. 481–543).

56. AGN, Inquisición, vol. 781, exp. 54, fs. 610–20, 627–30.

57. Aguirre Beltrán, *Medicina y magia*, 121–23, 138. San Nicolás Tolentino may have held a particularly important place in Afro-Mexican cosmology. The first black and mulatto confraternity established in Mexico was named in his honor in 1560 (Chávez Carbajal, "La gran negritud en Michoacán," 120).

58. Roque de los Santos, an Indian, also sang to invoke the Virgin Mary. He testified that he sang the following after prescribing the herb Rosa María to one of his patients, "How beautiful that the Rosa María comes, how beautiful that she comes, how beautiful that she and these others are coming, how beautiful that she comes, that she comes, how beautiful that Our Lady of Solitude is going." See AGN, Inquisición, vol. 848, exp. 1, fs. 12–13.

59. The author wishes to thank Kay Reed and Jane Rosenthal from the Religious Studies Department at DePaul University for their assistance in translating these verses. Any errors that remain in the translation are my own.

60. Sebastián provides a very interesting case study. Recall that Sebastián was a slave in the Hospital de San Juan de Dios in Zacatecas and therefore could have witnessed European/Catholic medicinal practices in action. Furthermore, he testified that he had learned to cure from an Indian. In both cases, his apprenticeship in curing would have represented the incorporation of indigenous and Catholic healing knowledge into an Afro-Mexican cosmology rather than a process through which he came to acquire a full

understanding of the cultures from which the materials, symbols, and beliefs originated.

61. AGN, Inquisición, vol. 781, exp. 54, fs. 637–40.

62. For the two cases that do not mention ritual purification, see Pedro Astacio (AGN, Inquisición, vol. 800, exp. 14, fs. 335–65); Diego Barajas (AGN, Inquisición, vol. 826, exp. 8, fs. 198–212).

63. Janzen, *Ngoma*, 64. For BaKongo practice in Brazil, see Karasch, *Slave Life in Rio de Janeiro*, 264–65. Similarly, one of the four professional offices of Nahua doctors was the *techichinani* (*chupador* or sucker) (Aguirre Beltrán, *Medicina y magia*, 56–58).

64. AGN, Inquisición, vol. 781, exp. 54, f. 640.

65. José Antonio Hernández and Juan Manuel Sánchez, both Spaniards, also claimed to have sucked illness and/or witchcraft from their patients. However, Juan and José made use of that practice in only one of the many cures attributed to each. Afro-Mexican curers, by contrast, undertook the symbolic action of removing foreign objects from a patient's body in numerous cures. See AGN, Inquisición, vol. 1210, exp. 4, vol. 1302, exp. 7.

66. Smoke appears to have continued to play a central role in indigenous/mestizo curanderismo. For example, see the case of María de Escobar, a mestiza (AGN, Inquisición, vol. 767, exp. 30, fs. 465–91), and the case of Roque de los Santos, an Indian (AGN, Inquisición, vol. 848, exp. 1, fs. 1–61). Roque had the witnesses of one of his cures smoke cigars and blow the smoke on the patient to counteract the witchcraft attacking her.

67. Aguirre Beltrán, *Medicina y magia*, 187–88.

68. Craemer et al., "Religious Movements in Central Africa," 469.

69. MacGaffey, *Religion and Society in Central Africa*, 142–45.

70. Janzen, *Lemba*, 197.

71. Bristol, *Christians, Blasphemers, and Witches*, 156. The physician Juan Esteynoffer (Steinhoffer) published a popular treatise on healing entitled *Florilegio medicinal*.

72. Aguirre Beltrán, *Medicina y magia*, 59–74. Aguirre based his conclusions on the writings of Melville Herskovits under whom he studied at the University of Chicago. However, Herskovits's works focus on Afro-American cultural formations that are based on a different African cultural foundation than that in Mexico. Haitian voodoo and Bahian *candomblé* are dominated by syncretic worship of *orishas* and *voduns* (deities) that were derived from the cultures of the Bight of Benin, not West Central Africa.

73. Karasch, "Central African Religious Tradition," 233–53; Karasch, *Slave Life in Rio de Janeiro*, 255–301. Karasch argues that West Central Africans in Rio de Janeiro did not convert to Catholicism or establish a syncretism between African gods and the European cult of the saints. Rather, they played an active

role in the creation of a new religious traditions based on the West Central African cultural foundation that I have been discussing in this chapter. That religious tradition included not only Catholic elements but also Dahomian/ Yoruba cultural elements characteristic of candomblé in Bahia.

74. For a discussion of West Central African, or Kongolese, Christianity in the Portuguese Atlantic world, see Sweet, *Recreating Africa*, 106–15.

75. For a discussion of the spread of Christianity throughout the region, see Thornton, "Religious and Ceremonial Life in Kongo and Mbundu Areas," 83–90. Thornton argues that Central African Christians could be found throughout the region, although conversion rates were not as high among them as among the Kongo.

76. Thornton, "The Development of an African Catholic Church in the Kingdom of Kongo," 151; Thornton, *The Kongolese Saint Anthony*, esp. ch 1.

77. Fetishes were important throughout Central Africa. In Loango, north of Kongo, fetishes were also called *nkisi*, while in the Kimbundu speaking areas south of Kongo they were known as *kiteke*. In each respective region the same term also referred to temples or shrines. See Thornton, "Religious and Ceremonial Life in Kongo and Mbundu Areas," 80; Vansina, *Kingdoms of the Savanna*, 31.

78. Frey and Wood, *Come Shouting to Zion*, 19; Hinton, *The Kingdom of Kongo*, 102, 184–85; Thornton, "The Development of an African Catholic Church in the Kingdom of Kongo," 157.

79. MacGaffey, *Art and Healing of the Bakongo*, 4–5, 33.

80. Craemer et al., "Religious Movements in Central Africa," 470; Janzen, *Ngoma*, 69, 142. Janzen found that particular musical instruments were associated with particular therapeutic rituals.

81. AGN, Inquisición, vol. 894, fs. 171, 193. Diego Barajas, a mulatto, also used music when he prescribed peyote and Rosa María. See AGN, Inquisición, vol. 826, exp. 8, fs. 198–212.

82. Interestingly, the single non-Afro-Mexican curing ceremony that included many of these elements was performed by an Indian named Roque de los Santos. He built an altar to Jesus and Saint Cayetano and two lit candles. He placed Rosa María and peyote on the altar that he perfumed in copal smoke. Then he gave his patient the herbs mixed in water to drink. He and the witnesses then smoked cigars and blew the smoke on the sick woman to counteract the witchcraft from which she suffered. He also sucked her palms so that the illness would pass from her to him. It is not surprising to find such consonance, for at least two reasons. First, indigenous and West Central Africans shared similar understandings of magic, curing, and illness. And second, magic continued to play a central role in the cosmological visions of both communities in the colonial context.

83. All denunciations and trials before the Mexican Inquisition are listed in the index for the Ramo de Inquisición. Using that index, I compiled a database of 279 accusations of witchcraft and curing during the eighteenth century that includes the year of the trial, the name of the accused, their crime(s), their sex, and their race. See table 3.1A in the appendix to this book.

84. Alberro, *Inquisición y sociedad en México*, 586; Ceballos Gómez, *Hechicería, brujería e Inquisición en el Nuevo Reino de Granada*, 85–86; Bristol, *Christians, Blasphemers, and Witches*, 172.

CHAPTER 4

1. AGN, Inquisición, vol. 531, exp. 73, fs. 591–602.

2. For a general discussion of blasphemy in colonial Mexico, see Villa-Flores, *Dangerous Speech*.

3. Bristol, "Negotiating Authority in New Spain," 170. Also see Tausig, *The Devil and Commodity Fetishism in South America*, 41–44. Blasphemy, some hypothesize, might have reflected a slave's rejection of the Christian ideology that justified his or her subjugation with the promise of redemption in the afterlife. Or the slave may have conferred onto the Christian god the same qualities that he or she gave to his master. Thus, a god who failed to protect even a slave was not fulfilling the role ascribed to it and therefore could be denounced. See Alberro, *Inquisición y sociedad en México*, 463; Palmer, *Slaves of the White God*, 152–53.

4. For studies that treat blasphemy as resistance, see Bristol, *Christians, Blasphemers, and Witches*, 116–17; McKnight, "Blasphemy as Resistance," 231; Villa-Flores, "To Lose One's Soul," 468.

5. An important question that speaks to intentionality and has yet to be adequately addressed in the historiography concerns how common this language was in New Spain. Were those few persons brought before the Inquisition as blasphemers exceptional in their use of such language, or do these cases speak to a larger issue in which blasphemous phrases were part of the vernacular? In at least one case of a slave blasphemer, witnesses testified that the accused commonly used phrases such as "by Jesus' entrails" (*por la entrañas del Cristo*), "by the Virgin's entrails" (*por las entrañas de la Virgen*), "by the baptism of God" (*por el bautismo de Dios*), and "by the Virgin's birth" (*por el parto de la Virgen*). This might suggest that blasphemy was more a part of the vernacular than previously assumed. See AGN, Inquisición, vol. 583, exp. 4, f. 407.

6. Genovese, *Roll, Jordan, Roll*, 598; Gorender, *A escravidão reabilitada*, 20. James Scott also argues that the attempts to define resistance reduce its effectiveness as an analytical tool (*Weapons of the Weak*, 291–93).

7. Morgan, *Slave Counterpoint*, xxii. For similar arguments, see Foner, "Review Essay"; Johnson, "On Agency," 116.

8. Lears, "The Concept of Cultural Hegemony," 573.

9. These instances of short-term flight, treated as mild protests against master power, are considered in depth in chapter 5.

10. AGN, Inquisición, vol. 586, exp. 6, fs. 375–76.

11. AGN, Inquisición, vol. 586, exp. 6, fs. 386–88.

12. AGN, Inquisición, vol. 586, exp. 6, fs. 373–410. Antonio was eventually sentenced to fifty lashes and two years service in an obraje for his transgressions.

13. AGN, Inquisición, vol. 464, exp. 6, f. 105.

14. AGN, Inquisición, vol. 464, exp. 6, fs. 103–48. Interestingly, one of the Indians working in the panadería offered Juanillo an unnamed root to dull the pain from the beating he was about to receive.

15. AGN, Inquisición, vol. 689, exp. 39, fs. 447–68. For another example, see AGN, Inquisición, vol. 438, exp. 7, fs. 285–89.

16. AGN, Inquisición, vol. 571, exp. 2, fs. 54–85. Villa-Flores argues that when slaves threatened to blaspheme prior to punishment they were actually transferring blame for the offense from themselves to their masters. In doing so, he suggests, slaves undertook an inversion of the colonial discourse that justified slavery by predicating the Christian salvation of African souls on the servitude of their bodies. In proceeding with the beating in the face of such a threat, he suggests, masters shouldered part of the responsibility for the sin of blasphemy, at least in the eyes of slaves, if not in those of the master and the Inquisition ("Defending God's Honor," 198). It should be noted, however, that the Inquisition never took action against a slave owner for causing a slave to blaspheme. In the eyes of the inquisitors, fault lay with the slave in question.

17. Their ability to do so undermines Scott's conception of public and private transcripts that made such public complaints by subordinate groups unlikely if not impossible (*Domination and the Arts of Resistance*, 5–6, 208–9).

18. AGN, Inquisición, vol. 1551, exp. 46, f. 617.

19. AGN, Inquisición, vol. 1551, exp. 46, fs. 614–25.

20. AGN, Inquisición, vol. 441, exp. 5, f. 535.

21. AGN, Inquisición, vol. 441, exp. 5, f. 505.

22. AGN, Inquisición, vol. 605, exp. 8, fs. 404–27.

23. AGN, Inquisición, vol. 526, exp. 27, fs. 594–605.

24. HL, Mexican Inquisition Papers, 1525–1822, no. 35131, vol. 37.

25. AGN, Inquisición, vol. 583, exp. 4, f. 407.

26. HL, Mexican Inquisition Papers, 1525–1822, no. 35131, vol. 37.

27. O'Gorman, "El trabajo industrial en la Nueva España a mediados del siglo XVII," 62.

28. HL, Mexican Inquisition Papers, 1525–1822, no. 35131, vol. 37, f. 27.
29. HL, Mexican Inquisition Papers, 1525–1822, no. 35131, vol. 37, fs. 15–17.
30. AGN, Inquisición, vol. 454, exp. 21, fs. 445–54.
31. AGN, Inquisición, vol. 441, exp. 5, fs. 503–42.
32. AGN, Inquisición, vol. 584, exp. 14, fs. 394–416.
33. AGN, Inquisición, vol. 605, exp. 11, fs. 451–73.
34. This conception owes in large part to the powerful effects of Frank Tannenbaum's arguments in his seminal *Slave and Citizen*.
35. *Las Siete Partidas*, 4.21.6.
36. "Ordenanzas acerca de la orden que se ha de tener en el tratamiento con los negros para la conservación de la política que han de tener (ca. 1545)," in Konetzke, *Colección de documentos*, 2:237–40. The ordinance reads "que todos los señores de negros tengan cuidado de hacer buen tratamiento a sus esclavos . . . no castigalles con crueldades, ni ponelles las manos, sin evidente razón, y que no puedan cortalles miembro ni lisiados."
37. "Instrucción sobre la educación, trato y ocupación de los esclavos," in Konetzke, *Colección de documentos*, 3:643–52.
38. Salmoral, *Los códigos negros de la América Española*, 119–21.
39. AGN, Inquisición, vol. 583, exp. 4, fs. 390–519.
40. Alejandro de la Fuente has found that the practice of "burning with different types of resins" was defined as abusive in Cuba in 1574 ("Slaves and the Creation of Legal Rights in Cuba," 670). Authorities in New Spain never pointed directly to that practice when assessing if a master was abusing his slaves or not.
41. Afro-Mexican slaves rarely fell within the jurisdiction of the General Indian Court in Mexico City, overseen by the viceroy, which served as the court of first instance for all civil and criminal cases initiated by Indians, even those involving non-Indian defendants, within the environs of the capital city. It also functioned as the appeals court for similar cases initiated outside that jurisdiction. See Borah, *Justice by Insurance*.
42. Lewis, *Hall of Mirrors*, 36–37.
43. As I note in chapter 3, the Provisorato was established to hear the religious transgressions of Indians (Greenleaf, "The Inquisition and the Indians of New Spain," 138–40). Also see Morena de los Arcos, "New Spain's Inquisition for Indians from the Sixteenth to the Nineteenth Century," 23–36. In theory, while actual control over Indian orthodoxy fell under episcopal authority in the form of the care of a provisor or vicar general, the Inquisition served as the fact-finding agency in cases regarding indigenous religiosity.
44. AGN, Inquisición, vol. 520, exp. 237, fs. 411–37.
45. Bristol, *Christians, Blasphemers, and Witches*, 245n9. Bristol uses Steve Stern's notion of "pluralizing patriarchs" to describe this process. We must try to

ascertain whether the slave's goal was to appear before the Inquisition or if the appearance was merely a repercussion of the act itself. Purposeful intentionality is significant when discussing these cases. Herman Bennett also argues that Afro-Mexicans developed a "heightened strategic consciousness" that allowed them to use colonial institutions and discourses to their advantage in ways the Spanish never imagined (*Africans in Colonial Mexico*, 193). Also see Stern, *The Secret History of Gender*, 99–103.

46. For a similar understanding of criminal cases, see Stern, *The Secret History of Gender*, 66.

47. Also see Gudmundson, "Negotiating Rights under Slavery"; Schwartz, "Resistance and Accommodation in Eighteenth-Century Brazil."

48. AGN, Inquisición, vol. 735, exp. 31, fs. 389–411.

49. AGN, Inquisición, vol. 735, exp. 31, fs. 389–411.

50. AGN, Inquisición, vol. 418, exp. 4, f. 339.

51. AGN, Inquisición, vol. 418, exp. 4, f. 333.

52. AGN, Inquisición, vol. 418, exp. 4, f. 363.

53. AGN, Inquisición, vol. 418, exp. 4, fs. 320–64. In a letter received by inquisitors on June 13, 1642, Ortega accused his slave Antonio of stealing over six thousands pesos on various occasions (f. 346).

54. AGN, Inquisición, vol. 454, exp. 14, fs. 253–92. For a more detailed discussion of Juan's case, see Alberro, "Juan de Morga and Gertrudis de Escobar."

55. AGN, Inquisición, vol. 454, exp. 14, fs. 270.

56. AGN, Inquisición, vol. 454, exp. 14, fs. 262–70.

57. AGN, Inquisición, vol. 572, exp. 13, fs. 187–214.

58. AGN, Inquisición, vol. 629, exp. 6, f. 514.

59. AGN, Inquisición, vol. 629, exp. 6, f. 517.

60. Equally important, both Juana's and Nicolás's cases involved violence against slaves by mistresses, potentially undermining the conception that women lacked equal access to coercive methods of social control as men, primarily physical and sexual violence. See Higgins, *"Licentious Liberty" in a Brazilian Gold-Mining Region*, 171, and Whitman, "Diverse Good Causes," 346, for the suggestion that women had less access to physical violence.

61. Only in thirteen of the sixty-four cases that describe what occurred after the blasphemy did masters stop beating their offending slave. In the other fifty-one masters continued to punish the slave, even intensifying the beating in a number of cases (Villa-Flores, "Defending God's Honor," 222).

62. AGN, Inquisición, vol. 477, exp. 23, fs. 238–55.

63. HL, Mexican Inquisition Papers, 1525–1822, no. 35131, vol. 37, f. 5.

64. Joan Bristol reports that of the thirty-eight slaves convicted of blasphemy by the Mexican Inquisition in the seventeenth century, eleven received one

hundred lashes and eleven received two hundred lashes as part of their official punishment (*Christians, Blasphemers, and Witches*, 245n18).

65. Barry Higman notes the "propensity" of African slaves to run away when compared to creole slaves (*Slave Populations and Economy in Jamaica*, 386–93). Similarly, Africans were much more rebellious than creoles for much of the history of slavery in the Americas. Nearer the end of slavery, however, historians highlight the importance of creole slaves as leaders in slave rebellions. See Genovese, *From Rebellion to Revolution*, 18–21.

66. The differences between the myriad forms of African slavery and slavery in the Americas were significant. The racialized nature of slavery in the Americas, economies based solely on monocrop agriculture and slave labor, the higher levels of violence and workloads slaves faced in monocrop production, and, the greater social distance between masters and slaves may have all been unexpected to Africans. See Lovejoy, and Trotman, "Experiencias de vida y expectativas." Furthermore, historians have taken great pains to connect specific instances of African rebelliousness in the Americas to historical processes in Africa. For example, see Kea, "When I die, I shall return to my own land," 160; Lovejoy, "Background to Rebellion"; Thornton, "African Dimensions of the Stono Rebellion."

67. Reis, *Slave Rebellion in Brazil*, 142; Wyatt-Brown, "The Mask of Obedience," 1232.

68. AGN, Inquisición, vol. 530, exp. 16, fs. 293–96.

69. AGN, Inquisición, vol. 530, exp. 16, fs. 293–96.

70. AGN, Inquisición, vol. 604, exp. 16, fs. 58–63.

71. AGN, Inquisición, vol. 765, exp. 15, fs. 182–97, quoted in Behar, "Sexual Witchcraft, Colonialism, and Women's Powers," 195–98.

72. AGN, Inquisición, vol. 561, exp. 1, fs. 1–22.

73. AGN, Inquisición, vol. 520, exp. 2, fs. 2–3.

74. AGN, Inquisición, vol. 444, exp. 4, fs. 431–75.

75. Behar, "Sex and Sin, Witchcraft and the Devil in Late-Colonial Mexico," 34–53; Stern, *The Secret History of Gender*, 108.

CHAPTER 5

1. AGN, Tierras, vol. 3543, exp. 1, f. 58.

2. Palenques were common throughout the colony. At least one other runaway community successfully entered into a series of negotiations with the state, which eventually granted the resident runaways their freedom and the right to establish the free town of San Lorenzo de los Negros. For a discussion of the San Lorenzo palenque, see Proctor, "Slave Rebellion and Liberty in Colonial Mexico," 24–27.

3. Carroll, "Mandinga," 494. Also see AGN, Tierras, vol. 3543, exp. 1–3; Carroll and Reyes, "Amapa, Oaxaca"; Taylor, "The Foundation of Nuestra Señora de Guadalupe de los Morenos de Amapa." Taylor includes a translated copy of the introduction to the baptismal book of Amapa (which is housed in the manuscript collection of the Zimmerman Library, University of New Mexico) recounting the founding of the pueblo.

4. Taylor, "The Foundation of Nuestra Señora de Guadalupe de los Morenos de Amapa," 443; Carroll, "Mandinga," 497.

5. David Geggus finds that this type of rumor of "unfulfilled emancipation" was quite common in the late eighteenth- and early nineteenth-century Caribbean. In fact, he argues that such rumors were implicated in twenty slave revolts from 1789–1832 in the Caribbean and as far away as upper Peru ("The Bois Caïman Ceremony," 250n19).

6. AGN, Tierras, vol. 3543, exp. 1, fs. 67, 78.

7. AMC, vol. 21, año 1735, fs. 3–5, quoted in Naveda Chávez-Hita, *Esclavos negros en las haciendas azucareras de Córdoba*, 133. Also see Carroll, *Blacks in Colonial Veracruz*, 97, who reports that as many as two thousand slaves participated in this uprising.

8. AGN, Tierras, vol. 3543, exp. 1, fs. 77–78.

9. Taylor, "The Foundation of Nuestra Señora de Guadalupe de los Morenos de Amapa," 444.

10. This number included the fifty-two listed in Mandinga as well as seventeen others who had been turned over to local authorities to be returned to their masters. See AGN, Tierras, vol. 3543, exp. 1, fs. 7, 111.

11. AGN, Tierras, vol. 3543, exp. 1, f. 111. Among the seventeen returned to their masters were three married couples, two single women, and two children.

12. AGN, Tierras, vol. 3543, exp. 2, f. 126. The followers of Yanga, who eventually established the free town of San Lorenzo de los Negros, offered a very similar set of proposals when applying for free status in 1608. See Proctor, "Slave Rebellion and Liberty in Colonial Mexico," 24.

13. AGN, Tierras, vol. 3543, exp. 2, fs. 29–30.

14. Taylor, "The Foundation of Nuestra Señora de Guadalupe de los Morenos de Amapa," 443.

15. Aguirre, *Agentes de su propia libertad*; Chalhoub, *Visões de liberdade*.

16. The origins of the debate lie with Eugene Genovese, who argues that the age of Atlantic revolutions (1775–1815) marks an important shift in the nature and goals of slave rebellion from escapist to revolutionary, when Afro-American slave revolts and maroon movements merged with the trans-Atlantic bourgeois-democratic revolutions of the late eighteenth century. In many ways what Genovese proposes is a transition from "pre-modern primitive rebellions" to modern revolutions (*Rebellion to Revolution*, 3,

82). Geggus warns against treating the impacts of European antislavery campaigns and the libertarian ideologies emanating out of the American, French, and Haitian revolutions as common phenomena and suggests that the former more frequently caused rebellions ("The Enigma of Jamaica in the 1790s," 299; "The Slaves and Free Colored of Martinique during the Age of the French and Haitian Revolutions," 298). For scholars who contend that "antislavery" rebellion could have emanated out of slavery itself and did not require external ideologies that the Enlightenment rhetoric of the Atlantic revolutions and abolitionism relied on, see Gaspar, *Bondsmen and Rebels*.

17. John Thornton, in his survey of slave resistance, attempts to eschew the "political/nonpolitical" debate as he isolates three levels of slave actions against owner interests: "day-to-day" resistance, *petite marronnage* (short-term flight), and *grande marronnage*, which included long-term flight, the creation of runaway communities, armed rebellions, and even revolution (*Africa and Africans in the Making of the Atlantic World*, 273). Day-to-day resistance and *petite marronnage*, on his view, were aimed at improving slaves' position within society, whereas the primary goal of *grande marronnage* was escape from the slave system. Thornton's typology complicates that of Richard Price's, which he outlines in his introduction to *Maroon Societies*.

18. Genovese, *Rebellion to Revolution*, 3, 82.

19. Gaspar, *Bondsmen and Rebels*, 172, 216, 256. Hilary Beckles asserts that the "fundamental ideological core of most West Indian slave rebellions" was slaves saying "We want to be free, and will pursue that freedom by all means necessary" (*Black Rebellion in Barbados*, 3).

20. For James Scott, rebellions represent moments when the private transcripts of oppressed groups are interjected into the public without disguise or subterfuge (*Domination and the Arts of Resistance*, 182, 224).

21. AGN, Inquisición, vol. 724, exp. 4, fs. 71–269.

22. In four other cases it is impossible to tell how the slave bigamists were separated from their first wives. In one final case, a slave woman married twice in the same city. For the three cases of slaves sold away from their spouses, see AGN, Inquisición, vol. 544, exp. 23, fs. 463–81, vol. 610, exp. 11, fs. 233–85, vol. 667, exp. 1, fs. 1–40.

23. In the remaining case, the slave in question married twice in Puebla, but she testified that she did not believe her first marriage had actually been formalized. See AGN, Inquisición, vol. 454, exp. 39, fs. 475–523. The cases included herein span the period from 1651 to 1752. Two in ten slave bigamists were black. That they were predominantly men reflects larger patterns among colonial bigamists. See Boyer, *Lives of the Bigamists*, 8.

24. For such hypotheses, see Palmer, *Slaves of the White God*, 57.

25. Before running away, half of slave bigamists were married to free women of African descent, nearly one in four were married to slave women, and the remaining were married to Indians or mestizas. Therefore, nearly three in four were married to free women, and nearly three in four were married to Afro-Mexican women. These marriage patterns are fairly consistent with those of slave men as discussed in chapter 2.

26. AGN, Inquisición, vol. 789, exp. 30, fs. 449–549.

27. However, the rate of one per two hundred may be inflated because these four censuses listed 5.9 percent of slaves as absent, compared to the general average of 3.7 percent I note in the text. Moreover, I did not include any censuses that did not include runaways in my calculations

28. AGN, Inquisición, vol. 483, exp. 7, fs. 285–89.

29. AGN, Inquisición, vol. 786, exp. 3, fs. 224–362.

30. AGN, Inquisición, vol. 802, exp. 1, fs. 1–35.

31. Bennett, *Africans in Colonial Mexico*, esp. ch. 6.

32. AGN, Inquisición, vol. 789, exp. 30, f. 472.

33. In only one case did inquisitors consider the possibility that claims of abuse by slaves might have been subterfuge to deflect their attention away from the crime of bigamy. However, in this case, the inquisitors dismissed the claims of abuse as the reason for flight, asserting instead that the slave ran away because of his desire to marry a second time, which seems unlikely from the case materials. See AGN, Inquisición, vol. 808, exp. 2, fs. 146–248.

34. AGN, Inquisición, vol. 789, exp. 30, fs. 497–99.

35. AGN, Inquisición, vol. 610, exp. 11, fs. 233–385; vol. 945, exp. 25, fs. 265–66.

36. AGN, Inquisición, vol. 439, exp. 13, fs. 65–74. Also see Boyer, *Lives of the Bigamists*, 147–48, who suggests that the two issues might be related, that Felipe's relations with his mayordomo were strained, perhaps owing to competition over his wife.

37. AGN, Inquisición, vol. 794, exp. 1, f. 2.

38. AGN, Inquisición, vol. 794, exp. 1, fs. 2–12.

39. For the third and forth examples, see AGN, Inquisición, vol. 813, fs. 59–93; vol. 911, exp. 5, fs. 39–131.

40. AGN, Inquisición, vol. 530, exp. 5, fs. 238–42.

41. AGN, Inquisición, vol. 502, exp. 5, fs. 430–51, vol. 808, exp. 2, f. 192.

42. AGN, Inquisición, vol. 865, fs. 450–62. Antonio testified before the Inquisition on April 21 and 23, 1738, but by the time the inquisitors attempted to reinterview him in January 1739, he had apparently gone mad. He was placed in the Hospital de San Hipólito, where he subsequently died. Suits like the one brought by Antonio against his owner Don Domingo de Rebellar are treated in depth in chapter 6.

43. Mentz, *Trabajo, sujeción y libertad en el centro de la Nueva España*, 382.

44. The slave population totaled 130 in 1708, 101 in 1728, and 104 in 1763. See AGN, Bienes Nacionales leg. 908, exp. 11, fs. 70–82, leg. 98, exp. 2; AGN, Tierras, vol. 1935, fs. 48–50. As I discuss in chapter 1, ingenios in central New Spain averaged sixty-eight slaves in the middle of the eighteenth century.

45. AGN, Criminal, vol. 135, exp. 56, fs. 1–21.

46. For a discussion of the 1612 slave rebellion, see Martínez, "The Black Blood of New Spain"; Proctor, "Slave Rebellion and Liberty in Colonial Mexico."

47. AGN, Criminal, vol. 135, exp. 56, f. 203.

48. Ana María was the only slave to explicitly state that the slaves' desire for a new owner motivated their flight. See AGN, Criminal, vol. 135, exp. 56, f. 213.

49. AGN, Criminal, vol. 135, exp. 56, f. 205.

50. "Real Cédula que los negros no trabajan los días de fiesta y guarden la fiesta como los cristianos (1544)," in Konetzke, Colección de documentos, 1:231.

51. AGN, Criminal, vol. 135, exp. 56, fs. 202–5.

52. AGN, Criminal, vol. 135, exp. 56, f. 205

53. AGN, Criminal, vol. 135, exp. 56, f. 213.

54. AGN, Criminal, vol. 135, exp. 56, fs. 203, 209.

55. AGN, Criminal, vol. 135, exp. 56, fs. 203, 209. While it seems hard to believe that slave owners might kill, or allow their mayordomo to kill, a number of their slaves, a letter written by Don Manuel suggests that he was responsible for the significantly increased levels of coercion on the hacienda.

56. Painter, "Soul Murder and Slavery," 133. Painter suggests that slave parents employed violence against their children to impress that particular reality of slave life on them.

57. AGN, Criminal, vol. 135, exp. 56, fs. 202, 213.

58. The demands articulated by the Calderón slaves are reminiscent of those made during a slave rebellion in Bahia in 1789. See Schwartz, "Sugar Plantation Labor and Slave Life," 39–64.

59. AGN, Criminal, vol. 135, exp. 56, f. 187.

60. AGN, Criminal, vol. 135, exp. 56, f. 187.

61. AGN, Criminal, vol. 135, exp. 56, f. 194.

62. AGN, Bienes Nacionales, vol. 131, exp. 10, fs. 1–5.

63. AGN, Bienes Nacionales, vol. 131, exp. 10, f. 2.

64. There appears to have been some confusion as to the names of the leaders. Joseph Hilario, Joseph Roberto, Ana María, Antonio Manuel Roque, and Tomas de Aquino were all questioned by the authorities, as was a slave who gave his name as Ramón Márquez (perhaps this is Francisco Ramón). However, Vicente Ferrer was not interrogated, nor did that name appear in the slave list generated on August 9. See AGN, Tierras, vol. 1935, exp. 7, f. 48.

65. AGN, Criminal, vol. 135, exp. 56, f. 199.

66. For example, see Tannenbaum, *Slave and Citizen*; Klein, *Slavery in the Americas*.

67. For some examples from the voluminous literature on indigenous peoples in colonial courts, see Kellogg, *Law and the Transformation of Aztec Culture*; Stern, *Peru's Indian Peoples and the Challenge of Spanish Conquest*. For discussions of the role of colonial judicial institutions in mediating patriarchy, see Seed, *To Love, Honor, and Obey in Colonial Mexico*; Stern, *The Secret History of Gender*.

68. Hobsbawm, "Peasants and Politics," 13.

CHAPTER 6

1. AGN, Civil, vol. 1862, exp. 6.

2. Catalina's opening petition tied Miguel's manumission to the monies that she claimed to be saving. She clearly indicated that she believed she had paid for his freedom. But Saravia's denial of any knowledge of those funds and the fact he granted Miguel's manumission gratis make it difficult to know exactly when she conceived of the idea to purchase her freedom and began saving to do so. She changed tact slightly with her second petition that focuses solely on Doña Isabel's heresy.

3. As late as December 1704, some forty-five years later, Miguel, Catalina's younger son, continued to press the case, in the name of his deceased mother and his brother, Felipe, against Aeta for the restitution of the money Catalina had entrusted to him. That same year he won a judgment against Saravia's estate for the 40 pesos in back wages.

4. Cutter, *The Legal Culture of Northern New Spain*, 36.

5. *Las Siete Partidas*, 4.21.13.

6. Hordes, "The Crypto-Jewish Community of New Spain," 262. My thanks to Robert Ferry, who pointed out the investigation of Aeta and Saravia to me.

7. Medina, *Historia del Tribunal del Santo Oficio de la Inquisición en México*, 290. Medina includes a long description of the investigation that resulted in Aeta and Saravia, among others, receiving reprimands.

8. In order to explore the relationship between freedom and slavery in New Spain, I consider all found cases, or parts thereof, between 1604 and 1769 in the AGN (twenty-seven), along with two similar cases from the AHN in Madrid, of supposed slaves (fifty-eight in all) who sued their masters over freedom. More cases of this type may become available when the Tribunal Superior de Justicia opens at the AGN in Mexico City.

9. For studies that consider that question, see Davis, *The Problem of Slavery in the Age of Revolution*; Davis, *The Problem of Slavery in Western Culture*;

Owensby, "How Juan and Leonor Won Their Freedom," 71; Patterson, *Freedom in the Making of Western Culture*; Patterson, "The Unholy Trinity."

10. Chaves, "Slave Women's Strategies for Freedom and the Late Spanish Colonial State"; Johnson, "A Lack of Legitimate Obedience and Respect"; Lavallé, *Amor y opresión en los Andes coloniales*, 236; Mallo, "La libertad en el discurso del estado, de amos y esclavos"; Soulodre-La France, "Socially Not So Dead!"; Townsend, "Half My Body Free, the Other Half Enslaved." For studies that explore the long colonial period, trying to find the origins of late colonial legal practice by slaves in the earlier period, see Bryant, "Enslaved Rebels, Fugitives, and Litigants"; de la Fuente, "Slave Law and Claims-Making in Cuba"; Premo, *Children of the Father King*, 211–42.

11. Blanchard, "The Language of Liberation," 500. Laurent Dubois hypothesizes that slave revolutionaries expanded French revolutionary ideology, which was heavily tilted toward property rights and hence ambiguous about slavery and slaves' right to liberty, into the full-fledged vision of human equality that we embrace today (*A Colony of Citizens*, 2, 69). Aline Helg argues that the Enlightenment ideals of the age of revolution had greater resonance among free people of African descent in Caribbean Colombia than among the enslaved (*Liberty and Equality in Caribbean Colombia*, 14, 108–18).

12. Davis, *Inhuman Bondage*, 144; Foner, "The Meaning of Freedom in the Age of Emancipation," 442; Owensby, "How Juan and Leonor Won Their Freedom," 73; Patterson, "The Unholy Trinity," 563.

13. Blackburn, *The Overthrow of Colonial Slavery*, 35, 55; Gaspar, "The Antigua Slave Conspiracy of 1736," 312; Gaspar, *Bondsmen and Rebels*, 216.

14. Davis, *Inhuman Bondage*, 122–23. For a similar argument, see Aguirre, *Agentes de su propia libertad*, 211–13.

15. Hünefeldt, *Paying the Price of Freedom*, 7, 203.

16. Díaz, *The Virgin, the King, and the Royal Slaves of El Cobre*, 13 (emphasis mine). Also see Díaz, "Of Life and Freedom at the (Tropical) Hearth," 19.

17. This clearly corresponds with "the 'negative' definition of freedom as the absence of external constraints on autonomous, self-directed individuals" (Foner, "The Meaning of Freedom in the Age of Emancipation," 446).

18. Patterson, *Freedom in the Making of Western Culture*, 1–5.

19. Haskell, review, 98.

20. Thus, for example, the Atlantic revolutions did not represent the advance of freedom over nonfreedom but rather the drowning out of sovereignal freedom by personal and civic notes.

21. Additionally, theologians and legal philosophers from the Spanish tradition clearly defined personal freedom as the antithesis of slavery well before the sixteenth century (Owensby, "How Juan and Leonor Won Their Freedom,"

77). The *Siete Partidas* defined liberty as "the power which every man has by nature to do what he wishes," so long as "the force or right of law or fuero does not prevent him" (4.22.1).

22. Eric Foner argues that the transformation of personal liberty from a privilege, which we might best understand as an advantage or immunity enjoyed by an individual beyond the usual rights and advantages of someone of the same social station, to a universal right in the United States was greatly influenced by the push toward universal (male) suffrage and the "rapid expansion of capitalism." In relation to the second, he argues that "the market revolution greatly encouraged the spread of liberal individualism, and broad dissemination of a 'negative' definition of freedom as the absence of external constraints on autonomous, self-directed individuals" ("The Meaning of Freedom in the Age of Emancipation," 444–46, quote, 446).

23. Owensby, *Empire of Law and Indian Justice in Colonial Mexico*, 130–66.

24. Owensby, *Empire of Law and Indian Justice in Colonial Mexico*, 161–62.

25. Palmer, *Slaves of the White God*, 116.

26. To date, the number of studies that focus on slaves' use of the colonial courts, particularly in pursuit of freedom during the period prior to the late eighteenth and early nineteenth centuries, is fairly limited. For a few examples that focus on both the Hapsburg and Bourbon periods, see Bryant, "Enslaved Rebels, Fugitives, and Litigants," 7–46; de la Fuente, "Slaves and the Creation of Legal Rights in Cuba," 659–92; Premo, *Children of the Father King*, 211–41. For the significant number of studies that focus on the Bourbon and independence periods, see notes 10 and 11.

27. Klein, *Slavery in the Americas*, 196; Tannenbaum, *Slave and Citizen*, 54. Tannenbaum does not use the term "coartación," but what he describes is much the same as what Klein describes.

28. de la Fuente, "Slave Law and Claims-Making in Cuba," 357.

29. The misconception that slaves enjoyed the right to manumission continues to influence the literature on the subject. For example, see de la Fuente, "Slave Law and Claims-Making in Cuba," 357. De la Fuente talks about the right to freedom being a conditional one that was enforced by the Spanish imperial bureaucracy over time.

30. *Las Siete Partidas*, 4.22.

31. *Recopilación de leyes de los reynos de las Indias*, 7.5.1–29; "Instrucción sobre la educación, trato, y ocupación de los esclavos (1789)," in Konetzke, *Colección de Documentos*, 3:643–52.

32. Bergad et al., *The Cuban Slave Market*, 122–42; de la Fuente, "Slaves and the Creation of Legal Rights in Cuba," 663.

33. The text reads "Ordenamos á nuestras Reales Audiencias, que si algun Negro, ó Negra, ó otros qualesquiera tenidos por esclavos, proclamaren á libertad,

los oygan, y hagan justicia, y provean que por esto no sean maltratados de sus amos" (*Recopilación de leyes de los reynos de las Indias*, 7.5.7).

34. *Las Siete Partidas*, 3.2.8.

35. *Las Siete Partidas*, 6.3.24. The law reads "Where a man is under obligations to several persons by reason of debts which he owes . . . and said party has all his property or the greater portion of it invested in slaves, and wishes to liberate them all in order to defraud those to whom he is indebted, he may not do so."

36. *Las Siete Partidas*, 3.2.8.

37. *Las Siete Partidas*, 3.5.4 (emphasis mine).

38. Surviving manumissions recorded in cartas de libertad and wills from all extant notary books in Mexico City for the periods 1673–76 and 1723–26 and in Guanajuato for the period 1699–1750 form the heart of my analysis. Data from Frederick Bowser's study of manumission in Mexico City between 1580 and 1650 is also presented for comparative purposes; see Bowser, "The Free Person of Color in Mexico City and Lima."

39. There was a significant reduction in the relative number of slaves freed in wills and a related rise in the number executed via cartas over time in New Spain. In 1673–76, just over 51 percent of manumissions were found in wills compared to just 37 percent in 1723–26. In Guanajuato for the period 1699–1750, 38 percent of manumissions were effected via wills.

40. Aguirre, *Agentes de su propia libertad*; Hünefeldt, *Paying the Price of Freedom*, 5.

41. AN, Mendoza, Lorenzo de, #378, vol. 394, exp. 17.

42. AN, Guerrero, Clemente José, #263, vol. 1701, fs. 673–75.

43. Inheritance in Spanish America was firmly established by legal tradition. All legitimate children inherited equally, with the exception that testators could set aside one-fifth of their estate and assign it as they pleased. Therefore, wills rarely included a complete list of belongings and assets but rather served as specific instructions for particular parts of property. See Couturier, "Women and the Family in Eighteenth-Century Mexico," 296.

44. For a few examples, see Bergad et al., *The Cuban Slave Market*, 139; Bowser, "The Free Person of Color in Mexico City and Lima," 348; Libby and Paiva, "Manumission Practices in a Late Eighteenth-Century Brazilian Slave Parish," 111; Patterson, *Slavery and Social Death*, 263.

45. In eighteenth-century Guanajuato, women sold 37 percent and purchased 24 percent of all slaves but freed 39 percent. Information on slave sales is drawn from all sales listed in the notarial books for Mexico City (AN, 1675 and 1725) and Guanajuato (AHGPC, 1699–1750).

46. These rates are higher than but still comparable to those found in other Latin American colonies. See Proctor, "Gender and the Manumission of Slaves in New Spain," 316.

47. See tables 6.1A and 6.2A in the appendix to this book.

48. The historical literature holds that gratis manumissions granted by men were "almost exclusively limited to cases in which masters were, in fact, liberating their own children or sexual partners" (Libby and Paiva, "Manumission Practices in a Late Eighteenth-Century Brazilian Slave Parish," 112), but if we analyze every gratis manumission granted by men, we find that less than one in seven (13–17 percent) of all slaves freed in New Spain could possibly have been children or sexual partners. Similarly, if sexual relations were a significant motivation to grant gratis manumissions to women and children we might expect men to have granted them at higher rates than women. Such was not the case, however, as male and female masters granted gratis manumissions at similar rates.

49. For a more in-depth discussion of the gendered nature of manumission, specifically as it relates to undermining the argument that amorous relations between slave women and their masters, and the resulting paternity by masters of slave children, best explains patterns of manumission, see Proctor, "Gender and the Manumission of Slaves in New Spain," 309–36.

50. AN, Díaz de Rivera, Juan, #199, vol. 1329, fs. 354–55, vol. 2506, fs. 354–55; AN, Morante, Baltasar, #379, vol. 2507, fs. 48–49.

51. AN, Piedras Cortés, Pedro de, #500, vol. 3372, fs. 332–33. For a similar example, see AN, Morante, Baltasar, #379, vol. 2594, fs. 136–38.

52. AN, Pacheco de Figueroa, Marcos, #499, vol. 3368, fs. 4–6.

53. AN, Morante, Baltasar, #379, vol. 2504, fs. 136–38; AN, Muñoz de Castro, Felipe, #391, vol. 2578, fs. 8–9. For a similar finding for colonial Peru, see Premo, *Children of the Father King*, 220.

54. Walter Johnson makes a similar argument about conceptions of slave rebellion in the historiography of the United States ("Time and Revolution in African America," 155).

55. Of twenty-nine found cases, twenty-one, involving forty-nine slaves, were "breach of promise" suits; two, involving three slaves, centered on violated "dominion"; two other suits sought to establish a "just price"; and two more had to do with claims of "free birth." Two final cases that could be classified as "just price" or "dominion" cases deserve clearer definitions. In one, a slave demanded the establishment of a "just price" to expedite the liberation of her daughter, who had already been promised future manumission by her recently deceased owner. In the other, a slave's advocate argued that a master had abused his "limited dominion" over a slave. That claim of "limited dominion" was initially grounded in the assertion that a previous owner had bequeathed the slave with a restriction that he be allowed to purchase his freedom at a later date, which meant that absolute dominion had not been passed from owner to owner.

56. Owensby, "How Juan and Leonor Won Their Freedom," 49.
57. AHN, Sección de Inquisición, vol. 1727, exp 2, fs. 1–174.
58. AGN, Inquisición, vol. 503, exp. 2, fs. 17–44.
59. Nineteen of those cases—involving some thirty-seven slaves—reached resolution, whereas ten case files remain incomplete. In two of the cases treated as complete, the courts established a "just price," but we cannot know if the price was actually paid and the slave freed because such information is not included in the case file. But in each case the court clearly concluded that the slave's case had merit. Among the nineteen completed cases thirteen were successful, resulting in the liberation of twenty-seven slaves. Six petitions, involving twelve slaves, were rejected. The fates of the nineteen slaves found in the ten incomplete case files remain unknown.
60. AHN, Seccíon de Inquisición, vol. 1737, exp. 13, fs. 79r–82v, cited in Ferry, "Don't Drink the Chocolate," 14n11.
61. AGN, Civil, vol. 1474, exp. 29.
62. AGN, Bienes Nacionales, vol. 381, exp. 25, f. 10.
63. AGN, Bienes Nacionales, vol. 381, exp. 25, f. 15. Ironically, the abbess then successfully renewed the attempt to sell María, charging that she was unwanted in the convent because she did not have the disposition to serve there. She supported that charge by claiming that María had voluntarily left the cloister on two separate occasions. Don Torres y Vergara, in essence contravening his first decision, ordered that María be relocated to the Santa Clara convent in Mexico City, where she was to live out the rest of her life (see fs. 38–40).
64. AGN, Bienes Nacionales, vol. 564, exp. 19.
65. This represents one of the few found instances of an Afro-Mexican owning slaves. The implications of that reality do not undermine my findings that free and enslaved Afro-Mexicans shared a sense of common cultural identity in seventeenth- and eighteenth-century New Spain. Rather, it highlights that a myriad of other identities could render that common identity less important at times.
66. AGN, Civil, vol. 753, exp. 11–14. Interestingly, after the court had found for Juan Esteban, de la Riva appealed. She submitted what appears to be a fraudulent bill of sale, dated June 7, 1738, stating that she bought Juan Esteban directly from Prados for 300 pesos. The court did not pay much attention to that evidence, as suggested by the fact that it did not seek to overturn the earlier finding.
67. AGN, Tierras, vol. 3170, cuaderno 4, fs. 1–18.
68. AGN, Bienes Nacionales, vol. 79, exp. 14.
69. AGN, Bienes Nacionales, vol. 79, exp. 14.
70. *Las Siete Partidas*, 7.9.46.

71. AGN, Bienes Nacionales, vol. 488, exp. 36, f. 1. Although this type of language situating the court, as representing the king, as ultimate patriarch was not common in seventeenth- and early eighteenth-century New Spain, it apparently become quite common in other Spanish colonies in the context of the Bourbon reforms and the Enlightenment in the last quarter of the eighteenth century. For example, see Premo, *Children of the Father King*, 137–39.

72. AGN, Bienes Nacionales, vol. 488, exp. 36, f. 13.

73. For three cases brought against living slaveholders by slaves without reference to a deceased master, see AGN, Civil, vol. 2243, exps. 3–4; AGN, Criminal, vol. 695, exp. 8, fs. 268–96; AGN, Inquisición, vol. 503, exp. 2, fs. 17–44. The fourth case, brought by a free person of color in the name of a slave, can be found in AGN, Civil, vol. 1474, exp. 29. For a similar trend in late colonial Buenos Aires, Argentina, see Johnson, "A Lack of Legitimate Obedience and Respect," 638.

74. AGN, Bienes Nacionales, vol. 79, exp. 12, fs. 1–13.

75. AGN, Bienes Nacionales, vol. 79, exp. 12, f. 8 The bill of sale did include a clause that if Juana's heirs could provide the original purchase price that Sánchez paid for Juan within three years, he would be required to sell him back. Sezeña then changed his argument slightly and suggested that by including this provision Juana had in fact pawned rather than sold Juan to Sánchez, and as a result he still did not receive absolute dominion. Therefore, Sezeña continued, Sánchez did not have the authority to brand Juan on the face and as such his client should be freed. That argument also proved unsuccessful.

76. This case serves as tantalizing evidence that speaks to the oft-stipulated connections between sex and manumission in Spanish and Portuguese America. Despite the evocative nature of this case, sex between male masters and their female slaves was not, as I have noted, as significant in patterns of manumission as we might think. See notes 48 and 49.

77. AGN, Bienes Nacionales, vol. 137, exp. 131, fs. 4–6.

78. AGN, Bienes Nacionales, vol. 137, exp. 131, fs. 13–15.

79. The *Siete Partidas* (4.22.1) required that a master freeing his or her slaves had to supply a notarized offer—either in the form of a last will and testament or a carta de libertad—or, in the case of verbal manumissions, had to have five witnesses to the manumission.

80. AGN, Civil, vol. 2243, exps. 3–4.

81. AGN, Civil, vol. 337, 2a parte, exp. 3, fs. 1–4. The slaves had paid Güemez the following amounts over the course of seven years: 414 pesos (Nicolás), 430 pesos (Ramón), 500 pesos (Gertrudis de Bocanegra), and192 pesos (Gertrudis de la Encarnación).

82. AGN, Civil, vol. 337, 2a parte, exp. 3, f. 32.
83. The final document in the case file is a petition from Alférez Güemez dated November 6, 1734; see AGN, Civil, vol. 337, 2a parte, exp. 3.
84. Owensby, "How Juan and Leonor Won Their Freedom," 46.
85. AHN, Seccíon de Inquisición, vol. 1727, exp. 6, fs. 4–5.
86. The Inquisition heard this case because control of the hacienda where Leonor labored apparently passed to the Holy Office owing to outstanding debts.
87. AGN, Tierras, vol. 2888, exp. 1, f. 125.
88. AGN, Bienes Nacionales, vol. 211, exp. 7, fs. 58–59. Valdez subsequently sold Marcos and his sister, who was also offered future manumission in Juana's will, for a total of 690 pesos.
89. AHN, Seccíon de Inquisición, vol. 1727, exp. 6, f. 22, quoted in Owensby, "How Juan and Leonor Won Their Freedom," 65.
90. AGN, Criminal, vol. 695, exp. 8, f. 270.
91. Higgins, *"Licentious Liberty" in a Brazilian Gold-Mining Region*, 171; Johnson, "A Lack of Legitimate Obedience and Respect," 642; Patterson, *Slavery and Social Death*, 220, 296.
92. AGN, Civil, vol. 2300, exp. 12.
93. AGN, Bienes Nacionales, vol. 211, exp. 7, f. 50.
94. AGN, Bienes Nacionales, vol. 564, exp. 19.
95. For studies that illuminate the ability of slaves to navigate colonial institutions, see Bennett, *Africans in Colonial Mexico*, 1–2; Bryant, "Enslaved Rebels, Fugitives, and Litigants," 21; Johnson, "A Lack of Legitimate Obedience and Respect," 635–6; Owensby, "How Juan and Leonor Won Their Freedom," 44.
96. Roseberry, "Hegemony and the Language of Contention," 362.
97. Such a conception helps us explain the absence of discourses of freedom in the master-slave conflicts explored in previous chapters and also helps us understand the increasing frequency with which slaves deployed such discourses in the Bourbon and independence periods, by which time they had become increasingly part of sociopolitical discourse, even in Spanish America.

CONCLUSION

1. Stern, *The Secret History of Gender*, 7.
2. Scott, *Weapons of the Weak*, 326.

Bibliography

Archives

Archivo de la Basílica Colegiata de Guanajuato Santa Fe, Guanajuato, Mexico (ABCG)

Archivo General de la Nación, México City, Mexico (AGN)
    Archivo Genealogía y Heráldica (AGH)
        Sagrario Metropolitano, Cuidad de México
        Sagrario, San Luis Potosí
    Archivo Histórico de Hacienda (HH)
    Archivo Histórico del Hospital de Jesús (AHHJ)
    Archivo del Tribunal Superior de Justicia del Distrito Federal
    Bienes Nacionales
    Clero Regular y Secular
    General de Parte
    Ramo Civil (Civil)
    Ramo Criminal (Criminal)
    Ramo de Inquisición (Inquisición)
    Ramo de Matrimonios (Matrimonios)
    Real Fisco de la Inquisición (RFI)
    Ramo de Tierras (Tierras)

Archivo Histórico de Guanajuato, Guanajuato, Mexico (AHG)
    Protocolos de Cabildo

Archivo Histórico Nacional, Madrid, Spain (AHN)
    Seccíon de Inquisición

Archivo Histórico de Notarias del Distrito Federal, Mexico City, Mexico (AN)

Archivo Municipal de Córdoba, Cordoba, Spain (AMC)

Huntington Library, San Marino, California (HL)
Mexican Inquisition Papers, 1525–1822

Published Primary Sources

Instrucciones a los hermanos jesuitas administradores de haciendas: Manuscrito mexicano de siglo XVIII. Edited by Francois Chevalier. México, DF: Universidad Nacional Autónoma de México, 1950.

Konetzke, Richard, ed. *Colección de documentos para la historia de la formación social de Hispanoamérica, 1493–1810.* 3 vols. Madrid: Consejo Superior de Investigaciones Cientificas, 1955–62.

Lucena Salmoral, Manuel. *Los códigos negros de la América Española.* Alcalá: UNESCO/Universidad de Alcalá, 1996.

O'Gorman, Edmundo. "El trabajo industrial en la Nueva España a mediados del siglo XVII: Visita a los obrajes de paños en la jurisdicción de Coyoacán." *Boletín del Archivo General de la Nación* 11, no. 1 (1940): 33–116.

Recopilación de leyes de los reynos de las Indias. 3 vols. Madrid: Consejo de la Hispanidad, 1943.

Ruiz de Alarcón, Hernando. *Treatise on the Heathen Superstitions That Today Live among the Indians Native to This New Spain.* Edited by and translated by J. Richard Andrews and Ross Hassig. Norman: University of Oklahoma Press, 1984.

Las Siete Partidas. Translated by Samuel Parsons Scott. Edited by Robert I. Burns. 5 vols. Philadelphia: University of Pennsylvania Press, 2001.

von Humboldt, Alexander. *Political Essay on the Kingdom of New Spain.* Translated by John Black. Edited by Mary Maples Dunn. New York: Knopf, 1972.

Secondary Sources

Aguirre, Carlos. *Agentes de su propia libertad: Los esclavos de Lima y la desintegración de la esclavitud, 1821–1854.* Lima: Fondo Editorial de Pontificia Universidad Católica del Perú, 1993.

Aguirre Beltrán, Gonzalo. "La esclavitud en los obrajes novoespañoles." In *La ortodoxia recuperada (en torno a Ángel Palerm),* edited by Susana Glantz, 249–59. México, DF: Fondo de la Cultura Económica, 1987.

———. *El negro esclavo en Nueva España: La formación colonial, la medicina popular y otros ensayos*. México, DF: Fondo de Cultura Económica, 1994.

———. *Medicina y magia: El proceso de aculturación en la estructura colonial*. México, DF: Fondo de Cultura Económica, 1963, 1992.

———. *La población negra de México: Estudio etnohistórico*. 3rd ed. México, DF: Fondo de Cultura Económica, 1989.

Alberro, Solange. *Inquisición y sociedad en México, 1571–1700*. México, DF: Fondo de Cultura Económica, 1988.

———. "Juan de Morga and Gertrudis de Escobar: Rebellious Slaves." In *Struggle and Survival in Colonial America*, edited by David G. Sweet and Gary B. Nash, 165–88. Berkeley: University of California Press, 1981.

Althouse, Aaron P. "Contested Mestizos, Alleged Mulattos: Racial Identity and Caste Hierarchy in Eighteenth Century Pátzcuaro, Mexico." *The Americas* 62, no. 2 (2005): 151–75.

Altman, Ida. *Transatlantic Ties in the Spanish Empire: Brihuega, Spain, and Puebla, Mexico, 1560–1620*. Stanford: Stanford University Press, 2000.

Anderson, Rodney D. "Race and Social Stratification: A Comparison of Working-Class Spaniards, Indians, and Castas in Guadalajara, Mexico in 1821." *Hispanic American Historical Review* 68, no. 2 (1988): 209–43.

Andrews, J. Richard, and Ross Hassig. Introduction. In Hernando Ruiz de Alarcón, *Treatise on the Heathen Superstitions That Today Live among the Indians Native to This New Spain, 1629*. Edited by and translated by J. Richard Andrews and Ross Hassig. Norman: University of Oklahoma Press, 1984.

Bakewell, Peter. *Silver Mining and Society in Colonial Mexico: Zacatecas, 1546–1700*. Cambridge: Cambridge University Press, 1971.

Barrett, Ward J. *The Sugar Hacienda of the Marqueses del Valle*. Minneapolis: University of Minnesota Press, 1970.

Barrett, Ward J., and Stuart Schwartz. "Comparación entre dos economías azucareras coloniales: Morelos, México y Bahía, Brasil." In *Haciendas, latifundios, y plantaciones en América Latina*, edited by Enrique Florescano, 532–72. México, DF: Siglo XXI, 1975.

Bauer, Arnold J. "Rural Workers in Spanish America: Problems of Peonage and Oppression." *Hispanic American Historical Review* 62, no. 3 (1979): 34–63.

Bazant, Jan. "Evolution of the Textile Industry of Puebla, 1544–1845." *Comparative Studies of Society and History* 7, no. 1 (1964): 56–69.

Beckles, Hilary McD. *Black Rebellion in Barbados: The Struggle against Slavery, 1627–1838*. Bridgetown, Barbados: Antilles Publications, 1984.

———. *Natural Rebels: A Social History of Enslaved Black Women in Barbados*. New Brunswick: Rutgers University Press, 1994.

Behar, Ruth. "Sex and Sin, Witchcraft and the Devil in Late-Colonial Mexico." *American Ethnologist* 14, no. 1 (1987): 34–53.

———. "Sexual Witchcraft, Colonialism, and Women's Powers: Views from the Mexican Inquisition." In *Sexuality and Marriage in Colonial Latin America*, edited by Asunción Lavrin, 178–208. Lincoln: University of Nebraska Press, 1992.

Bennett, Herman L. *Africans in Colonial Mexico: Absolutism, Christianity, and Afro-Creole Consciousness, 1570–1640*. Bloomington: University of Indiana Press, 2003.

Bennett, Herman L. "Lovers, Family and Friends: The Formation of Afro-Mexico, 1580–1810." PhD diss., Duke University, 1993.

Bergad, Laird W. *Slavery and the Demographic and Economic History of Minas Gerais, Brazil, 1720–1888*. Cambridge: Cambridge University Press, 1999.

Bergad, Laird W., Fe Iglesias García, and María del Carmen Barcia. *The Cuban Slave Market*. Cambridge: Cambridge University Press, 1995.

Berlin, Ira. *Many Thousands Gone: The First Two Centuries of Slavery in North America*. Cambridge, MA: Harvard University Press, 1998.

———. *Slaves without Masters: The Free Negro in the Antebellum South*. New York: The New Press, 1974.

Berlin, Ira, and Philip D. Morgan. "Labor and the Shaping of Slave Life in the Americas." In *Cultivation and Culture: Labor and the Shaping of Slave Live in the Americas*, 1–48. Charlottesville: University Press of Virginia, 1993.

Berthe, Jean-Pierre. "Xochimancas: Les travaux et les jours dan une *hacienda* sucrière de Nouvelle-Espagne au xviie siècle." *Jahrbuch für Geschichte von Staat, Wirtschaft und Gesellschaft Lateinamerikas* 3 (1966): 88–117.

Binder, Wolfgang, ed. *Slavery in the Americas*. Würzburg, DE: Königshausen and Nuemann, 1993.

Blackburn, Robin. *The Overthrow of Colonial Slavery, 1776–1848*. London: Verso, 1988.

Blanchard, Peter. "The Language of Liberation: Slave Voices in the Wars of Independence." *Hispanic American Historical Review* 82, no. 3 (2002): 499–523.

Borah, Woodrow. *Justice by Insurance: The General Indian Court of Colonial Mexico and the Legal Aides of the Half-Real*. Berkeley: University of California Press, 1983.

Borah, Woodrow, and Sherburne F. Cook. "Marriage and Legitimacy in Mexican Culture: Mexico and California." *California Law Review* 54, no. 2 (1966): 946–97.

Bowser, Frederick P. *The African Slave in Colonial Peru, 1524–1650*. Stanford: Stanford University Press, 1974.

———. "The Free Person of Color in Mexico City and Lima: Manumission and Opportunity, 1580–1650." In *Race and Slavery in the Western Hemisphere:*

Quantitative Studies, edited by Stanley L. Engerman and Eugene D. Genovese, 331–65. Princeton: Princeton University Press, 1975.

Boyer, Richard. "Caste and Identity in Colonial Mexico: A Proposal and an Example." *Latin American Studies Consortium of New England*, occasional paper no. 7 (1997): 1–17.

———. *Lives of the Bigamists: Marriage, Family and Community in Colonial Mexico.* Albuquerque: University of New Mexico Press, 1995.

Brading, D. A. *Haciendas and Ranchos in the Mexican Bajío: León, 1700–1860.* Cambridge: Cambridge University Press, 1978.

Bristol, Joan Cameron. *Christians, Blasphemers, and Witches: Afro-Mexican Ritual Practice in the Seventeenth Century.* Albuquerque: University of New Mexico Press, 2007.

———. "Negotiating Authority in New Spain: Blacks, Mulattos, and Religious Practice in the Seventeenth Century." PhD diss., University of Pennsylvania, 2001.

Brockington, Lolita Gutiérrez. *The Leverage of Labor: Managing the Cortés Haciendas in Tehuantepec, 1588–1688.* Durham: Duke University Press, 1989.

Bryant, Sherwin K. "Enslaved Rebels, Fugitives, and Litigants: The Resistance Continuum in Colonial Quito." *Colonial Latin American Review* 13, no. 1 (2004): 7–46.

Burke, Peter. *History and Social Theory.* Ithaca: Cornell University Press, 1992.

Byrd, Alexander X. "The Slave Trade from the Biafran Interior to Jamaica: Commerce, Culture Change, and Comparative Perspective." Paper presented at the International Seminar on the History of the Atlantic World, 1500–1800, Harvard University, 1998.

Cáceres, Rina, ed. *Rutas de la esclavitud en África y América Latina.* San José, Costa Rica: Editorial de la Universidad de Costa Rica, 2001.

Calvo, Thomas. *Guadalajara y su región en el siglo XVII: Población y economía.* Guadalajara: Ayuntamiento de Guadalajara, 1992.

———, ed. *Historia y población en México (siglos XVI–XIX).* México, DF: El Colegio de México, 1994.

Carmagnani, Marcelo. "Demografía y sociedad: La estructura social de los centros mineros del norte de México, 1600–1720." In Calvo, *Historia y población en México*, 122–62.

Carrera, Magali. *Imagining Identity in New Spain: Race, Lineage, and the Colonial Body in Portraiture and Casta Paintings.* Austin: University of Texas Press, 2003.

———. "Locating Race in Late Colonial Mexico." *Art Journal* 57, no. 3 (1998): 36–45.

Carroll, Patrick J. *Blacks in Colonial Veracruz: Race, Ethnicity, and Regional Development.* Austin: University of Texas Press, 2001.

————. "Black Laborers and Their Experience in Colonial Jalapa." In Frost et al., *El trabajo y los trabajadores en la historia de México*, 119–32.

————. "Mandinga: The Evolution of a Mexican Runaway Slave Community." *Comparative Studies in Society and History* 19, no. 4 (1977): 488–505.

————. "Los mexicanos negros, el mestizaje y los fundamentos olvidados de la 'raza cósmica': Una perspectiva regional." *Historia Mexicana* 44, no. 3 (1995): 403–38, iii–xvi.

Carroll, Patrick J., and Aurelio de los Reyes. "Amapa, Oaxaca: Pueblos de Cimarrones (Noticias Históricas)." *Boletín del Instituto Nacional de Antropología e Historia de México* 2, no. 4 (1973): 43–50.

Castleman, Bruce A. "Social Climbers in a Colonial Mexican City: Individual Mobility within the *Sistema de Castas* in Orizaba, 1777–1791." *Colonial Latin American Review* 10, no. 2 (2001): 229–49.

Castro Rivas, Jorge A., Matilde Rangel López, and Rafael Tovar Rangel. *Desarrollo socio demográfico de la cuidad de Guanajuato durante el siglo XVII*. Guanajuato, México: Universidad de Guanajuato, 1999.

Ceballos Gómez, Diana Luz. *Hechicería, brujería e Inquisición en el Nuevo Reino de Granada: Un duelo de imaginarios*. Bogotá, Columbia: Editorial Universidad Nacional, 1994.

Cervantes, Fernando. *The Devil in the New World: The Impact of Diabolism in New Spain*. New Haven: Yale University Press, 1994.

Chalhoub, Sidney. *Visões de liberdade: Uma história das últimas décadas da escravidão na corte*. São Paulo: Companhia das Letras, 1990.

Chambers, Douglas B. "Ethnicity in the Diaspora: The Slave-Trade and the Creation of African 'Nations' in the Americas." *Slavery and Abolition* 22, no. 3 (2001): 25–39.

————. "'My own nation': Igbo Exiles in the Diaspora." *Slavery and Abolition* 18, no. 1 (1997): 72–97.

Chance, John K., and William B. Taylor. "Estate and Class in a Colonial City: Oaxaca in 1792." *Comparative Studies of Society and History* 19, no. 3 (1977): 454–87.

Chaves, María Eugenia. "Slave Women's Strategies for Freedom and the Late Spanish Colonial State." In *Hidden Histories of Gender and the State in Latin America*, edited by Elizabeth Dore and Maxine Molyneux, 108–26. Durham: Duke University Press, 2000.

Chávez Carbajal, María Guadalupe. "La gran negritud en Michoacán, época colonial." In *La presencia africana en México*, edited by Luz María Martínez Montiel, 79–131. México, DF: Consejo Nacional para la Cultura y las Artes, 1995.

Christian, William A., Jr. *Apparitions in Late Medieval and Renaissance Spain*. Princeton: Princeton University Press, 1981.

————. *Local Religion in Sixteenth-Century Spain*. Princeton: Princeton University Press, 1981.

Clendinnen, Inga. *Ambivalent Conquests: Maya and Spaniard in Yucatan, 1517–1570*. Cambridge: Cambridge University Press, 1987.

Cook, Sherburne F., and Woodrow Borah. *The Indian Population of Central Mexico, 1531–1610*. Berkeley: University of California Press, 1963.

Cope, R. Douglas. *The Limits of Racial Domination: Plebian Society in Colonial Mexico City, 1660–1720*. Madison: University of Wisconsin Press, 1994.

Cortés Jácome, María Elena. "La memoria familiar de los negros y mulatos: Siglos XVI–XVIII." In *La memoria y el olvido*, edited by Segundo Simposio de Historia de las Mentalidades, 125–33. México, DF: Instituto Nacional de Antropología e Historia, 1985.

————. "Negros amancebados con indias, siglo XVI." In *Memoria del primer simposio de Historia de la Mentalidades, Familia, Matrimonio y Sexualidad en Nueva España*, 285–93. México, DF: SEP, 1982.

Couturier, Edith. "Women and the Family in Eighteenth-Century Mexico: Law and Practice." *Journal of Family History* 10, no. 3 (1985): 294–304.

Craemer, Willy de, Jan Vansina, and Renée C. Fox. "Religious Movements in Central Africa: A Theoretical Study." *Comparative Studies in Society and History* 18, no. 4 (1976): 458–75.

Craton, Michael. "Changing Patterns of Slave Families in the British West Indies." *Journal of Interdisciplinary History* 10, no. 1 (1979): 1–35.

Cutter, Charles R. *The Legal Culture of Northern New Spain, 1700–1810*. Albuquerque: University of New Mexico Press, 2001.

da Costa, Emilia Viotti. *Crowns of Glory, Crowns of Blood: The Demerara Slave Rebellion of 1823*. New York: Oxford University Press, 1994.

Davis, David Brion. *Inhuman Bondage: The Rise and Fall of Slavery in the New World*. New York: Oxford University Press, 2006.

————. *The Problem of Slavery in the Age of Revolution, 1770–1823*. Ithaca: Cornell University Press, 1975.

————. *The Problem of Slavery in Western Culture*. Ithaca: Cornell University Press, 1966.

Deans-Smith, Susan. "Creating the Colonial Subject: Casta Paintings, Collectors, and Critics in Eighteenth-Century Mexico and Spain." *Colonial Latin American Review* 14, no. 2 (2005): 169–204.

de la Fuente, Alejandro. "Slave Law and Claims-Making in Cuba: The Tannenbaum Debate Revisited." *Law and History Review* 22, no. 2 (2004): 339–68.

————. "Slaves and the Creation of Legal Rights in Cuba: *Coartación* and *Papel*." *Hispanic American Historical Review* 87, no. 4 (2007): 659–92.

Delgado, Daniel Lemus. *Concepto y práctica medicinal en el México precortesiano*. Guadalajara: Instituto Jalisciense de Antropología y Historia, 1992.

Díaz, María Elena. "Of Life and Freedom at the (Tropical) Hearth: El Cobre, Cuba, 1709–73." In *Beyond Bondage: Free Women of Color in the Americas*, edited by David Barry Gaspar and Darlene Clark Hine, 19–36. Urbana: University of Illinois Press, 2004.

———. *The Virgin, the King, and the Royal Slaves of El Cobre: Negotiating Freedom in Colonial Cuba, 1670–1780*. Stanford: Stanford University Press, 2000.

Dubois, Laurent. *A Colony of Citizens: Revolution and Slave Emancipation in the French Caribbean, 1787–1804*. Chapel Hill: University of North Carolina Press, 2004.

Esteynoffer, Juan de. *Florilegio medicinal*. Edited by María del Carmen Anzures y Bolaños. México, DF: Academia Nacional de Medicina, 1978.

Evans-Pritchard, Evans E. "Witchcraft." *Africa* 8, no. 4 (1935): 417–22.

Farriss, Nancy M. *Maya Society under Colonial Rule: The Collective Enterprise of Survival*. Princeton: Princeton University Press, 1984.

Ferry, Robert. "Don't Drink the Chocolate: Domestic Slavery and the Exigencies of Fasting for Crypto-Jews in Seventeenth-Century Mexico." *Nuevo Mundo–Mundos Nuevos* (2005), http://nuevomundo.revues.org/document934.html.

Few, Martha. *Women Who Live Evil Lives: Gender, Religion, and the Politics of Power in Colonial Guatemala*. Austin: University of Texas Press, 2002.

Fields, Barbara Jeanne. "Slavery, Race and Ideology in the United States of America." *New Left Review*, May–June 1990, 95–118.

Florescano, Enrique. "La formación de los trabajadores en la época colonial, 1521–1750." In *La clase obrera en la historia de México de la colonia al imperio*, 7th ed., edited by Enrique Florescano, Isabel González Sánchez, Jorge González Angulo, Roberto Sandoval Zarauz, Cuauhtémoc Velasco A. and Alejandra Moreno Toscano, 58–79. México, DF: Siglo Veintiuno, 1996.

Foner, Eric. "The Meaning of Freedom in the Age of Emancipation." *Journal of American History* 81, no. 2 (1994): 435–60.

———. "Review Essay: Putting New World Slavery in Perspective." Review of *Inhuman Bondage: The Rise and Fall of Slavery in the New World*, by David Brion Davis. *Slavery and Abolition* 28, no. 2 (2007): 277–88.

Foucault, Michel. *Discipline and Punish: The Birth of the Prison*. Translated by Alan Sheridan. New York: Vintage Books, 1995.

Fox-Genovese, Elizabeth. *Within the Plantation Household: Black and White Women of the Old South*. Chapel Hill: University of North Carolina Press, 1988.

Frey, Sylvia R., and Betty Wood. *Come Shouting to Zion: African American Protestantism in the American South and the British Caribbean to 1830*. Chapel Hill: University of North Carolina Press, 1998.

Frost, Elsa Cecilia, Michael C. Meyer, and Josefina Zoraida Vázquez, with the collaboration of Lilia Díaz. *El trabajo y los trabajadores en la historia de México*. México, DF: Colegio de México, 1979.

Gaspar, David Barry. "The Antigua Slave Conspiracy of 1736: A Case Study of the Origins of Collective Resistance." *William and Mary Quarterly*, 3rd ser., 35, no. 2 (1978): 308–23.

———. *Bondsmen and Rebels: A Study of Master-Slave Relations in Antigua, with Implications for Colonial British America.* Baltimore: Johns Hopkins University Press, 1985.

Geggus, David Patrick. "The Bois Caïman Ceremony." In *Haitian Revolutionary Studies*, 81–92. Bloomington: Indiana University Press, 2002.

———. "The Enigma of Jamaica in the 1790s: New Light on the Causes of Slave Rebellions." *William and Mary Quarterly*, 3rd ser., 44, no. 2 (1987): 247–99.

———. "The Slaves and Free Colored of Martinique during the Age of the French and Haitian Revolutions: Three Moments of Resistance." In *The Lesser Antilles in the Age of European Expansion*, edited by Robert L. Paquette and Stanley L. Engerman, 280–301. Gainesville: University Press of Florida, 1996.

Genovese, Eugene D. *From Rebellion to Revolution: Afro-American Slave Revolts in the Making of the Modern World.* Baton Rouge: Louisiana State University Press, 1979.

———. *Roll, Jordan, Roll: The World the Slaves Made.* New York: Vintage Books, 1972.

Germeten, Nicole von. *Black Blood Brothers: Confraternities and Social Mobility for Afro-Mexicans.* Gainesville: University of Florida Press, 2006.

Gibson, Charles. *The Aztecs under Spanish Rule: A History of the Valley of Mexico, 1519–1810.* Stanford: Stanford University Press, 1964.

Ginzburg, Carlo. *The Cheese and the Worms: The Cosmos of a Sixteenth-Century Miller.* Translated by John and Anne Tedeschi. Baltimore: Johns Hopkins University Press, 1992.

Glassman, Jonathon. "The Bondsman's New Clothes: The Contradictory Consciousness of Slave Resistance on the Swahili Coast." *Journal of African History* 32, no. 2 (1991): 277–312.

Gorender, Jacob. *A escravidão reabilitada.* São Paulo: Atica/Secretaria de Estado da Cultura, 1990.

Gosner, Kevin. *Soldiers of the Virgin: The Moral Economy of a Colonial Maya Rebellion.* Tucson: University of Arizona Press, 1992.

Greenleaf, Richard E. "The Inquisition and the Indians of New Spain: A Study in Jurisdictional Confusion." *The Americas* 22, no. 2 (1965): 138–66.

———. "The Obraje in the Late Mexican Colony." *The Americas* 23, no. 3 (1967): 227–50.

Gruzinski, Serge. *The Conquest of Mexico: The Incorporation of Indian Societies into the Western World, 16th–18th Centuries.* Translated by Eileen Corrigan. Cambridge, UK: Polity Press, 1993.

——. *Man-Gods in the Mexican Highlands: Indian Power and Colonial Society, 1520–1800.* Stanford: Stanford University Press, 1989.

Gudmundson, Lowell. "Negotiating Rights under Slavery: The Slaves of San Geronimo (Baja Verapaz, Guatemala) Confront Their Dominican Masters in 1810." *The Americas* 60, no. 1 (2003): 109–14.

Gutiérrez, Ramón A. *When Jesus Came the Corn Mothers Went Away: Marriage, Sexuality, and Power in New Mexico, 1500–1846.* Stanford: Stanford University Press, 1991.

Hall, Gwendolyn Midlo. "African Ethnicities and the Meanings of 'Mina.'" In Lovejoy and Troutman, *Trans-Atlantic Dimensions of Ethnicity in the African Diaspora,* 43–65.

Hanke, Lewis. *The Spanish Struggle for Justice in the Conquest of America.* Philadelphia: University of Pennsylvania Press, 1949.

Haskell, Thomas L. Review of *Freedom in the Making of Western Culture,* vol. 1 of *Freedom,* by Orlando Patterson. *Journal of Interdisciplinary History* 25, no. 1 (1994): 95–102.

Helg, Aline. *Liberty and Equality in Caribbean Colombia, 1770–1835.* Chapel Hill: University of North Carolina Press, 2004.

Henningsen, Gustav. *The Witches' Advocate: Basque Witchcraft and the Spanish Inquisition (1609–1614).* Reno: University of Nevada Press, 1980.

Hernández Sáenz, Luz María. *Learning to Heal: The Medical Profession in Colonial Mexico, 1767–1831.* New York: Peter Lang, 1997.

Heywood, Linda M., ed. *Central Africans and Cultural Transformations in the American Diaspora.* Cambridge: Cambridge University Press, 2002.

Higgins, Kathleen J. *"Licentious Liberty" in a Brazilian Gold-Mining Region: Slavery, Gender, and Social Control in Eighteenth-Century Sabará, Minas Gerais.* University Park: Pennsylvania State University Press, 1999.

Higman, B. W. "African and Creole Slave Family Patterns in Trinidad." *Journal of Family History* 3, no. 2 (1978): 163–80.

——. "Household Structure and Fertility on Jamaican Slave Plantations: A Nineteenth-Century Example." *Population Studies* 27, no. 3 (1973): 527–49.

——. *Slave Population and Economy in Jamaica, 1807–1834.* Cambridge: Cambridge University Press, 1976.

——. *Slave Populations of the British Caribbean, 1807–1834.* Baltimore: Johns Hopkins University Press, 1984.

Hinton, Anne. *The Kingdom of Kongo.* Oxford: Clarendon Press, 1985.

Hoberman, Louisa Schell. *Mexico's Merchant Elite, 1590–1660: Silver, State, and Society.* Durham: Duke University Press, 1991.

Hobsbawm, Eric J. "Peasants and Politics." *Journal of Peasant Studies* 1, no. 1 (1973): 1–20.

Hordes, Stanley M. "The Crypto-Jewish Community of New Spain, 1620–49: A Collective Biography." PhD diss., Tulane University, 1980.

Horn, Rebecca. *Postconquest Coyoacan: Nahua-Spanish Relations in Central Mexico, 1519–1650.* Stanford: Stanford University Press, 1997.

Hünefeldt, Christine. *Paying the Price of Freedom: Family and Labor among Lima's Slaves, 1800–1854.* Berkeley: University of California Press, 1994.

Jaén, Didier T. Introduction. In José Vasconcelos, *The Cosmic Race: A Bilingual Edition.* Baltimore: Johns Hopkins University Press, 1997.

Janzen, John M. *Lemba, 1650–1930: A Drum Affliction in Africa and the New World.* New York: Garland, 1982.

———. *Ngoma: Discourses of Healing in Central and Southern Africa.* Berkeley: University of California Press, 1992.

Johnson, Lyman L. "'A Lack of Legitimate Obedience and Respect': Slaves and Their Masters in the Courts of Late Colonial Buenos Aires." *Hispanic American Historical Review* 87, no. 4 (2007): 631–57.

Johnson, Walter. "On Agency." *Journal of Social History* 37, no. 1 (2003): 113–24.

———. "Time and Revolution in African America: Temporality and the History of Atlantic Slavery." In *Rethinking American History in a Global Age,* edited by Thomas Bender, 148–68. Berkeley: University of California Press, 2002.

Joseph, Gilbert M., and Daniel Nugent, eds. *Everyday Forms of State Formation: Revolution and the Negotiation of Rule in Modern Mexico.* Durham: Duke University Press, 1994.

Karasch, Mary C. "Anastácia and the Slave Women of Rio de Janeiro." In *Africans in Bondage,* edited by Paul E. Lovejoy, 79–105. Madison: University of Wisconsin Press, 1986.

———. "Central African Religious Tradition in Rio de Janeiro." *Journal of Latin American Lore* 5, no. 2 (1979): 233–53.

———. *Slave Life in Rio de Janeiro, 1808–1850.* Princeton: Princeton University Press, 1987.

Kea, Ray A. "'When I die, I shall return to my own land': An 'Amina' Slave Rebellion in the Danish West Indies, 1732–34." In *The Cloth of Many Colored Silks: Papers on History and Society, Ghanaian and Islamic, in Honor of Ivor Wilks,* edited by John Hunwick and Nancy Lawler, 159–93. Evanston: Northwestern University Press, 1996.

Kellogg, Susan. *Law and the Transformation of Aztec Culture, 1500–1700.* Norman: University of Oklahoma Press, 1995.

Klein, Herbert S. *Slavery in the Americas: A Comparative Study of Virginia and Cuba.* Chicago: University of Chicago Press, 1967.

Knab, Timothy. *La guerra de los brujos de la sierra de Puebla: Un viaje por el inframundo de los aztecas contemporáneos.* Translated by Gustavo Pelcastre. México, DF: Diana, 1998.

Konrad, Herman W. *A Jesuit Hacienda in Colonial Mexico: Santa Lucía, 1576–1767.* Stanford: Stanford University Press, 1980.

Landers, Jane G. "*Cimarrón* and Citizen: African Ethnicity, Corporate Identity, and the Evolution of Free Black Towns in the Spanish Circum-Caribbean." In *Slaves, Subjects, and Subversives: Blacks in Colonial Latin America,* edited by Jane G. Landers and Barry M. Robinson, 111–45. Albuquerque: University of New Mexico Press, 2006.

Lanning, John Tate. *The Royal Protomedicato: The Regulation of the Medical Profession in the Spanish Empire.* Edited by John Jay TePaske. Durham: Duke University Press, 1985.

Lavallé, Bernard. *Amor y opresión en los Andes coloniales.* Lima: Instituto Francés de Estudios Andinos; Instituto de Estudios Peruanos, 1999.

Law, Robin. "Ethnicity and the Slave Trade: 'Lucumi' and 'Nago' as Ethnonyms in West Africa." *History in Africa* 24 (1997): 205–19.

Lears, T. J. Jackson. "The Concept of Cultural Hegemony: Problems and Possibilities." *American Historical Review* 90, no. 3 (1985): 567–93.

Lewis, Laura. *Hall of Mirrors: Power, Witchcraft, and Caste in Colonial Mexico.* Durham: Duke Univ. Press, 2003.

Libby, Douglas Cole. "Proto-Industrialization in a Slave Society: The Case of Minas Gerais." *Journal of Latin American Studies* 23, no. 1 (1991): 1–35.

Libby, Douglas Cole, and Clotilde Andrade Paiva. "Manumission Practices in a Late Eighteenth-Century Brazilian Slave Parish: São José d'El Rey in 1795." *Slavery and Abolition* 21, no. 1 (2000): 96–127.

Libby, Douglas Cole, and Zephyr Frank. "Exploring Parish Registers in Colonial Minas Gerais, Brazil: Ethnicity in São José do Rio das Mortes, 1780–1810." *Colonial Latin American Historical Review* 14, no. 3 (2005): 213–44.

Lockhart, James. *The Nahuas After the Conquest: A Social and Cultural History of the Indians of Central Mexico, Sixteenth Through Eighteen Centuries.* Stanford: Stanford University Press, 1992.

Lohse, Russell. "Slave-Trade Nomenclature and African Ethnicities in the Americas: Evidence from Early Eighteenth-Century Costa Rica." *Slavery and Abolition* 23, no. 3 (2002): 73–92.

Lokken, Paul. "Marriage as Slave Emancipation in Seventeenth-Century Rural Guatemala." *The Americas* 58, no. 2 (2001): 175–200.

Love, Edgar F. "Marriage Patterns of Persons of African Descent in a Colonial Mexico City Parish." *Hispanic American Historical Review* 51 (1971): 79–91.

Lovejoy, Paul E. "Background to Rebellion: The Origins of Muslims Slaves in Bahia." *Slavery and Abolition* 15, no. 2 (1995): 151–80.

———. "Ethnic Designations of the Slave Trade and the Reconstruction of the History of Trans-Atlantic Slavery." In Lovejoy and Troutman, *Trans-Atlantic Dimensions of Ethnicity in the African Diaspora*, 9–42.

———. "Identifying Enslaved Africans in the African Diaspora." In *Identity in the Shadow of Slavery*, 1–29. London: Continuum, 2001.

Lovejoy, Paul E., and David V. Trotman. "Experiencias de vida y expectativas: Nociones Africanas sobre la esclavitud y la realidad en América." In Cáceres, *Rutas de la esclavitud en África y América Latina*, 379–403.

———. eds. *Trans-Atlantic Dimensions of Ethnicity in the African Diaspora*. London: Continuum, 2003.

MacGaffey, Wyatt. *Art and Healing of the Bakongo, Commented by Themselves: Minkisi from the Laman Collection*. Stockholm: Folkens Museum-Etnografiska, 1991.

———. *Religion and Society in Central Africa: The BaKongo of Lower Zaire*. Chicago: University of Chicago Press, 1986.

MacLachlan, Colin M., and Jaime E. Rodríguez O. *The Forging of the Cosmic Race: A Reinterpretation of Colonial Mexico*. Berkeley: University of California Press, 1980.

Mallo, Silvia C. "La libertad en el discurso del estado, de amos y esclavos: 1780–1830." *Revista de Historia de América* 112 (1991): 121–46.

Martin, Cheryl English. *Rural Society in Colonial Morelos*. Albuquerque: University of New Mexico Press, 1985.

Martínez, María Elena. "The Black Blood of New Spain: *Limpieza de Sangre*, Racial Violence, and Gendered Power in Early Colonial Mexico." *William and Mary Quarterly*, 3rd ser. 61, no. 3 (2004): 479–521.

Martínez Montiel, Luz María. "Integration Patterns and the Assimilation Process of Negro Slaves in Mexico." In *Comparative Perspectives on Slavery in New World Plantation Societies*, edited by Vera Rubin and Arthur Tuden, 446–54. New York: The New York Academy of Sciences, 1977.

———. *Negros en América*. Madrid: MAPFRE, 1992.

———, ed. *La presencia africana en México*. México, DF: Consejo Nacional para la Cultura y las Artes, 1995.

McAlister, Lyle N. "Social Structure and Social Change in New Spain." *Hispanic American Historical Review* 43, no. 3 (1963): 349–70.

McCaa, Robert. "*Calidad, Clase*, and Marriage in Colonial Mexico: The Case of Parral, 1788–90." *Hispanic American Historical Review* 64, no. 3 (1984): 477–501.

McCaa, Robert, Stuart B. Schwartz, and Arturo Grubessich. "Race and Class in Colonial Latin America: A Critique." *Comparative Studies of Society and History* 21, no. 3 (1979): 421–33.

McKnight, Kathryn Joy. "Blasphemy as Resistance: An African Slave Woman before the Mexican Inquisition." In *Women in the Inquisition: Spain and the New World*, edited by Mary E Giles, 229–53. Baltimore: Johns Hopkins University Press, 1999.

Medina, José Toribio. *Historia del Tribunal del Santo Oficio de la Inquisición en México*. México, DF: Consejo Nacional para la Cultura y las Artes, 1991.

Menard, Russell R., and Stuart B. Schwartz. "Why African Slavery? Labor Force Transitions in Brazil, Mexico, and the Carolina Lowcountry." In *Slavery in the Americas*, edited by Wolfgang Binder, 89–114. Würzburg, Germany: Königshausen and Neumann, 1993.

Mentz, Brígida von. *Trabajo, sujeción y libertad en el centro de la Nueva España: Esclavos, aprendices, campesinos y operarios manufactureros, siglos XVI a XVIII*. México, DF: CIESAS, 1999.

Miller, Joseph C. "Central Africa during the Era of the Slave Trade, c. 1490s–1850s." In Heywood, *Central Africans and Cultural Transformations in the American Diaspora*, 21–70.

Miño Grijalva, Manuel. *La protoindustria colonial Hispanoamericana*. México, DF: Colegio de México, 1993.

Moreno de los Arcos, Roberto. "New Spain's Inquisition for Indians from the Sixteenth to the Nineteenth Century." In *Cultural Encounters: The Impact of the Inquisition in Spain and the New World*, edited by Mary Elizabeth Perry and Anne J. Cruz, 23–36. Berkeley: University of California Press, 1991.

Moreno Fraginals, Manuel, Herbert S. Klein, and Stanley Engerman. "The Level and Structure of Slave Prices on Cuban Plantations in the Mid-Nineteenth Century: Some Comparative Perspectives." *American Historical Review* 88, no. 5 (1983): 1201–18.

Morgan, Philip D. *Slave Counterpoint: Black Culture in the Eighteenth-Century Chesapeake and Lowcountry*. Chapel Hill: The University of North Carolina Press, 1998.

———. "The Cultural Implications of the Atlantic Slave Trade: African Regional Origins, American Destinations and New World Developments." *Slavery and Abolition* 18, no. 1 (1997): 122–45.

Morin, Claude. *Michoacán en la Nueva España del siglo XVIII: Crecimiento y desigualdad en una economía colonial*. México, DF: Fondo de Cultura Económica, 1979.

Mörner, Magnus. *Race Mixture in the History of Latin America*. Boston: Little, Brown, 1967.

Mullin, Michael. *Africa in America: Slave Acculturation and Resistance in the American South and the British Caribbean, 1736–1831*. Urbana: University of Illinois Press, 1994.

Naveda Chávez-Hita, Adriana. *Esclavos negros en las haciendas azucareras de Córdoba, Veracruz, 1690–1830*. Xalapa: Universidad Veracruzana, Centro de Investigaciones Históricas, 1987.

———. "Trabajadores esclavos en las haciendas azucareras de Córdoba, Veracruz: 1714–1763." In Frost et al., *El trabajo y los trabajadores en la historia de México*, 162–81.

Nazzari, Muriel. "An Urgent Need to Conceal: The System of Honor and Shame in Colonial Brazil." In *The Faces of Honor: Sex, Shame, and Violence in Colonial Latin America*, edited by Lyman Johnson and Sonya Lipsett-Rivera, 103–26. Albuquerque: University of New Mexico Press, 2002.

Ngou-Mve, Nicolás. *El África Bantú en la colonización de México (1595–1640)*. Madrid: Consejo Superior de Investigaciones Científicas, 1994.

O'Neil, Mary. "Magical Healing, Love Magic and the Inquisition in Late Sixteenth-Century Modena." In *Inquisition and Society in Early Modern Europe*, edited by Stephen Haliczer, 88–114. Totowa, NJ: Barnes and Noble Books, 1987.

O'Toole, Rachel Sarah. "Inventing Difference: Africans, Indians, and the Antecedents of 'Race' in Colonial Peru (1580s–1720s)." PhD diss., University of North Carolina, 2001.

Owensby, Brian P. *Empire of Law and Indian Justice in Colonial Mexico*. Stanford: Stanford University Press, 2008.

———. "How Juan and Leonor Won Their Freedom: Litigation and Liberty in Seventeenth-Century Mexico." *Hispanic American Historical Review* 85, no. 1 (2005): 39–79.

Painter, Nell Irvin. "Soul Murder and Slavery: Toward a Fully Loaded Accounting." In *U. S. History as Women's History: New Feminist Essays*, edited by Linda K. Kerber, Alice Kessler-Harris, and Kathryn Kish Sklar, 125–46. Chapel Hill: University of North Carolina Press, 1995.

Palmer, Colin A. "From Africa to the Americas: Ethnicity in Early Black Communities of the Americas." *Journal of World History* 6, no. 2 (1995): 223–35.

———. *Slaves of the White God: Blacks in Mexico, 1570–1650*. Cambridge, MA: Harvard University Press, 1976.

Patterson, Orlando. *Freedom in the Making of Western Culture*. Vol. 1 of *Freedom*. New York: Basic Books, 1991.

———. *Slavery and Social Death: A Comparative Study*. Cambridge, MA: Harvard University Press, 1982.

———. "The Unholy Trinity: Freedom, Slavery, and the American Constitution." *Social Research* 54, no. 3 (1987): 543–77.

Perrone, Bobette, H. Henrietta Stockel, and Victoria Krueger. *Medicine Women, "Curanderas," and Women Doctors*. Norman: University of Oklahoma, 1989.

Perry, Mary Elizabeth. *Gender and Disorder in Early Modern Seville*. Princeton: Princeton University Press, 1990.

Pitkin, Hanna F. "Are Freedom and Liberty Twins?" *Political Theory* 16, no. 4 (1988): 523–52.

Poole, Stafford. *Our Lady of Guadalupe: The Origins and Sources of a Mexican National Symbol.* Tucson: University of Arizona Press, 1997.

Premo, Bianca. *Children of the Father King: Youth, Authority, and Legal Minority in Colonial Lima.* Chapel Hill: University of North Carolina, 2005.

Price, Richard. "Introduction: Maroons and Their Communities." In *Maroon Societies: Rebel Slave Communities in the Americas,* 1–32. Baltimore: Johns Hopkins University Press, 1979.

Proctor, Frank T., III. "Afro-Mexican Slave Labor in the Obrajes de Paños of New Spain, Seventeenth and Eighteenth Centuries." *The Americas* 60, no. 1 (2003): 33–58.

———. "La familia y comunidad esclava en San Luis Potosí y Guanajuato, México, 1640–1750." In Cáceres, *Rutas de la esclavitud en África y América Latina,* 223–50.

———. "Gender and the Manumission of Slaves in New Spain." *Hispanic American Historical Review* 86, no. 2 (2006): 309–36.

———. "Slave Rebellion and Liberty in Colonial Mexico." In Vinson and Restall, *Black Mexico,* 21–50.

———. "Slavery, Identity, and Culture: An Afro-Mexican Counterpoint, 1640–1763." PhD diss., Emory University, 2003.

Quezada, Noemí. *Enfermedad y maleficio: El curandero en el México colonial.* México, DF: Universidad Nacional Autónoma de México, 1989.

Rabell, Cecilia. "Matrimonio y raza en una parroquia rural: San Luis de la Paz, Guanajuato, 1715–1810." In Calvo, *Historia y población en México,* 163–204.

Reis, João José. *Slave Rebellion in Brazil: The Muslim Uprising of 1835 in Bahia.* Translated by Arthur Brakel. Baltimore: Johns Hopkins University Press, 1993.

Risse, Guenter B. "Medicine in New Spain." In *Medicine in the New World: New Spain, New France, and New England,* edited by Ronald L. Numbers, 12–63. Knoxville: University of Tennessee Press, 1987.

Roddock, Rhoda E. "Women and Slavery in the Caribbean: A Feminist Perspective." *Latin American Perspectives* 12, no. 1 (1985): 63–80.

Roseberry, William. "Hegemony and the Language of Contention." In Joseph and Nugent, *Everyday Forms of State Formation,* 355–66.

Rousse, Joseph. "Power/Knowledge." In *The Cambridge Companion to Foucault,* edited by Gary Gutting, 95–123. New York: Cambridge University Press, 2005.

Rust, Philip F., and Patricia Seed. "Equality of Endogamy: Statistical Approaches." *Social Science Research* 14, no. 1 (1985): 57–79.

Salvucci, Richard J. *Textiles and Capitalism in Mexico: An Economic History of the Obrajes, 1539–1840.* Princeton: Princeton University Press, 1987.

Sandoval, Fernando B. *La industria de azúcar en Nueva España.* México, DF: Instituto de Historia, 1951.

Scharrer Tamm, Beatriz. *Azúcar y trabajo: Tecnología de los siglos XVII y XVIII en el actual Estado de Morelos.* México, DF: CIESAS, 1997.

Schwartz, Stuart B. "Resistance and Accommodation in Eighteenth-Century Brazil: The Slaves' View of Slavery." *Hispanic American Historical Review* 57, no. 1 (1977): 69–81.

———. "Sugar Plantation Labor and Slave Life." In *Slaves, Peasants, and Rebels: Reconsidering Brazilian Slavery*, 39–64. Urbana: University of Illinois Press, 1996.

———. *Sugar Plantations in the Formation of Brazilian Society: Bahia, 1550–1835.* Cambridge: Cambridge University Press, 1985.

Scott, James C. *Domination and the Arts of Resistance: Hidden Transcripts.* New Haven: Yale University Press, 1990.

———. Foreword. In Joseph and Nugent, *Everyday Forms of State Formation*, vii–xii.

———. *Weapons of the Weak: Everyday Forms of Peasant Resistance.* New Haven: Yale University Press, 1985.

Seed, Patricia. "'Are These Not Also Men?': The Indians' Humanity and Capacity for Spanish Civilisation." *Journal of Latin American Studies* 25, no. 3 (1993): 629–52.

———. *To Love, Honor, and Obey in Colonial Mexico: Conflicts over Marriage Choice, 1574–1821.* Stanford: Stanford University Press, 1988.

———. "Social Dimensions of Race: Mexico City, 1753." *Hispanic American Historical Review* 62, no. 4 (1982): 569–606.

Simpson, Lesley Byrd. *Many Mexicos.* 4th ed. Berkeley: University of California Press, 1966.

Slenes, Robert. "'*Malungu, ngoma vem*': Africa coberta e descoberta do Brazil." *Revista Universidão de São Paulo* 12 (1991–92): 48–67.

Socolow, Susan Migden. *The Women of Colonial Latin America.* Cambridge: Cambridge University Press, 2000.

Soulodre-La France, Renée. "Socially Not So Dead! Slave Identities in Bourbon Nueva Granada." *Colonial Latin American Review* 10, no. 1 (2001): 87–103.

Stark, David M. "Discovering the Invisible Puerto Rican Slave Family: Demographic Evidence from the Eighteenth Century." *Journal of Family History* 21, no. 4 (1996): 395–418.

Stern, Steve J. *Peru's Indian Peoples and the Challenge of Spanish Conquest: Huamanga to 1640.* 2nd ed. Madison: University of Wisconsin Press, 1993.

———. *The Secret History of Gender: Women, Men, and Power in Late Colonial Mexico.* Chapel Hill: University of North Carolina Press, 1995.

Super, John C. "Querétaro Obrajes: Industry and Society in Provincial Mexico, 1600–1810." *Hispanic American Historical Review* 56, no. 2 (1976): 197–216.

Sweet, James H. *Recreating Africa: Culture, Kinship, and Religion in the Afro-Portuguese World, 1441–1770*. Chapel Hill: University of North Carolina Press, 2003.

Tadman, Michael. "The Demographic Cost of Sugar: Debates on Slave Societies and Natural Increase in the Americas." *American Historical Review* 105, no. 5 (2000): 1534–75.

Tannenbaum, Frank. *Slave and Citizen: The Negro in the Americas*. Boston: Beacon Press, 1992.

Tausig, Michael T. *The Devil and Commodity Fetishism in South America*. Chapel Hill: University of North Carolina Press, 1980.

Taylor, William B. "The Foundation of Nuestra Señora de Guadalupe de los Morenos de Amapa." *The Americas* 26, no. 4 (1970): 439–46.

———. *Landlord and Peasant in Colonial Oaxaca*. Stanford: Stanford University Press, 1972.

———. "The Virgin of Guadalupe in New Spain: An Inquiry into the Social History of Marian Devotion." *American Ethnologist* 14, no. 1 (1987): 9–33.

Thornton, John K. *Africa and Africans in the Making of the Atlantic World, 1400–1800*. 2nd ed. Cambridge: Cambridge University Press, 1998.

———. "African Dimensions of the Stono Rebellion." *American Historical Review* 96, no. 4 (1991): 1101–13.

———. "The Development of an African Catholic Church in the Kingdom of Kongo, 1491–1750." *Journal of African History* 25, no. 2 (1984): 147–67.

———. *The Kingdom of Kongo: Civil War and Transition, 1641–1718*. Madison: University of Wisconsin Press, 1983.

———. *The Kongolese Saint Anthony: Dona Beatriz Kimpa Vita and the Antonian Movement, 1684–1706*. Cambridge: Cambridge University Press, 1998.

———. "Religious and Ceremonial Life in Kongo and Mbundu Areas, 1500–1700." In Heywood, *Central Africans and Cultural Transformations in the American Diaspora*, 71–90.

Townsend, Camilla. "'Half My Body Free, the Other Half Enslaved': The Politics of the Slaves of the Guayaquil at the End of the Colonial Era." *Colonial Latin American Review* 7, no. 1 (1998): 105–24.

Urquiola, José Ignacio. "Empresas y empresarios." In *Los obrajes en la Nueva España*, edited by Carmen Viqueira and José Ignacio Urquiola, 239–300. México, DF: Consejo Nacional para la Cultura y las Artes, 1990.

Valdés, Dennis N. "The Decline of Slavery in Mexico." *The Americas* 44, no. 2 (1987): 167–94.

Vansina, Jan. "Equatorial Africa and Angola: Migrations and the Emergence of the First States." In *Africa from the 12th to the 16th century*, vol. 4 of *General History of Africa*, edited by DjiBril T. Niane, 551–77. Berkeley: University of California Press, 1984.

————. Foreword. In Heywood, *Central Africans and Cultural Transformations in the American Diaspora*, xi–xiii.

————. *Kingdoms of the Savanna*. Madison: University of Wisconsin Press, 1968.

————. "The Kongo Kingdom and its Neighbors." In *Africa from the Sixteenth to the Eighteenth Century*, vol. 5 of *General History of Africa*, edited by Bethwell A. Ogot, 546–87. Berkeley: University of California Press, 1992.

————. *Paths in the Rainforests: Toward a History of Political Tradition in Equatorial Africa*. Madison: University of Wisconsin Press, 1990.

————. "Western Bantu Expansion." *Journal of African History* 25, no. 2 (1984): 129–45.

Van Young, Eric. *Hacienda and Market in Eighteenth-Century Mexico: The Rural Economy of the Guadalajara Region, 1675–1820*. Berkeley: University of California Press, 1981.

————. "Mexican Rural History since Chevalier: The Historiography of the Colonial Hacienda." *Latin American Research Review* 18, no. 3 (1983): 5–61.

Vasconcelos, José. *The Cosmic Race: A Bilingual Edition*. Baltimore: Johns Hopkins University Press, 1997.

Velázquez, María Elisa. *Mujeres de origen africáno en la capital novohispana, siglos XVII y XVIII*. México, DF: Universidad Nacional Autónoma de México, 2006.

Villa-Flores, Javier. *Dangerous Speech: A Social History of Blasphemy in Colonial Mexico*. Tucson: University of Arizona, 2006.

————. "Defending God's Honor: Blasphemy and the Social Construction of Reverence in New Spain, 1520–1700." PhD diss., University of California, San Diego, 2001.

————. "'To Lose One's Soul': Blasphemy and Slavery in New Spain, 1596–1669." *Hispanic American Historical Review* 82, no. 3 (2002): 435–68.

Villanueva, Margaret A. "From Calpixqui to Corregidor: Appropriation of Women's Cotton Textile Production in Early Colonial New Spain." *Latin American Perspectives* 12, no. 1 (1985): 17–40.

Vinson, Ben, III. *Bearing Arms for His Majesty: The Free-Colored Militia in Colonial Mexico*. Stanford: Stanford University Press, 2001.

Vinson, Ben, III, and Matthew Restall, eds. *Black Mexico: Race and Society from Colonial to Modern Times*. Albuquerque: University of New Mexico Press, 2009.

Wade, Peter. *Race and Ethnicity in Latin America*. London: Pluto Press, 1997.

Whitman, Stephen. "Diverse Good Causes: Manumission and the Transformation of Urban Slavery." *Social Science History* 19, no. 3 (1995): 333–69.

Wyatt-Brown, Bertram. "The Mask of Obedience: Male Slave Psychology in the Old South." *American Historical Review* 93, no. 5 (1988): 1228–51.

Index